Land of the High Flags

For 1600 years or more two gigantic Buddhas, once brilliant with gold leaf and frescos and surrounded by monastic cells hewn into the mountainside,

towered benignly over the Bamian Valley. The gold and the monks and pilgrims are long gone; and now the great Buddhas are gone too. [BILL WOODBURN]

The Minaret at Jam, sole remant of the once-vast Ghorid empire. [YOLANDE CROWE]

LAND *OF THE* HIGH FLAGS

AFGHANISTAN
WHEN THE GOING WAS GOOD

ROSANNE KLASS

Editors: Albert Erskine, this edition, Andrew Coe

Library of Congress Catalog Card Number has been requested:
ISBN: 978-962-217-786-4

Published by Odyssey Books & Guides, 903 Seaview Commercial Building
21–24 Connaught Road West, Sheung Wan, Hong Kong
www.odysseypublications.com

Production by Twin Age Ltd, Hong Kong
E-mail: twinage@netvigator.com

Distributed in the USA by
W.W. Norton & Company, Inc
500 Fifth Avenue, New York, NY 10110, USA
Tel: 800-233-4830; Fax: 800-458-6515 ; www.wwnorton.com

Unless otherwise noted, all photos author's collection.
Front/back cover photos by Bill Woodburn: *On the road from Kabul to Bamian*;
Buzkashi being played at Kabul.
Opposite: *An Afghan.* [ROLAND & SABRINA MICHAUD/WOODFIN CAMP]

Printed in Hong Kong

*To Suzanne Baskin and
the friends who fill these pages.*

Author's Note

When this book was written, not many people knew much about Afghanistan—not even where it was. So I wrote a brief introductory note giving them a few facts. But since 1980, Afghanistan has constantly been in the world's headlines, and I no longer need to explain that it's not in Africa, or that it's pretty big (slightly larger than France and only looking relatively small on a map by comparison with its larger neighbors: Iran [old Persia], Pakistan, and the "-istans" of Central Asia that used to be part of the vast Soviet Union). With millions killed and driven out as refugees since 1978, its population today is probably around twelve to fifteen million, though often reported as much larger.

The major languages are still the two dialects of Pushto, dominant in the south and other Pushtun areas, and the Afghan dialect of Farsi (Persian)—which scholars like to call Dari. Farsi is the lingua franca in Kabul and everywhere else. Dozens of other languages and dialects are spoken locally in various parts of the country. (Arabic is *not* one of them. Sometimes Arabs who fought in Afghanistan are called Afghans, but this is just slang—Arabs have never formed an ethnic group in Afghanistan; in fact, Arabs have never been popular there.)

Many Afghans identify themselves by their ethnic groups, which are mostly Indo-European, Iranian, and Turkic in origin. But in this book, the term "Afghan" is used to mean any citizen of Afghanistan of whatever ethnic origin; its other, older uses are explained. Whatever their origins, Afghans are characteristically strong, colorful personalities – proud, dignified, even melodramatic, generous, quixotic, often exasperating, sometimes brutal, and quite unforgettable.

All these different peoples are here because this tangle of mountains and desert, which bestrides the few routes between Central Asia and the Indian Ocean, has been much fought over and marched across since time lost in the mists of prehistory, and some of the invaders and travelers stayed. Balkh, now a layer cake of archeological ruins, was an already-ancient "mother of cities" back when Zoroaster called this "a land of high flags." It has been a trade route for millennia and still is: three thousand years ago, Afghan lapis lazuli adorned the sarcophagus of the Egyptian pharaoh Tutankhamen, and today a pipeline is being planned to carry natural gas from Central Asia to India. In short, it has always been one of the great crossroads of the world—and until God moves the mountains it will continue to be so.

Under various names it has been a province of the ancient empires of Persia and India and conquerors like Alexander the Great and Genghis Khan, pulled back and forth among them like the prize in its national game of *buzkashi*. And what is now Afghanistan has itself been the seat of empire in its turn, so that India's mothers warned their children to be good "or the Afghan will come and get you."

It is not true that Afghanistan has never been conquered, though Afghans like to think so; but it *is* true that it was never conquered by any of the ambitious 19th century European colonial powers. The modern country of Afghanistan emerged in 1747, carved out of the collapsing empires of Persia and Moghul India just as the great age of European colonial empire-building was approaching its zenith. This highly strategic route to India and the sea was coveted by the empires of Russia, expanding across Central Asia, and Great Britain, then ruling what are now Pakistan and India.

Afghanistan survived as an independent country primarily because those two great modern empires did not want to confront each other face to face. From the 18th century on, Russian czars and commissars coveted Afghanistan as a pathway to the Indian Ocean but hesitated to confront the military power of the British Empire directly. The British were primarily concerned to keep Russia away from the borders of India, the jewel in its Victorian imperial crown; they fought two wars in Afghanistan to make sure that Russia did not encroach there. But Britain was satisfied to install friendly rulers in Kabul, subsidize them, and maintain an "advisory" role over Afghanistan's foreign relations. And when a modernizing king balked at that influence and started a third war in 1919, London, weakened by World War I and already on the way to giving up its Indian empire, pretty much washed its hands of Afghanistan.

After the British left India in 1947 and Pakistan was created, most of the world simply forgot about it.

Of course, as we now know, Russia never did. Reportedly, the first Russian plans to invade Afghanistan were drawn up under Catherine the Great in 1791. Two centuries later, Moscow had never lost interest, and with Britain gone and the rest of the world oblivious, began taking one cautious step after another toward those mountain passes and the sea—first via influence and pressure, then through subversion, and, when those failed, with the Red Army.

I list this summary amalgam of information here to answer questions I am still asked, and to correct some common misinformation not mentioned elsewhere in this book, or—for the most part—in the headlines. What the world has seen on the evening news for the past three decades is a brutal tangle of raw wild mountains echoing with the sounds of gunfire and battle, and ragged impoverished people struggling to survive amid violence.

But it has not always been thus.

Except for an upheaval in the wake of an ill-conceived attempt to modernize overnight, throughout most of the 20th century

Afghanistan was relatively calm, reaching out to the modern world after its long enforced isolation and eager to make progress. The decades between World War II and the first covert communist coup of 1973 were an optimistic time, when Afghanistan was a stable constitutional monarchy and was even moving toward a democratic elected government.

I was lucky enough to meet the Afghans during those hopeful years. This book is not meant to be instructional and does not pretend to be comprehensive. It is meant to tell how things were for one particular person at one particular time. This is how it was for me.

—New York, 2007

Above: *Atop one of the mountain spurs that thrusts into the city, the Baala Hissar fortress, once the palace of kings, has brooded over Kabul for almost 1500 years. In the 1940s, the ancient ramparts were strung with electric lights. At night, power might fail and the entire city might go dark but the lights along the parapets of Baala Hissar always remained undimmed, the first thing a traveler to Kabul saw from afar.* [BILL WOODBURN]

Following pages:*One of the lakes of Band-I-Amir—just suddenly there, icy blue, in the midst of the desert mountain landscape of the Hazarajat.*

[BILL WOODBURN]

1

Once upon a time—that is, several years ago—chance took me to Afghanistan, and for more than two years I lived there among the mountains of Central Asia and taught English to young men from its villages. When I left, there was in my hands an Ariadne's thread of friendship to guide me back someday across the labyrinthine gulfs of time and place, back again to those harsh splendid hills.

But the beginning was not auspicious.

The torpid heat of Karachi in September lies upon the city like a heavy hand. Asia was to me first of all that stifling heat and brilliant glassy sunlight. By night, while our ship lay offshore in the harbor

Left: *Lorries and buses were always over-loaded inside and out, and elaborately decorated in garish colors.*

[ROLAND & SABRINA MICHAUD/WOODFIN CAMP]

waiting for the dawn in order to unload its passengers and cargo, the lights studded along the boundary between the darkness of the city and that of the sea glittered welcomingly. But in the humid glare of morning the dockside was, like any dockside, shabby and hectic, and the tin roof of the long customs shed reflected the heat in shimmering waves. I tried to make myself understand that I was truly standing on a piece of Asia, teetering on the doorstep of its immensity—but what should *I* be doing in Asia? This was a place to find in the newspapers, the atlases, the geography books; it had never counted in my personal world.

Then how could I be here, surrounded by thin sweating faces under grimy turbans, beneath a strange sky glazed with heat? Six months before, I had not even imagined this; but circumstances had swept me along and, like a tide, deposited me here on this pier with my new husband, waiting for a travel agent to meet us. He would take our affairs in hand and see us through until we were securely settled on the train that would take us north to Peshawar, the last stop before the Afghan border. I could think no further yet than the end of that ride.

The agent, an officious, ineffectual young man, arrived at last and quickly created so much confusion that we had to go to the central customs house to straighten out our affairs. I was handed into a horse-drawn tonga, where I sat, looking around me in disbelief, while the baggage was piled onto a camel cart. I suddenly remembered a movie I had seen years before in which ladies in elegantly ruffled white silk, holding parasols, sat in a tonga chatting with coolly tailored gentlemen in white topees. That picture—the India of Kipling's stories, locked safely onto printed pages—seemed real: my presence in this noisy reality seemed like a dream.

Around me on the open piers sweating coolies pushed and shoved crates and baggage back and forth, shouldering bales onto camel carts. Slings full of baskets filled with potatoes were swung down from the hold of our ship, where they had been stowed at Naples. The travel agent scurried back and forth amid the confusion, scolding and prodding and arguing with the customs men until he had seen our baggage onto a cart and on its way into the city. Then he jumped into the tonga, tossed some money to the coolies, and, in the midst of their outraged protests, ordered the driver to set off. He turned to me.

"They are all ungrateful robbers, madame," he said. "You must pay no attention to what they say."

Embarrassed, I stared away silently at the city around me.

"You are in India," I told myself again, and again I did not believe it. Strictly speaking, of course, I was not: I was a few years too late for that. I was in Pakistan. And in 1951 the marks of India's partition and the wracked confusion that followed in its wake were still very apparent in Karachi. Ramshackle refugee huts were scattered along the wide streets, which were filled with a confusion of small cars, tongas, handcarts, and the big lumbering goods carts pulled at a snail's pace by imperturbable camels. Heavily loaded coolies plodded along the sidewalks. Sellers of fruit and gram occasionally squatted down and set forth their baskets of wares, while now and then a woman wrapped in a *burqa*—hidden, huddled-looking—moved quietly along.

On the curbs and in the gutters there were large reddish splotches. I shuddered. They were of course only betel-nut juice, but I was too apprehensive even to inquire. My imagination leaped to another conclusion: the streets were still marked with the bloody terror of Partition riots. In my mood, the strangeness of every sight was magnified, and the nervous prickings of fear began to find their way through my dreamy sense of unreality.

Thanks to the ineptitude of the agent, the customs inspection turned into a day-long ordeal and it was late afternoon before our things were finally dispatched to the railway station.

I had spent much of the day sitting on a crate in the sunlight of the customs-house yard, watching while workmen with claw hammers and bonding wire took apart and resealed all the crates and trunks that had been so carefully packed to sustain us for two years of the unknown. My clothing was glued to me. I hardly noticed any more the trickles of perspiration that ran steadily down my face. We had not had anything to eat or drink all day.

With relief close to tears we finally walked into the fan-cooled office of the travel bureau to pick up mail and currency. Its genial director, a florid, gray-haired Englishman, reassuringly announced that he would advise us on the basis of his thirty years' experience "out here."

He looked at me sympathetically. "You look a bit tired," he said. "How would you like a cup of tea?"

I could have blessed him.

He opened a drawer of his desk and, to my surprise, took out a small primus stove, a kettle, and a bottle of distilled water. After putting the kettle on to boil, he brought forth from another drawer a canister of tea, a teapot, cups, saucers, sugar, and spoons, and set them out carefully on the desk top.

"But, can't you just send out for tea?" I asked.

"Oh, I would never do that," he said firmly. "You can't trust anything out here unless you prepare it yourself. The water is practically poisonous, you know. Best way to kill yourself. Some people chance it, of course," he added thoughtfully, shaking his head at such foolhardiness, "but I've been around too long. Seen the *results*. I always brew my own tea. Fix my own food, too. You can't trust any of these people to do it."

"But what about on the train?" I asked, horrified. "What are we going to do on the train?"

"Oh, you can eat on the train if you want to," he declared, "but you do it at your own risk, you know. Myself, I wouldn't try it."

He poured the tea, handed me a spoon, and settled back comfortably.

"Better watch out for that water," he went on, with a certain relish. "I could tell you . . . well, I know a couple of people who wouldn't listen—thought I was an old woman, you know—insisted on washing in their compartment lavatories. Went *blind*! The water." He shook his head again, in sad resignation. "That's Asia for you. That's it. I've traveled all over, I've lived everywhere from Bengal to Baluchistan, and it's the same everywhere you go. You can do as you like, of course—that's your decision.

"I suppose," he added as a melancholy afterthought, "that the food on the train is about as safe as anything you'll ever get in this part of the world."

Nothing more was needed. The process of demoralization, initiated by naïveté, heat, and exhaustion, was now complete. We finished our tea in silence.

With a hearty air of futility our host then offered his good wishes for our journey and his hopes for our ultimate survival, and sent us on our way to the station.

We were just in time. The *Frontier Mail* was almost ready to leave on its fast run to Peshawar, the capital of the Northwest Frontier Province, the gateway to the Khyber Pass and our immediate destination. The travel agent, uniformly incompetent to the end, overlooked our reservation for air-conditioning and ushered us into the wrong compartment. The door was shut, the latch was thrown. The train drew slowly out of the central Karachi station, paused for a moment at the cantonment depot, and then, gathering its forces, shot out and away into the darkening countryside.

As it drew free of the last sprawling remnants of the city, I saw for the first time the beautiful dusk and nightfall of the Indic plains.

On either side of us the land stretched out, hazy with dust, softly colored in a multitude of grays and purples. The sun, a red disk hung at the edge of the horizon, threw its last rays onto the tops of the dusty trees scattered among the fields. Underbrush, peasant huts, and village walls were already lost in a shadowhood of duns and grays. The air was softened, as though the heat itself lay panting with exhaustion.

The twilight was long. Its hazy quality seemed unchanging. Then suddenly the night closed down like a shutter and the landscape was swallowed in utter darkness. A single bulb lit the little universe of the compartment and the only sign of the world outside was the desert wind, chilling and dry, that suddenly sprang up. When the sun disappeared the heat vanished, too, and the night was bitterly cold. The travel agency had promised to see to everything. Among the items they neglected was bedding, and I shivered the night through under a light coat, curled up on the cold leatherette of the berth. The hours of darkness and discomfort seemed interminable as I tossed and dozed, hungry, thirsty, exhausted, and shivering.

Then the sun rose, its brilliance pulling me wide awake again, and as soon as it was above the treetops the unrelenting heat began once more. If the night had been wretched, the day was worse.

As I watched the countryside fall away behind us, mile on endless mile, with its leafless twiggy underbrush and the little mud houses crumbling and windowless, I wondered desperately if this was what I had come to live in—and if it was, how I could bear it. It is difficult for me, even now, to realize that in season this land blooms and is fruitful. I grew up among the rich farmlands of the Middle West where the earth is black and the fields welcome a nourishing sun. Here, sky and earth seemed enemies glaring bitterly at one another, locked in a dogged struggle.

The sun burned down ferociously, beating at the earth, cracking and parching it, firing it like clay in a kiln; while the earth, stretched out like a great fragment of aged potsherd, stubbornly, bitterly resisted, holding up its dry underbrush and dusty trees as a defiant gesture. And on the margin of the struggle, along the borderline of the two elements, life trod cautiously: a bullock standing impassively in a field, a farmer with turban and shirt as dusty as the earth he walked, a child bending over a thread of water in a ditch.

Always, without relief, there was the heat. This world was an oven, unchanging, stifling. Even the wind created by the train as it rushed across the brown land was like a hot breath, and it brought in the dust—everlastingly, the dust. Dust that filtered into eyes and nostrils and between the teeth, that lay gritty on the hands and coated the eyelashes. Even closing the windows—if you could bear that—could not keep it out. Dust of the Sind desert, and then dust of the Punjab.

The train stopped frequently at boxy little stations whose platforms suddenly overflowed with vendors hawking fruits, sweetmeats, and bright syrupy drinks. Clusters of men leaned against the water tanks and gazed at the train. If I looked out the window they gazed at me. Their unflinching stares seemed ominous and my worried husband insisted that I stay in the compartment, even though I longed to get out and stretch my legs. Somehow it never occurred to us that these were simply small-town folk who, as everywhere else in the world, like to come down to the station to watch the crack express come through—and that their scowls came from squinting against the sunlight.

At each stop the waiter came along from the Spencer dining car to take orders, but with the Englishman's warning still fresh, we were afraid to order anything but tea. We had to have something to drink, and after much hesitation, we had theorized that tea might conceivably be safe because it was boiled. The Spencer-wallah appeared surprised at our capacity but made no comment. Unknown to him, we were taking no chances: we were not only living on tea in that baking heat, we were washing with it, brushing our teeth with it, and mingling bits of tea leaves with the grit that clung to our skins.

Darkness had fallen when we pulled into the big redbrick station at Lahore. A triumphantly Victorian edifice, at once grandiose and stodgy, all ells and cupolas and jutting lintels, it swarmed with the bustle and excitement of a major railway junction. The glare of bare bulbs alternated with pools of darkness under the arches of the roofed platform. From high hidden corners little gecko lizards, casting distorted dragon shadows, darted out to snap up the insects that flocked to the lights.

Twice each day the arrival of the *Frontier Mail* was the signal for a spurt of activity. Coolies, conductors, foodsellers shouting their wares, passengers unloading their baggage, other passengers hunting for their compartments—all rushed about among a confusion of bundles and bedrolls and tiffin tins and suitcases, dodging the clusters of families with sleepy children in their arms who had come down to greet or wave off various travelers. Through screen doors one could glimpse brightly lit waiting rooms and something that looked like a shop.

By now we were too miserable to continue to be fools. My husband pushed his way through the crowd and returned with a can of pears and a can of tomato juice. As the train pulled out again into the night, we opened them with a nail file and the back of a hair brush and for the first time in forty-eight hours had something to eat.

There was another night ahead of cold, comfortless dozing under a skimpy coat. It seemed by now that I had always been on this train, rushing through baking day and frigid night, and would go on so forever, but the morning promised to bring us to Peshawar. Beyond that lay the Khyber Pass—and Afghanistan.

We had yet to cross the Indus River and enter the Northwest Frontier Province, the domain of the Pushtuns—which is to say, the Afghans, for the two names are interchangeable and synonymous. Indians and Westerners call them the Pathans, but no matter. Whatever name one uses, they are the same people—tough, proud, willful, independent—who fought the British to a draw in western India and gave their name to the country to which I was going: Afghan-istan, the land of the Afghans. Whatever the jurisdiction of governments, from the Indus to the Oxus (the Amu) their spirit dominates, and nothing on either side of them is quite like it.

Somewhere in the last hours of that black night we rumbled across the Indus and thus, unknowing, into the world that I have never since completely left. As I slept restlessly, the great fort at Attock slipped by; built by the emperor Akbar, the greatest of the Great Moguls, it guards the river-crossing which has forever divided the plains of Hindustan from the lands of the Pushtuns. Across the Attock Bridge, then, cold and fitfully dreaming, and we had left behind the soft poetic cadences of Urdu and come into the homeland of that austere and sinewy tongue, Pushto. We had not come to the modern international boundary which formally states to mapmakers and customs men and sovereign states, There lies the land of the Afghans. That line lies beyond the Khyber Pass, already deep in Pushtun tribal territory. But we had come among the people who, on either side of that line, live by the same hard and ancient code. So, sleeping, we arrived in their world, and woke to the clear cool sunlight of fresh morning as the *Frontier Mail* pulled into Peshawar.

This was the end of the run. The train emptied out, other passengers gathered their belongings and hurried away. As we stood uncertainly, surrounded by our trunks and boxes, an arresting figure peered through the wrought-iron gates, then hurried across the platform to us: a white-clad, white-bearded Pushtun, his turban tied with a stiff flourish.

"You want to go to Dean's Hotel?" he asked, and then, without waiting for a reply, "You want a tonga? I have a very good tonga. Take care of everything. Come this way, please."

He deftly maneuvered us out through the gate and into the carriage, and disappeared back onto the platform. A few minutes later he reappeared, shepherding a cluster of coolies who had piled our baggage on a two-wheeled handcart. Ostentatiously threatening and directing them, he saw them off down the street, climbed up to the driver's seat of the tonga, and picked up the reins. But before he clucked to his horse he turned around, his eyes flashing in his tanned, shrewd old face, his white beard a badge of impeccable dignity.

"My name is *Johnson*, sahib," he announced. "Mohammed Akbar *Johnson*. My card—you may keep it. I am the best tonga-wallah in Peshawar. Do not worry about anythings. We will see your goods at Dean's Hotel."

With a flourish of the reins he roared an imprecation at his dutiful horse and we set off, clopping along the streets of the beautiful city.

We rode for half an hour or more that morning along curving boulevards lined with low sprawling loggiaed bungalows. Each was surrounded by green lawns set off from the street by low walls of stone which were covered with a profusion of blossoming vines still damp with dew—bougainvillaea, roses, jasmine. Peshawar was one of the gracious cities of the world, and that morning its beauties were succor to my parched and fearful spirit. We passed along the Mall and down broad streets lined with bookshops and big general-provisions stores which were still shuttered; we drove through other streets where the cigarette stalls and teahouses had already unbuckled their night-time armor and opened their nook-

and-cranny premises for the morning's business. Smoke and wisps of steam rose around samovars where men wearing the high Pushtun turbans squatted on their heels to enjoy a cigarette, a cup of tea, and friendly banter. This was the cantonment, the modern section of the city: it was clean, it was sweet, and if it lacked the fascination of the old city, it was green and blossomy and lovely.

At last the tonga turned in at a neatly graveled drive that swept around to the portico of a low rambling building surrounded by lawns and rose gardens: Dean's Hotel. Mohammed Akbar Johnson was right: the coolies, though on foot, had already arrived with our luggage. This was not, however, as remarkable as it seemed. Before another hour had passed we learned that Dean's was only a block or so from the station and that Johnson (who had adopted his name from a long-vanished, much-cherished employer) specialized in transporting greenhorns who could be carted halfway around town in contented ignorance. Still, his routes were so charming and his rascality so unabashed that I always took pleasure in being his dupe; and since age had dimmed his ability to recognize previous passengers, we were able to hoodwink one another quite happily on numerous subsequent occasions.

Dean's Hotel was then an island of unchange in a shifting world. Time had stopped there, I would guess, somewhere around 1936, when a sufficient quantity of cretonne and golden oak had been acquired. It reflected admirably the British gift for transmuting dowdiness into a comfortable style which was, I believe, known in India as "Home." The dim lounge had several hand-tinted portraits of the Royal Family for decoration, while a few aged copies of *The Illustrated London News* and *Country Life* were strewn about for those guests who required amusement.

At the reservations desk, which was tucked into a cubbyhole under the portico, there was a bulletin board where various letters were tacked up, waiting for the day when their destined recipients might conceivably arrive. Dean's was a sort of postal exchange for every wayfarer in North India, Pakistan, and Afghanistan. Some of the envelopes had the weary look of great age. They may well have been there for years and if they have not been claimed, are probably there yet. If I were to walk into Dean's tomorrow, I would not be surprised if the desk clerk—an imperturbable young man—were to say to me, "There's a letter here for you, madame. It came several years ago and I thought of sending it on, but I knew you would be in sooner or later to get it."

The hotel's one major drawback was the apparent assumption on the part of the management that no one bathes except between the hours of six and seven in the morning, or the hours of six and seven in the evening. Only during those hours was hot water available. Arriving for the first time too late to make the morning bath hours, disheveled and layered with grime as I was, it was dismaying to find that there was no hot water to be had. My misery must have been quite heartrending, for the sympathetic clerk had some heated specially and lugged in. It was enough to make a tepid tub, but, even so, my baths—I needed several—were unsatisfactory affairs. I was ready to peel off my dusty skin.

By the time we entered the cavernous dining room the lesson of two days' wretchedness had sunk in: one could go about in fear of strangeness and be constantly unhappy in surroundings that were consistently strange, or one could say the hell with it. There were long months of Asia ahead; there was only one choice; breakfast was delicious.

A friend from college days had been an instructor at the Teachers' College in Kabul for several years. We were going to stay with him, and a letter was waiting for us amid the clutter on the bulletin board. He advised us to cadge a ride to Kabul with someone going up by car; the trip was less than two hundred miles, but the bus took two days to do it. He also suggested that we arrange for our household goods to be sent up by Mr. K. A. Gai, a Peshawar merchant.

We found Mr. Gai's store on the main street. It looked large, but not lively. On the front veranda an elderly clerk sat at a desk piled high with a confusion of papers, ledgers, and books. Searching for the owner, we peered into the interior of the store, a dim cavern lined with shelves half empty now that import restrictions and the withdrawal of the British had reduced both the supply and demand for English marmalade, Scottish oatmeal, and Major Grey's chutney.

Finding no one, we turned to the clerk, who seemed immersed in a book. He wore an old-fashioned shirt, its detachable collar missing and the top stud unfastened, the sleeves caught with black garters. He looked up at us thoughtfully through steel-rimmed glasses. It was Mr. Gai. The book he put down on the desk as he turned to us was a study of comparative religious philosophies in German. We had just met a most remarkable man in a land known for remarkable men.

K. A. Gai appeared to be in his early sixties when I met him, but he might have been ten years older—or younger; there was about him a quality of burgeoning old age, of age coming but never arrived. As long as I knew him this never changed: his hair was graying but never grayer, his face was lined but never wrinkled, and his look was sharp and penetrating.

He had known, or so it seemed, everyone of interest on the Frontier for fifty years and more—viceroys, poets, archaeologists, soldiers, scholars, Afghan kings. Later, when I visited his home, I saw their photographs, affectionately inscribed, lining the walls of his library, and tokens of their friendship and respect had turned his home into a breath-taking gallery of Asian art.

The house itself was set in a spacious garden where flowers and shrubs grew in well-tended, elegant profusion. Fragile-looking black-and-gray cranes stalked haughtily beneath the leaves, and a pair of tiny delicate Chinese deer ran about, their necks encircled by turquoise-studded collars whose golden bells, tinkling, revealed their presence—now here, now there—among the blossoms. Around the house, facing this garden, swept a pillared veranda and against each pillar there stood a piece of sculpture—a Buddha from central China, perhaps, or a choice Gandhara piece—brought to him by his friends over the years, presentation pieces for a connoisseur. Here, when the business of the day was done, Gai devoted himself to his favorite interests, comparative religion and philosophy, amid a library as choice and rare as his home.

At his store, however, there was nothing unusual about his appearance; he seemed to be an ordinary, prosperous merchant—unless one noticed the stack of philosophical works in half a dozen languages which cluttered his desk. He quickly arranged to take care of our baggage, wished us a pleasant good morning and a happy journey, and returned to his reading.

Back at the hotel, several Americans were gathered over drinks in the lounge—members of the staff of the embassy in Kabul who had been down on a holiday and were returning the next morning. They had two station wagons and cheerfully offered a ride.

They were cheerful people. They seemed at their most cheerful in describing the discomforts of life in Kabul, invariably adding with discouraging relish, "Of course, you'll get used to it."

"No refrigerators," one young woman confided to me. "No refrigerators at all! And half the time, no ice."

2

*T*he first daylight brought our little caravan together. Besides the embassy people, we were joined by Mr. H—, a tall, bespectacled, elderly American mining engineer in a dark-blue pin-stripe suit and a dark-blue homburg, who was to ride up in our car. He had been in Kabul the year before, he explained, and was returning now to help get some coal mines going in the north. I found him very encouraging. Not only his placid demeanor but his wardrobe suggested that this was not going to be such a rough trip as I had imagined.

The drivers piled the luggage into the cars, and the hotel bearers emerged from the dining room with box lunches and gin bottles full of water for each of us. Mr. H— squeezed his way into the station wagon and settled himself comfortably on the back seat amid a stack of suitcases. He removed his bifocals, polished them, and replaced them. Then he took off his homburg and placed it carefully on his lap, where he carried it throughout the entire journey.

As we set out, I stubbornly pushed out of sight my real feelings: if this was adventure, I had no desire to be adventurous. I would not admit even to myself that I was frightened, I wanted to cling to familiarity, I wanted to go home. Just as I had begun to feel a little bit at ease in Peshawar, here we were, speeding along the road to the Khyber Pass, the city already behind us.

The highway ran straight west into the foothills of the Safed Koh range, a black ribbon of macadam crossing the Peshawar plain between plowed fields and high-walled mud-brick villages, drab among a scattering of trees. In the fields, water buffalo were already at work, treading in patient circles to turn the Persian wheels that dipped endlessly into the wells and spilled their water into little irrigation ditches.

Ten miles or so from the city, where the ground begins to heave and roll toward the hills, stolid old Fort Jamrud came into view, guarding the boundary between the Administered Districts of British India and the independent tribal territories which stretch through Khyber to the border. This is the entry to the classic Border country, the domain for centuries of the Afridi tribesmen—disputed, for a brief futile interlude, by the Khyber Rifles and Kipling's favorites, the Guides.

On that first morning, of course, the landmarks meant almost nothing to me. What little I knew about the Border and the Pass was a smattering of romantic fact so closely mixed with romantic fiction that it would be difficult to disentangle the two. But that is inevitably true of information about the Border, even when it has become familiar. What is true is often so far-fetched and incredible that it picks up by a sort of magnetism a further encrustation of fiction, and the two are so indistinguishable that you can never presume to be sure just where one leaves off and the other begins. It is simplest to believe everything or nothing, and one usually alternates between the two choices.

The Pushtuns probably possessed the Pass when Alexander the Great sent part of his army this way on his march to India. At least as long as history records, they have held its barren heights. Unable to wrest a living from the ungracious rock, they depended for centuries on tribute extorted from the merchant caravans which wound their way along the great trade route between India and Central Asia and thence both east and west; or they might rob the caravans, or raid the cities of the plain. But they returned always to the rugged mountains for which, again and again, they fought off every would-be conqueror. The very names of the clans echo in the mind like drums of battle: Afridi, Mohmand, Yusufzai.

It is easy, of course, to see the strategic advantage which possession of the Pass would give to any ruler of the surrounding lands, especially if he had pretensions to conquest. But to hold the mountains, and the mountains alone—that is bitter booty. So here one can begin to learn that men may love and die for a barren land which offers them nothing but struggle, that they may stubbornly refuse to relinquish it at any price—simply because they are born of it, and it is theirs.

The British finally gave up trying to conquer them and managed, at most, to keep the tribes from raiding by a combination of cash subsidies, constant military action, and skillful agents to handle their grievances. Pakistan continued the system. So the Pass is safe—that is, most of the time, and by daylight, and barring the unusual. But high in the hills are hidden forges where the tribesmen turn out precise duplicates of modern rifles, complete down to the serial numbers; and under any regime, let a finger be laid upon their freedom and the tribes rise in their pride and fight.

In Peshawar I had heard a vague story that, by treaty, twenty yards or so on either side of the road was protected but beyond that, you were on your own. I looked at the tall, sunburnt men who strode along the roadside, unable to decide whether they actually looked murderous or just dignified. I didn't really know what would happen to anyone who ventured twenty-one yards from the road, but I had a mental picture, undoubtedly left over from those childhood games where someone drew a line in the dust with a stick and dared you to step across it. Perhaps (I imagined)—perhaps as one's foot moved across that invisible boundary, a rifle would crack from a secret watch point on the mountainside and the foolhardy trespasser would fall, a victim of his own temerity. Still, I would have liked to edge my toe up to that mark: given the chance, I could not have resisted tempting fate within, perhaps, the inch, although I would have wanted to be sure of my measuring rod.

As Fort Jamrud fell behind us the road began to climb. Gradually the hills rose higher on either side and turned into mountains; a valley fell away between them, and the road wound along the rocky slope. Below the highway I saw a dirt trail, where occasionally a man prodded a string of donkeys along. I was alert now, watching for my first glimpse of the Khyber Pass. I had never seen pictures of it, but I could imagine it vividly: the road turning downward, the mountains rising up on either side of a low saddle, and thus, its fabled walls at last.

As the road twisted along the mountainside, still climbing, my attention was suddenly caught by a series of tablets set into the face of the rock. Speeding past, I could glimpse only fragments of the inscriptions: . . . *Her Majesty's First . . . defended in 184 . . . Black Watch Regiment* . . . Suddenly I felt a stir of excitement: these were the troops who had fought for the Pass; we must be close to it now.

I turned to the driver, a heavy-set, good-natured Peshawari. "When will we get to the Khyber Pass?" I asked.

He looked surprised and then amused.

"Khanum-sahib," he said politely, "we are in Khyber. We come in Khyber a long time ago." Without taking his eyes from the twisting road, he nodded, indicating the landscape around us. "Is all Khyber here."

I was stunned. In the Khyber and not knowing it? But where was that cleft I had imagined, parting the mountains like the waters of the Red Sea? This the legendary Khyber, and that little dirt track below us the ancient caravan route! For a moment I resented the mountains because they did not conform to my imagination, and the highway because it made the Pass seem so modern and easy.

By the time I had adjusted myself to the reality of the Khyber, we were nearly at its end. The massive heap of the ranges towering around us began to subside. The road curved past the railhead at Landi Kotal and a few miles further on, below the cliffs of Torkhum, the Pakistani customs post stood at the border. I did not need to ask where that was: on this side the customs bungalow was an oasis set among shady trees on a grassy terrace, on the far side lay a desert plain, and between the two the black macadam highway stopped as abruptly as though it had been sliced off with a knife. This was the line on the map and here it was a clear line on the earth as well.

While our passports were being checked we sat down to tea and pilau with a motley group of wayfarers who were sitting on their heels on the bungalow veranda. This was my first experience of being the only woman in a situation where women would normally not take part. Soon I would be used to living and working that way, day in and day out, but this time I was very much aware of being invited to join in as a courtesy because I was a foreigner. For the first time, too, and hesitantly, I dipped into a common food bowl.

My hosts were amused and tolerant as the grains of rice slipped and scattered between my untrained fingers. They passed the water-pipe to me too as it went around the circle, and chuckled when I took a puff, cupping my hand the way they did over the mouthpiece and trying not to choke on the powerful blast that burned my throat. It was lovely under the trees, the little bowls of tea were filled and refilled, and I was hardly eager to see the customs officer emerge with our papers completed, to wave us on.

Several yards down the road, smartly uniformed guards stood at attention by their sentry boxes, their berets set at a rakish angle. The famous sign was gone now, and had been for years—the sign that said: IT IS ABSOLUTELY FORBIDDEN TO CROSS THIS BORDER INTO AFGHAN TERRITORY. But someone invariably takes care to mention it to travelers. The fact that it had been posted by the British and not by the Afghans seemed to me to make it less an indication of inhospitality, but no more comforting. Why, I wondered, had it been so absolutely forbidden? There was no one to explain the intricacies of British policy, and so I was left to ponder the possibilities.

This was truly the border. The paved road ended and the desert began, guarded in its turn by Afghan militiamen. Even the trees of the customs-house yard cast no shade here, as though that too were somehow halted by jurisdictional fiat. The sun poured its full blaze upon a brown barren land that seemed to stretch away to the distant mountains without relief: no tree, no shadow, only the earth, the heat, the light. An uneven straggle of rocks marked the track across the desert which was the road, washed out with the floods of every spring.

A few miles beyond the border we pulled off to the Afghan customs station, a cluster of mud-brick buildings baking in the sunlight. Inside, however, the rooms were cool, and while we waited for clearance we struck up an acquaintance with an Englishman who had arrived a few moments ahead of us. This was a mistake.

He was enthusiastically setting out to drive to Istanbul in a battered old sedan. It was our ill luck to have him on the road before us, for every few miles his car broke down. Then we would find him standing at the roadside, cheerfully waving to us for help, and in that desert we could hardly pass him by.

As the day wore on I began to hate him. He could have flagged down one of the lorries which sometimes passed us on the way; one of them would have towed him to the nearest town. But his stubborn determination to drive it, which seemed to him to be the old bulldog spirit, seemed to me to be only an excuse for letting our driver do his tinkering and pushing. As a result of his undaunted fervor, we did not get rid of him till nearly midnight and he turned our trip into a twenty-hour ordeal.

Although we left Dakka long before noon, what with pushing and pulling the old sedan, and the roughness of the road itself, it was midafternoon before we reached Jalalabad, about sixty miles away. The interval was spent on that rutted track across the plains, littered with shale and rock and pebbles as a meadow might be with flowers. There must have been life and movement—a bus and several lorries passed us on the way—but the sense of empty desolation was overwhelming. A mile or two away, out of sight of the road, the Kabul River wound along, lined with fertile fields— for wherever there is water in Afghanistan, there is greenness and growth. Occasionally along the ranges to the left of us we caught a glimpse of a high-walled village and a hint of green around it. But around us the landscape was as barren as granite. Heat waves danced up from the burning earth and dust-devils rose whirling alongside the road. The sun burned down mercilessly; every breath of air came laden with heat and dust.

Why, I wonder, are deserts like this so seldom seen in paintings? Does their blasted brilliance defy capture in paint? Even the medieval saints in their painted deserts are not face to face with the raw earth;

ascetic though they may be, they dwell in mere wildernesses. No, deserts are usually left to photographers, and photographers most frequently choose sand dunes, the waves of an earthen sea.

So one has no previous preparation for this confrontation of the elements, stripped of any comfort or cover. Here on the plain of Batikot each rock and pebble stood alone in the glare of midday. This land had not even the passive stubborn look of the earth in the Punjab; this land had a sort of ferocious defiance, a rocky power that forced itself upon you. It demanded all of your strength just to face it; it yielded nothing.

The water in our gin bottles was lukewarm and we could see that we had not brought enough. Conversation had long since ceased, drowned in the heat and the roar of the motor. Mr. H— sat imperturbably holding his homburg on his lap; occasionally he murmured some attempted pleasantry and then gave up again. His only concession to the heat was the removal of his suit jacket, which he folded neatly and placed under the homburg, across his knees.

The journey had assumed a sort of pattern: steady irregular bumping, broken by swerves (down into a gully and then, motor straining, up the other side) where spring torrents had torn away the roadbed; there was the noise of the motor, the heat, the burning light that shone red through closed eyelids, the carefully measured sips of water, the futile search for some sort of comfort. Stop for the Englishman. Stretch every aching muscle. Long for some end to the endless. Get in again: suit jacket refolded, homburg replaced, guesses exchanged about our progress. Then on across the arid plain.

The fields and orchards of Jalalabad coming into view looked like a paradise; for the first time I began to understand what an oasis could mean. The city has an ancient and illustrious history, but I cared only that it was green. Set in a bend of the Kabul River, its streets were shaded by acacias, cool to the eyes, and in the garden of the hotel where we stopped to rest, there were bright marigolds and stiff scarlet cannas.

Our driver sent at once for watermelons and as soon as they were brought, thumped, and judged, he split one open. Afghanistan, he said, has the best melons in the world. I have often heard that stated, and I am inclined to think it is true. We quenched our thirst happily on this one and he loaded the others into the back of the station wagon. Then we were on our way again, leaving Jalalabad's cool citrus groves behind us.

Beyond the line of mountains which had bounded the horizon all day, snow-capped peaks had occasionally sprung into view; but the foothills themselves were brown and bare, folded, gullied, and humped, with a desolate prehistoric look. Now the road began to rise among them, climbing to the Sarobi gorge of the river. The afternoon wore on, the sun moved lower, the air became clear, though the heat remained. When we were well into the hills the road dipped sharply down a cleft where a hidden spring poured its stream down the mountainside. This was, though I did not know it then, one of the classic ambush points of the old road.

The driver suggested we take a rest here and finish the melons. While he put them in the stream to cool, and filled the water bottles, I examined the lifeless slopes rising around us. There was the spring, bursting forth like a beneficence, but around it was nothing—not a tree or a shrub, not a house or a trail or a sign of life. It might all have been a mirage.

I took off my shoes and went wading, grateful for the icy shock of the water. I splashed my face and arms and sat down on a rock to dabble my feet in the current. I looked up again, to see a row of armed men squatting motionless, high up on the mountainside, watching us.

Where had they come from? When, and how? There was nothing to offer concealment, not even a boulder—nothing larger than the shingles of rock littering the slopes. The land was utterly barren and there had been no sign of life for miles. Suddenly, silently, they had materialized. There they sat, on their heels, stern, unmoving, rifles slung across their shoulders and bandoliers across their chests, as though they were graven into the mountain rock.

The driver, following my eyes, noticed them and shrugged casually.

They watched us as we ate our melons. They watched as we got back into the car and set out again. They never moved. As we drove off, the tribesmen were still sitting, following us only with their eyes. I looked back a moment later; they had vanished.

At sunset we passed through the Sarobi gorge, where the Kabul River rushed through its deep channel far below us. Across the river lay a scene that seemed miraculous after the parched day: the green fertility of the Eastern Province. In the quiet evening light, rows of poplars stretched between the glimmering green rice fields, and the bleating of flocks floated to us across the valley. It looked utterly placid, a soothing haven of peaceful farmland; it is the home of some of the toughest of the Pushtun tribes.

The village of Sarobi itself, where a German engineering firm was building a power dam, had an incongruous cluster of neat little stone houses with a stolid Middle European look to them--the homes of the administrative staff. Though they actually clung to the cliffs as precariously as the adobe Afghan buildings around them, they had an air of nestling cozily against the rock. As a goodwill gesture, the company had built a new mosque for the local citizens, and although it scrupulously imitated the Islamic mode, this too had a curious aura of the Schwarzwald, as though the muezzin might suddenly yodel.

Beyond Sarobi we began the long tortuous climb over the hump of the Lataband Pass.

"Kabul is beyond Lataband," the driver told me, and, encouraged, I imagined that we were almost there. Still uneducated in the ways of mountains, I thought we would soon pass a razorback, glide downward, and arrive. Instead, as night fell we wound on, climbing and twisting, hour after hour, in a blackness cut only by the channel of our headlights. They shone on the rough, narrow dirt road— just wide enough for our car—which was hewn into the gigantic mountainside; they caught the face of the mountain itself as the road bent back and forth and its barren flanks rose up to face us.

There was no moon, and the stars shed no light. We had been traveling since sunrise. Exhaustion had sapped away all feeling. Only the driver and Mr. H— seemed to feel any assurance that we were going to arrive anywhere, ever. The imperturbable engineer, dusty now but still firmly gripping his hat, nodded peacefully in the back seat as we jolted along. It occurred to me that sartorially, he had turned out to be a pretty false prophet. I hardly cared any more.

Near midnight, at an isolated teahouse, we finally rid ourselves of the Englishman, who reluctantly surmised that his jalopy might not make it after all, and after that we could at least go on steadily. From time to time the driver murmured encouragement to me: "Not so long now, khanum-sahib. Soon. Almost at the top now."

The headlights picked out a little hut beside the road, with whitewashed stones scattered about it and a tattered rag or two dangling listlessly from poles stuck into the ground. The driver stopped, jumped out, and disappeared into the hut. In a moment he was back. That was, he explained, the dwelling of a very holy hermit who lived at the top of the Pass. One must never pass by without giving alms, in gratitude for a safe journey—and in hopes of completing it.

The night wore on, midnight was long past, and still the road wound along, dipping and climbing, although now we did seem to be heading generally downward. Then suddenly, ahead and below us, a thin spangle of lights swung across the darkness in a narrow line, as though outlining the upper wings of a butterfly. The driver pointed to them.

"Kabul," he said cheerfully.

We were not there yet. The road turned and the lights in the valley disappeared; it twisted around and there they were again, tantalizingly close and yet still beyond us. There was nothing to indicate the city but that single line of light, and I puzzled over its peculiar shape. I could think of only one structure with that shape but it was a stimulating thought: a roller coaster. Surely, if Kabul had an amusement park it must be a fairly sophisticated city.

"What are those lights?" I demanded.

"Kabul."

"Yes, but what in Kabul? What do they light?"

"Nothing, khanum. Just lights. Kabul lights."

We continued this colloquy until I wearied of it. Obviously he could not or would not understand. The lights must light something but I could not guess what, and apparently the driver was not going to tell me.

But he had. They were, as he said, just lights, lighting nothing. They marched along a medieval wall crowning the mountain which splits Kabul into two sections. Nothing else is on that hilltop, and the ancient, crumbling wall itself was constructed by some long-forgotten king to hold off an equally long-gone enemy— Tamerlane, some say, or the White Huns. Its shattered crenellations cut like irregular teeth into the blue sky over the city from whatever angle you look up at it. A few years before, a municipal official had decided to stimulate civic pride by stringing lights along the parapets, and there they were, a beacon to the countryside for many miles around. Power might fail in the city and every house be plunged into darkness, but from your window you could look up in frustration to see them gleaming undisturbed along the ridge. I eventually became quite fond of them.

Being in an unimaginative mood that night, however, I could not guess at any of this, so I puzzled wearily over the roller coaster until we reached the floor of the Kabul Valley and began the drive into the city.

Kabul was almost completely in darkness, except for the mountain lights and a few main streets. I first knew we were in the sleeping city when the headlights picked up high mud walls on either side of us. Ditches lined with slender trees ran along the edges of the unpaved streets. Occasionally a stray dog, awakened by the car, slunk away from the headlight beams. Otherwise the city was motionless and silent: it was past two o'clock.

The station wagon turned down a wide paved business street, sporadically lit by pole lamps, and stopped in front of a building that bore the sign "Hotel-i-Kabul." After the day-long roar of the motor, the absolute silence struck my ears thunderously.

Knocking on the hotel door, the driver roused a porter and returned at last to inform the awakened Mr. H—that there were no rooms available; but in view of the lateness of the hour, a cot could be set up for him in the hallway. The engineer pronounced himself eminently satisfied with this arrangement and, gathering his things together, he carefully put on his hat and coat, expressed his pleasure at having had our company throughout the trip, shook hands all around, and disappeared into the building.

The driver checked his gas gauge and announced that he would have to go for petrol before he could continue on to our friend's home. Then he too vanished into the night.

Exhausted, we sat silently in the car on the silent street. Aside from the lighted window of the hotel, the only sign of life was a booted, uniformed policeman who paced slowly up and down the street, pausing on each turn to peer wordlessly through the car window into my face before resuming his round. The air was cool and fresh, but the breeze brought with it the pervasive, pungently sweet odor of artemesia—wormwood—which is burned for fuel in the autumn. It began to annoy me, and then to obsess me: I smelled it, tasted it, felt it; it was too much, it was the last straw, it would surely drive me mad. Winding up the windows was no help; even a drink of water seemed to me to taste of it. I was, one might say, at the end of my rope.

The door of the hotel opened again and Mr. H— reappeared on the steps. He had removed his jacket and shirt and, with his suspenders pulled up over his undershirt, his homburg still firmly set upon his head, had come back to say good night. He did so, and with unruffled composure returned to his hall cot. I never saw him again.

The gas tank refilled at last, we drove through more tunnels of walled streets until the driver pulled up before a big green gate on which was chalked, in enormous letters, GUL BAZ KHAN. Underneath, in much smaller letters, was the name of our friend. The driver got out and pounded resoundingly on the gate. A raucous barking was set up inside. We waited.

At last a small door in the gate opened and a fierce-looking unshaven face appeared, ornamented with bristling mustachios. The man exchanged a few words in Persian with the driver and then the door was abruptly shut again. When it reopened, another, sterner face appeared. This time the driver motioned to us to get out, and he began to unload the suitcases.

The owner of the stern visage stood aside, holding the door open wordlessly, and, stooping, I stepped past him into a garage filled with heaps of sawdust and piles of wood. He went over to another door at one side, opened it a crack, and shouted what was apparently some sort of password: "Jimmee bast-ast?"

"Bali, sahib," came a sleepy answer. "Jimmeee bast-ast!"

At this, the man flung open the door, and, still without a word exchanged, I passed through into a pitch-black courtyard.

I could discern the corner of a building to my right, and beyond it a square of light streamed out across the ground. As I came around the corner I saw a short flight of steps leading up to a small porch. The light came from a glassed door, through which I saw our friend coming out into the hallway, sleepily wrapping his bathrobe around him.

I stumbled up the steps and into the brightly lit hallway. I was exhausted. I was frightened. I was utterly miserable and near tears. I could not stand another minute of it all.

I was home.

3

Morning always comes, and a proper breakfast and a pot of coffee are touchingly sufficient to improve my point of view in most circumstances.

I found that the sunlight in the cool mountain air of Kabul was an illumination instead of the bombardment it had been on the plains below. The dismal shadows of the night before began to dissolve themselves into a comfortable household and—reluctantly—I began to feel at ease. Most of the day had passed, however, before I realized that I was actually enjoying myself.

The stern man who had ushered us into the house last night was identified as the head of the household staff: Gul Baz Khan, bearer, a Pushtun from Peshawar whose preeminent listing on the front gate was supported by his severe dignity. He was overwhelmingly, impeccably efficient. He spoke only when spoken to. His crisp instructions to the other servants brought immediate action. He awed me. He meant to.

Our host was planning to return to America soon, and it occurred to me that the bearer might be demonstrating his skill with such punctilio so that I would decide to keep him on. I was wrong. Behind that poker face Gul Baz was casing the situation and deciding whether he would keep us.

Shuffling about in command of the kitchen was a tall, balding older man who in shape and face very closely resembled a thoughtful walrus. This was Mohammed Ilyas, also a Peshawari, and a master of the tepid cuisine which, so far as I can gather, the British voluntarily imposed upon themselves in India. A shy, gentle man, Ilyas would peer anxiously around the corner of the dining-room doorway as we ate. When noticed, he would smile in embarrassment and, touching a finger to his karakul hat in a quick respectful gesture, he would murmur, "I hope Madame is pleased," and back hastily out of sight.

The owner of the fiercely unkempt visage which had first greeted our arrival was a former *batcha*—a houseboy—name unknown and unneeded, for he was departing that very day for his village. His place had already been taken by a red-haired, not very clever young man named Mohammed Kalim, the first of a series of not very clever young men who pumped the water, chopped the wood, opened the gate, and performed similar necessary but undemanding tasks under the commanding eye of Gul Baz Khan.

If little could be said against Kalim, little could be said for him, either, except that he was consistently good-natured and had no objection to killing chickens for the cook. He observed me covertly as he went about with his twig broom, glancing away sheepishly if I happened to catch his eye. I don't recall that he ever spoke to me directly.

Finally, there was the object of the mysterious password exchanged the night before: Jimmy, an evil-tempered mongrel who invariably bit anyone he could reach. "Jimmee bast-ast?" was nothing more obscure than an urgently necessary inquiry as to whether he was securely locked up. Through a window I could see him, tied in a corner of the compound, gazing balefully around the yard and grumbling to himself.

The house itself was small but comfortable, having been built by its owner along lines suggested by our friend. Radiating from the entry hall were a living room, dining room, sunroom, bedroom, bath, and kitchen; outside, along one wall of the compound, was a row of servants' rooms and storerooms. In the kitchen Ilyas managed with a smoky wood stove; but there was a galvanized iron sink with running water from a tank atop the house, pumped full throughout the day by the indefatigable Kalim. The bathroom had imported fixtures. A large wood-burning water heater could, on forty-five minutes' notice, provide enough boiling water to fill the big tin tub. The thunderous gargle of the overhead tank of the w.c. was painfully indiscreet; but at least all of the plumbing functioned well enough.

There were no closets in the house. Instead, tall Elmira cupboards—known by a process of linguistic sea-change as *al-marees*—stood in the bedroom, the hall, and the kitchen. A surprising upside-down effect was created by paneled wood ceilings and plaster floors.

Every room had wide casement windows, their sills as deep as window seats because of the thick walls of adobe brick. Like many Afghan homes, this house was set at such an angle that the windows would not get the full force of the hot summer sun, but would catch enough of the winter sunlight to heat the rooms throughout most of the day. I had seen such an arrangement once before, in a

Wisconsin home, where it was exhibited as a demonstration of the unique ingenuity of Frank Lloyd Wright. In Kabul, it seemed, it was a standard procedure.

A neat marble fireplace added a decorative touch to the living room, and, all in all, my fears about primitive living were assuaged by a brief inspection.

My social life got under way at once.

It was quite common in Kabul, when a newcomer was expected, to issue an invitation against the possibility that he or she might arrive in time to accept it. Thus there was waiting for me an invitation to have tea that very afternoon with a group of women from the small American teachers' colony. The party was on the other side of the city. It meant venturing out alone, without a word of Persian in my repertory.

I was given detailed instructions which I was totally unable to commit to memory, and a map of the route as well, with the thoughtful addition of a crudely phonetic travel vocabulary. *"Dusty rust,"* it read, "means turn right. *Dusty chop* means turn left. *Rooburroo* means go straight. *Bahss* means stop."

"That should get you there," my host said encouragingly.

Meanwhile Gul Baz had sent for a *gawdi*—the Afghan name for a tonga—and by way of precaution was engaged in giving the driver detailed instructions himself. Nervously clutching my map in one hand while I clung to the uncomfortable seat with the other, I set off.

Kabul spreads out on either side of the intruding mountain rather like the legs of a drafting compass. I was in Shahr-i-nau, a modern residential district of embassies and prosperous homes, midway along one leg. I was going to Carta Char, another new section, about as far along the other leg, and my route lay along the main streets of the city. As the skinny horse clopped placidly down the unpaved residential streets I could see nothing of the homes and gardens. Afghanistan is an orthodox Muslim country, and because purdah— the seclusion of Afghan women—was then still mandatory, high walls surrounded every compound with complete and inviolable privacy.

We turned onto a broad paved avenue that curved past government buildings and the main cinema and led to the river. This street was crowded with buses, gawdis, and, above all, pedestrians, who looked at me curiously while I as curiously looked back at them. Gradually I became aware that I was a phenomenon, a woman alone, riding openly through streets filled with an exclusively masculine population. Afghan women, shrouded in the shapeless, dull, all-enveloping *chadri*, were only shadowy, undifferentiated figures emerging occasionally from a shop or waiting at the bus-stops. The stares turned on me were neither hostile nor discourteous, just curious; later, I was to learn that my dark hair and eyes sometimes caused speculation as to whether I was indeed a foreigner or, conceivably, a daring local woman.

Shops lined the streets, their full façades open to reveal the wares piled up inside or hung from the open shutters: cigarettes, candy, pharmaceuticals, embroidered golden sheepskin coats, teapots, bolts of cloth, cones of sugar wrapped in bright colored paper, karakul hats, photographic supplies, radios. The low buildings had a worn, weather-beaten look. The plaster was often chipping off the brick at the corners, and most of them needed a fresh coat of paint. Flamboyant posters in front of the Cinema-i-Kabul advertised a romantic Indian film.

Along the stone parapets that edged the river bank, beautiful crimson carpets were hung for sale and karakul skins were spread out to bleach in the sunlight. The river at this season was a mere trickle meandering down the center of its dry bed between the walls. At the main bridge, marked by a large white mosque, the road turned the point of the mountain into the other leg of the compass and led out to Carta Char.

I had been nervously reading and rereading my instructions as we rattled along. The driver seemed to know where he was going, but I felt I should participate if only as a matter of form. After practicing the various phrases under my breath, I brought out an explosive *rooburroo*—"go ahead." That seemed fairly safe, since we were heading down a long straight avenue. It was fortunate that I had not waited longer to make my contribution, for a moment or so later the driver turned, and by the time I had consulted my map, the gawdi had stopped in front of a gate—the right one.

Most of the American teachers were living in Carta Char. Their wives had foregathered that afternoon to begin preparation for a program of Christmas carols which they hoped to present to the assembled American colony at the appropriate time. I was introduced to a dozen or more young women who immediately impressed me as the sort of ladies I was accustomed to see at certain social functions where they were usually engaged in selling crocheted pot-holders and appliquéd aprons, or serving macaroni casseroles. When I had been welcomed, we were all called upon to identify ourselves as sopranos, second sopranos, and altos. Song books were distributed, the hostess seated herself at an upright piano in one corner of the living room, and we spent half an hour or so on our feet working out the kinks in "O Come, All Ye Faithful."

Adjourning to comfortable armchairs—the house was furnished with mail-order Early American—we then got better acquainted over a quite splendid array of jelly sandwiches and angel food cake.

The ladies went out of their way to be helpful to a newcomer. They were kind: not one of them referred to the fact that I was wearing lipstick, although it was quite apparent that every one of them noticed it. They recomposed themselves with remarkable speed when I thoughtlessly lit a cigarette. And their inquiries as to my denominational preference were, if not subtle, discreet.

Out of their accumulated experience they were able to offer me considerable experience in facing the problems of housekeeping in Kabul. *E pluribus unum:* though many, these were in essence one: nothing was done properly in Afghanistan. If you really put your mind to it, however, and saw to everything yourself, life in Kabul could be almost, if not quite, just like home.

None of the women were teachers themselves: this domestic effort fully consumed their time. The availability of numerous servants only increased their burdens, since they somehow found that most servants were incompetent and all of them were dishonest. I was strongly advised to check my supply of tea and sugar daily, for that was where the thievery began.

I absorbed all of this with fascination, and when I returned to Shahr-i-nau at the end of the afternoon, I found I had a large store of interesting information to consider. It had been an instructive afternoon, though not perhaps precisely in the way intended.

That evening I visited Carta Char again for another social introduction. This time the hosts were an American-educated Afghan, a dean at the university, and his American wife—one of several American women married to Afghans who had been mentioned in lowered tones by the ladies that afternoon.

Big pots of tea were set about on low marble tables, along with bowls of pistachio nuts and an abundance of ash trays. There were only half a dozen people sitting around on the cushion-strewn couches, but the room seemed crowded. This impression was being created single-handedly by one of the guests, a dynamic man in his early thirties who was holding forth fervently on one or possibly several topics when he was interrupted by our arrival.

This was Dr. Abdul Kayeum, the director of Darul Mo'Allamein, the boarding school to which students came from all over the country to be trained as teachers. Kayeum had spent ten years or so in the United States, garnering an abundance of degrees in a variety of subjects from an assortment of major universities. He was poetically eloquent and overwhelmingly charming, with an aquiline nose and a high widow's peak that gave him somewhat the look of a benevolent Mephistopheles.

A strikingly lovely brunette sitting on one of the sofas turned out to be his wife Joan. She was an intelligent young woman from Chicago, with a delicate face, a quiet, gentle manner, and great poise, behind which lay a witty sense of humor and an endless supply of solid common sense. She promptly made a place for me next to her, and, sharing a bowl of pistachios between us, we tacitly established a friendship and settled down to enjoy the fireworks.

It was not so much that Kayeum dominated the conversation. Rather, everyone else preferred to sit back and let him keep going, occasionally interjecting a few words of stimulus whenever he showed signs of flagging. The room became smokier, the teacups were repeatedly refilled, and cigarette butts and pistachio shells piled up in the ash trays as he leaned forward from the edge of his chair, moving from one subject to another with brilliance and wit, and occasionally arguing four sides of a question with himself.

He wore a black karakul hat, which he pushed back and forth on his head in a characteristic gesture that served as a sort of punctuation to whatever he was saying. Cocked forward, it indicated a full stop or a significant conclusion; shoved to the back of his head again, it meant that he was off on another line of thought.

Everyone in the little group was in some way connected with education or with the various development programs getting under way, so the potentialities of the Afghan future were the recurring theme of the conversation. There was an edge of excitement in their talk, a glimpse of possibilities just waiting to be grasped.

Listening to them all, I began to be aware of a combination of qualities which I have since come to think of as typically Afghan— sharp intelligence, humor, eloquence, passionate patriotism, a great capacity for friendship, ill-disguised sentimentality, and a gift for astute, even sardonic, self-criticism which can pass into despair and out again as swiftly as a summer storm. By the end of the evening I had been caught up in a vision of an energetic, exasperating people about to burst into greatness unless, of course, they fell flat on their collective face. Nothing in between—nothing in the way of comfortable mediocrity—seemed conceivable.

While I have had occasion since to alter this judgment in certain details, it still serves, I think, as well as any.

The excitement lay in that sense of splendid hopes and significant accomplishments lying just ahead, within momentary reach, and a feeling that hands were already being stretched out to achieve them. In that one night Afghanistan ceased to be only a landscape to me: it became a people, a past, and, above all, a future.

My first day in Kabul had been a remarkably full one. Within less than twenty-four hours I had met the two people who were to shape most significantly the entire direction of my experience in Asia: Gul Baz Khan, under whose suave tyranny I lived, and Abdul Kayeum, for whom I taught and from whom I learned.

There were many others, of course, whom I met later and who were important; but within one day the picture was beginning to take shape.

Whatever qualms remained, I knew that I had not traveled halfway around the world in order to pretend that I had never left home. Actually, I had traveled farther that day than in all the weeks before.

4

*D*ring my first months in Kabul there was time to look about. Outside of the household I had no responsibilities; and I could not easily meddle in household affairs without treading upon Gul Baz's sensitive and efficient toes. I had expected to be teaching: my husband was busy at the university and the Teachers' Training College: but for reasons which no one could have anticipated, I had turned into an uncomfortable problem for the officials of the Royal Afghan Ministry of Public Education.

Some weeks before we left the United States the Ministry had hired me, through the cultural attaché of the Afghan Embassy in Washington. I was to teach at a lycée in Kabul, where the principal and several of the teachers were Americans. For many years Kabul had had several such schools, where European staff members were employed to teach modern languages and to introduce new educational techniques. Before the Second World War there were lycées employing French, Germans, British, and Indians. After the war had brought American achievements into high repute, the Ministry decided to add American teachers. The oldest and most prestigious school in the country was put under American direction and later, new technical schools as well.

At one time a few of the teachers at the lycée had been women. It was a boys' school, of course. There was no coeducation, and as yet there was no foreign staff in any of the girls' schools. But the students were city boys, many of them from middle-class families. Their environment was perhaps a bit more worldly and less conservative than that of the provinces. At least they were accustomed to seeing foreign women in the city, without the chadri, and so the introduction of women as teachers had been accomplished without much real difficulty. The Ministry therefore had no reservations about hiring me.

The contracts had been signed, passage booked, and tickets bought; household effects had been shipped off. Friends and relatives were all but gathered for farewells at the pier when the cultural attaché called unhappily from Washington. He had just received a cable from Kabul canceling my appointment immediately for the one reason which no one had foreseen because no one had imagined it possible: the director of the school—the *American* director of the school—had flatly refused to have a woman on the staff. He had apparently threatened to resign if one were forced upon him.

The Ministry was caught completely off guard and in a rather nasty box. They would have expected some difficulty if the principal had been, say, a conservative Afghan of oldfashioned views, but they had simply assumed that there would be no problem with an American. Now, quixotically, while the orthodox Muslim administration was willing to accept change as progress, the standard-bearer of enlightened progress was adamant against it. His resistance caught them off guard and left them nonplused. And embarrassed. On the one hand, he was behaving presumptuously. On the other, he had just recently been appointed to a prestige position which was not only an important concern of the Ministry but, as a matter of fact, indirectly of interest to the American Embassy as well. Neither his resignation or discharge, nor an open dispute would have been pleasant—especially in the fairly limited confines of official and diplomatic circles, where rumor and gossip were, if not the lifeblood, at least the adrenalin in the social veins.

They were annoyed; they were regretful; but perforce they cabled Washington to head me off. As the attaché was aware, it was too late. We were ready to sail. He was an amiable man who was genuinely distressed by the news he brought, and he tried to soften the blow by being hopeful. He was sure that there would be other positions available for me once I got to Kabul. He would write to the Ministry about it at once. All in all, he was as reassuring as he could manage to be, by long distance, and with cautious diplomatic noncommitment.

Thus, within a day or two of arriving in Afghanistan, I was sitting in the office of the Minister of Education, asking about a job. He received me very graciously, but I do not suppose that he could really have been very glad to see me, for, it turned out, there was simply no job available. The Ministry had limited foreign currency with which to hire teachers, and that had already been allotted. My actual arrival in Kabul—my incontestable, corporeal presence—was, I soon realized, an embarrassment and a nuisance to the Ministry, the American Embassy, and in sum to practically everyone concerned except, presumably, the man who had refused to have me hired. He apparently felt that if I chose to exist and to perpetrate that existence in Kabul, that was quite my own responsibility.

The Minister was more concerned, he was sympathetic, he even tried to be optimistic. Although there were no openings at present, he assured me that he would do his best to search one out and something would certainly be found. Not, perhaps, immediately, of course, since the school year was drawing to a close. But as the long vacation began in December and lasted till the beginning of March, I could not be teaching then anyway. And he thought it was likely— indeed, he was hopeful—that some arrangement could be made for me when the new term opened in the spring. The difficulty was that there were so few schools with staff openings for Americans (which meant, funds). Of these, only the lycée had ever had women on the faculty and unfortunately that staff was now . . . well . . . full. The technical school was completely masculine, and devoted to machines and motors anyhow. Perhaps someone might decide to leave a position somewhere—although of course as yet there was no indication of that. Or, just possibly the university might have a place for me and might be able to arrange the funds—yes, that seemed like a good idea.

At any rate, he was very hopeful and he would see to the matter as soon as possible. And in the meantime I should not worry myself about it, because the problem was certain to be solved.

It occurred to me privately that, as I was now there on the spot, he entertained some hope of persuading the American director to change his mind after all. But the Minister had already labored through that issue. This was strictly my own illusion, and I was quickly disabused of it.

Within a week of our arrival the director of the school came to call. His purpose was, ostensibly, to visit our host, who had been slightly ill in bed for a day or two, and to welcome the newcomers, but he pointedly made it clear that I would not under any circumstances work at his school as long as he had any say in the matter.

We were of course very cordial and took an immediate dislike to one another. He was an affable, self-assured, close-shaven man in his late thirties, with that rehearsed charm which is cultivated by people who decide to get ahead in life: the sort of charm which is mustered by visible effort and yet turns out to be no more than what ordinarily passes as common courtesy. One was tempted to suspect that he smiled at himself in the mirror every morning for just a moment or two too long.

He made no reference to the canceled contract, and on the whole we remained within the boundaries of conventional comments on the rigors of the trip from Peshawar. But he did manage to discourse with great vigor on the well-known truth that woman's duty is *Kinder, Kirche, Küche.* He was vibrantly enthusiastic over his own good fortune in having married a woman who recognized that fact and didn't go running about trying to do all sorts of things that were beyond her. It was certainly true that she did not go running about: she rarely appeared even at such ladies' teas as the one that had greeted me, and he usually came to parties alone, explaining with a rueful smile that his wife had decided to stay at home with the children. It seemed that they too did not trust servants.

So, with unwavering amiability and fathomless mutual animosity, we both knew exactly where we stood. It was perfectly clear that there was nothing for me to do but wait and hope, visiting the Ministry of Education from time to time as the weeks and then the months went by, to see if something had indeed turned up, or soon would. It never had; it was always about to. The leaves turned yellow and dropped; the gardens were withered with frost; the ground froze and the dull skies of approaching winter overhung the city. And I remained at liberty.

I explored the city, and went to parties, and tried to learn something about this land in which I suddenly found myself a visitor, and in which I was apparently unable to be of much use. One morning a sudden unexpected quivering of me and, to my surprise, everything around me reminded me that this was an earthquake zone. It was my first earthquake, mild enough to do no harm but strong enough to engage my interest. I immediately consulted Gul Baz Khan on the subject of earthquakes and he obligingly told me all he knew, which ran to vivid details of the terrible shock which razed the city of Quetta, where, as it happened, he had been at the time. This sent me hurrying down to the U.S. embassy library, where I looked up the history of the area as thoroughly as I could; I then came home and went about the house stringing up a complicated system of little bells, designed to sound the alarm in case the house came tumbling down in the middle of the night. I found myself lying awake for the next several nights, straining to hear that crucial first faint tinkle; so I went around the house again taking down these nuisances and consigning my future to the fates.

It was time to get ready for winter. Every day the skies seemed to settle more heavily over the mountains. The light was gray; the sky was gray; the city was gray and bare. In the bazaars, men wrapped themselves away in heavy coats. I got a pair of knee-high Turkoman boots as supple as slippers and was enormously pleased with them. Gul Baz ordered sawdust for the big black heating stoves and set them up, ugly but cozily efficient, in the house, and the woodseller came to negotiate our winter supply. This was a contest calling for sharp wits and sharper eyes. It required every member of the household, straining alertness to the utmost, to keep the woodman and his two helpers from robbing us in a dozen different ways. They short-weighted, juggled the scales, put a surreptitious foot on the wood to weigh it down, even tried to resell the same faggots to us over and over if we would let them, and had a new trick to replace every one we discovered. It was a game, and all in the highest good spirits, except for Gul Baz's management of our team. When we caught the woodseller cheating, he laughed heartily and it was our point; when we didn't, I imagine he must have laughed even harder. The transaction took most of a day. Then we shook hands all around and he retired with his winnings.

It was for me one of the satisfactions of life in Kabul to be made aware of the reality of the earth and its seasons and to be forced to shape life to their demands. The cords of kindling stacked neatly in the garage were tangible assurance of security against the coming winter. I hate the cold, and yet it pleased me that as the grasses withered with frost and the small animals were driven to their burrows, we too were forced to provide, so that like them we might emerge again into the first tentative sunlight of spring. Even the shiverings of the earthquake, which were echoed in uneasiness, gave me a strange satisfaction. Not that I wished for tragedy, of course; but for me the pride and pleasure of being human are more fully savored when they are set off against that vast realm the earth, its latent power, its unheeding courses. Our triumphs and disasters take on fresh shape and color when we feel the forces we live with, which the insulation of our lives now often contrives to conceal.

A forgotten part of me came back to life as I became aware of the delight of being sheltered, or observed the world responding to the changing year. There was a reawakening of perspective and with it a different sense of life, as though I had become aware of my own pulse and heartbeat.

But I felt that I was idling, which I have never learned to do gracefully. With every passing day I fretted more about my sense of uselessness. So I was glad for a chance to do some private tutoring.

An Afghan Jew, an energetic young businessman who had handled some matter or other for us, used to stop by from time to time to polish up his conversational English. He was planning to emigrate soon to the United States, living meanwhile with two uncles who had similar plans. All three of them had sent their families ahead to visit with relatives in Israel and had taken up bachelor quarters together. One day he explained to me that his elder uncle knew very little English and wished to know if I could give him lessons. I immediately agreed, and invited him to bring his uncle Shaban to tea the next day so that we could meet.

They arrived promptly at the appointed time, which was rather unusual in Kabul, where one could be as much as an hour late without being considered discourteous. Shaban Ibrahim was completely unlike his ebullient nephew: a dignified man in his early fifties, unobtrusively well tailored, soft-spoken, almost courtly in his courtesy, and very reserved. One could guess from his manner that he was customarily self-assured, so that he was shy and ill at ease at finding himself awkwardly walled off by language. For, despite his nephew's earlier assurances, he really knew no English at all, beyond a few words of greeting. His own sense of unease seemed to surprise and disturb him, as if an attack of vertigo had unexpectedly dislocated his equilibrium.

It was obvious that he was no bazaar shopkeeper; nor was he a crafty manipulator of the money-changer mentality which permeates much of the business world in the Near East. A wealthy import and export dealer, Shaban had the same look of solid estimable substance and judicious self-esteem which you may see gazing out steadfastly from the eighteenth-century portraits of worthy New England merchants. Indeed, for many years he had been the doyen of the Jewish community in Afghanistan, respected alike both in his own community and in the wider circles of business and government in which he moved.

There have been Jews in Afghanistan for centuries, for at least the thousand years of its Islamic history and—who knows?—perhaps long before that, perhaps since the days of Cyrus, or beyond.

Everything in this land stretches one hand into the present while the other reaches backward into an infinite past. It is as though each time one glanced at a flower, the earth were to fall away to reveal its web of roots twining down into dark unknown crevices. Certainly the communities of Herat and Kabul were ancient, and most Afghan Jews were native-born, as were their forefathers as far back as they knew. Others had fled to Afghanistan after the Soviet take-over in Bokhara and Tashkent, and during the Second World War there were even a few refugees from the Nazi terror who made their way across the Middle East to sanctuary here.

By and large their fortunes paralleled those of the nation as a whole: the Muslim world had traditionally been more hospitable to them than Europe. Although Afghanistan is constitutionally an Islamic state and they had to put up with some restrictions which affected all non-Muslims there (for there are small Sikh and Hindu groups, too), they were citizens, and many of them had prospered. The war which broke out between the newborn state of Israel and its Arab neighbors did not disturb their position. Afghanistan is not an Arab country, and the Afghans did not consider it at all their war. As a Muslim nation, it murmured the requisite formalities of sympathetic solidarity with its Muslim brethern and then went its own way, unconcerned.

But Israel did have an unsettling effect within the Jewish community itself. For the Jews of Afghanistan, devout and traditional, the creation of Israel was the ancient dream come true; the ancient promise so often recited had been kept, and many of them left to find their places in the Promised Land. This had led our friends to think of emigration, but they were unusual in choosing to go to America.

Shaban, his nephew explained for him, hoped to leave within a few months, as soon as he could wind up his business affairs, so he needed to learn English quickly. I promised to do my best and produced a textbook for him. He seemed pleased with the arrangements for lessons and, in turn, invited us to come to dinner on the following Friday evening.

When their servant ushered us into the ill-lit, cavernous living room of the silent house they shared, we found our three hosts sitting stiffly in a row on an ugly uncomfortable sofa, as though they had been ready and waiting for hours. At once they stood up, all together, bowed, shook hands, murmured greetings, and sat down again. They offered cigarettes, a drink. Then the conversation collapsed, exhausted while everyone tried to think of some way to revive it.

The room baldly displayed their enforced bachelorhood. They were prosperous men and not unworldly, but there was not a single object there which suggested comfort—nothing beyond the irreducible necessities of graceless sofas and empty marble-topped tables. Even the flowers stuck into vases here and there in honor of the occasion seemed as stiff and uncomforting as bunches of stalagmites. With their families gone, they had pooled their loneliness without diminishing it, moving together into the big empty house with only a rather gruff manservant to take care of them. I had a sudden vision of them huddling together, as it were, for comfort on some cold night, like the Gish sisters in peril. The temporary quality of their lives, their almost daily expectation of departure, their dependence on the postal service, which brought disembodied snatches of life to them from their pretty wives and children—all locked them into a forlorn limbo.

They rarely entertained, and they seemed almost surprised to have a woman at their table again; they all but drowned me in solicitude. The dinner was very good although the conversation was a strain. Shaban refused to attempt English. His painfully shy brother seemed to know none at all. The nephew was kept hectically busy throughout the meal trying to sustain a social exchange which involved a great many repetitions of, "What? What did he say?" and long explanations of every explanation. As we sat over coffee, the three men consulted briefly in Persian and he turned again to explain.

"It is Sukkoth, you know," he said. (I did not know, but I nodded politely.) "There is a family across the street—they have built a Sukkoh in their garden. Would you like to go there to see it? They have invited."

Sukkoth, the harvest festival. I had not seen a Sukkoh for years, although when I was small I always thought that they were very pretty: the little booths of trellis, trimmed with leaves and pieces of fruit, put up to symbolize the arbors in the harvest fields of Judaea so many centuries ago. It would be pleasant to go—and, anyhow, ungracious to refuse. Besides, our conversation seemed to have reached its uttermost limits. So we all went out into the shadowy street, and the men led the way to a gate some yards away. At their knock, we were let into a dark courtyard and led through a house, its rooms well lighted but vacant. Then we stepped through another outer door and I stood still, astonished.

I was in a large pavilion, perhaps twenty feet square or more, set up in a courtyard. Its high framework was of straight peeled saplings set into the earth. Overhead, fresh green boughs were thickly interwoven into a fragrant roof. The walls were deep-red carpets, hung like tapestries from the outer roof poles. They glowed in the warm yellow light of oil lamps, while more carpets covered the hard-packed earth into a floor. Around the sides of the room bright cushions and smaller rugs were profusely heaped and great brass trays were set out before them, filled with steaming pilaus, fresh fruits, pomegranates, dates, and almonds.

Family and friends, aunts and uncles, grandparents, the youngest children—all were sitting about on the cushions, eating, talking, laughing. As we entered they looked up and paused, and in that moment, before they rose to greet us, two thousand years slipped away and I might have been standing in the ancient fields of Judaea.

For at the end of the room, amid the cushions, a young woman knelt beside a child, her face turned to us. And that face was the face of Rebecca at the well, it was Rachel, it was Sarah, it was Ruth gleaning the fields beneath the eyes of Boaz; for that face Jacob labored seven years, and yet another seven, in the service of Laban. Eugéne Delacroix painted that face; William Blake saw it in his Visions; and Solomon sang of it. But I had never known that they were not dreaming.

She was perhaps less than twenty years old, but queenly and tall: *like the cedars of Lebanon:* the words seem to shape themselves. Her face was oval; her skin, smooth and faintly olive; her nose was high, arched, and aquiline; and her eyes—enormous eyes, shining, incredibly dark and liquid, utterly serene—were such eyes as I have never seen before or since, except only in a book of the carvings from the palace of Ashurnasirpal, and those were not gentle, like hers.

Her black hair lay smooth and glossy, drawn back under a flowing head scarf. When she rose, I saw that she was seven or eight months with child; but as she moved across the pavilion to welcome us, she held herself with such grace that her heavy body, in flowing robes, seemed even to enhance the beauty of her movements and there was a richness, as of poetry, about her.

She was mistress of this house. Around her were gathered her younger sisters, the smallest perhaps seven or eight years old; and each of them turned to us that same face. Her parents were there, and other relatives, but in none of their faces was there a sign of that proud unaware beauty. Her husband looked at us from time to time, to see if we had recognized her splendor, and threw admiring glances at her of which she was apparently oblivious. We were warmly welcomed; our plates were heaped with fruit. The company took up the thread of the evening again, singing and talking. Incongruously, one of the men brought out a short-wave radio and everyone was hushed as he tuned in a program of music from Israel.

As the children grew sleepy, they curled up quietly on their cushions, for the family lived in this Sukkoh throughout the long holiday. A breath of wind occasionally stirred the leaves overhead and swayed the hanging carpets. The sweet scent of ripe fruit and contentment overhung the warmth of the room. The young wife moved about, attending to the wants of her guests: a presence, an aura of a dream.

Outside again, in the frost-touched midnight, the desert stars glittered faintly, far away, and the chalky light of the pale full moon froze the streets and the high walls into a vista of ancient memory. And I thought: I have seen Ur of the Chaldees, I have sat in the tents of Abraham.

5

*T*he household had quickly fallen into a pattern of comfortable familiarity under the suave management of Gul Baz Khan, who ran domestic affairs with a practiced hand—making allowances, of course, for the eccentricities of those who dwelt therein but never, never allowing the reins to slip from his accomplished fingers. He respectfully agreed to do things my way, continued to do them his way, and we ignored the difference. Of the half-dozen people who lived and worked within the compound, he was the only one who was completely indispensable.

I never formally hired him. When illness forced our host to return to America, Gul Baz simply did not depart, and we never discussed the subject of his employment. To raise it would have put both of us in a delicate position which could lead only to unwanted disaster: if the question came up, my status as employer would require me to tell him I had decided to hire him. On the other hand, his status as the best bearer on either side of the Border required that *he* make the decision. Therefore, if I declared that I would keep him on, he would be forced to decline to be kept. The only solution to the impasse was not to mention the matter at all, and so we never did— except on one or two crisis occasions.

These occurred mysteriously and unpredictably, for reasons which he never coherently explained and which I have therefore never understood in the slightest. In the apparent clutch of some black mood, Gul Baz once or twice decided that some incredibly delicate barometer totally unknown to us had hinted at a faint lack of complete satisfaction with every aspect of his services. After brooding on this briefly, he would announce (invariably during lunch) that his services were obviously no longer wanted and so he was leaving for Peshawar at once.

When this occurred, I intuitively took the only possible course of action: I promptly burst into tears, rushed from the room, and flung myself weeping on the bed. This immediately demolished his resolve. There were a few minutes of uproar, while he swore that no power on earth could tear him from our service and I sobbed that he had never been less than perfect in the performance of his duties. Of course neither of us bothered to listen; as in the ancient Greek tragedies, this ritual drama performed the function of catharsis. It gave him an excuse to stay on, while it warned us that he was feeling touchy. When we had both subsided, he would disappear into the kitchen to put on the kettle, I would mop my eyes, we would have a cigarette together over a fresh cup of tea, and no more would ever be said about the whole incident.

For the most part, however, our relationship was smooth and cheerful and our positions were quite clear: he had hired me to be his employer, for which I was happy and grateful. I had good reason to be. He ran the house; he ran us; he took care of every problem, ministered to every need before it arose; he played Dutch uncle, arranged charming surprises, advised us on money, personal affairs, social demeanor, and a general philosophy of life; and he kept us thoroughly well-informed on all the local gossip. Did an American gentleman shoot and/or possibly poison his wife? Less than an hour after the event, Gul Baz was hovering over the dining table, serving up the details of the massacre with the mashed potatoes. Did an ambassador issue a dinner invitation? Gul Baz was ready with advice: "Please to be careful, khanum. His cook spits in the soup."

If his scope was amazing, his accuracy was uncanny.

Gul Baz Khan, of Nevekali Village, near Peshawar, was about forty years old when I met him. He was not sure of his exact age, since his birth had not been recorded, but he had heard that he was born shortly before the First World War, and pepperings of gray had begun to show in his black hair. He was a slender, wiry, handsome man of middle height and meticulously neat, even natty, appearance. His face was tanned and deeply lined and, despite a lifetime of self-disciplined stoicism, revealing: the lines between his brows came from a stern scowl which he habitually assumed, while the creases in his cheeks derived equally from severity and—like the crow's-feet about his eyes—from the exuberant laughter which lay just under his austere surface. He usually wore a small trim mustache, which he occasionally shaved off for a day or two just for the sake of change.

It was a shrewd, intelligent, worldly face; he was a shrewd, intelligent, worldly man, at once sophisticated and ingenuous.

Life had molded his features as wind and water carve a sandstone outcropping into significant form, but as he was a man of will and intensity, the essential molding force came from within, and his penetrating gaze always seemed to be measuring the world around him against the private yardstick of his own character. His dignity was unassailable; but his equilibrium was not. Despite his most earnest efforts to maintain a stern façade, his warmth, his laughter, his kindness and high temper were constantly breaking through. He loved nonsense, and he often doubled over with silent laughter— retreating to the kitchen, if necessary, to avoid compromising his dignity before guests. He was a quixotic man, a temperamental man of many contradictions; but tying them all together were the two threads of his unswerving sense of duty and his unbending pride.

These qualities led him eventually to request that I dismiss Ilyas, his friend of many years, his fellow villager, and his senior. He had brought Ilyas to Kabul and recommended him for the job, but when he suspected that the older man was cheating on the household accounts, no matter how slightly, his sense of honor made it unbearable to him.

Unlike Gul Baz Khan, Mohammed Ilyas could read and write, and in English—slowly, awkwardly, with great effort, but with greater pride; and he insisted on writing out his accounts. Every afternoon he would sit down at the kitchen table with a schoolboy's penny copybook and a stub of pencil, and laboriously mark down his purchases for the day. Then he would present the book to me for my approval, hovering anxiously in the doorway while I deciphered the list.

"Is correct, madame?" he would ask. "Tomatoes very high this week."

I did not enjoy the ritual. Ilyas's spellings were peculiar and sometimes incomprehensible, but I didn't want to tell him so and tried to struggle through them silently. Moreover, I did not know the prices in the bazaar, the sums struck me as modest anyhow, and, finally, I preferred to trust him. But both men insisted that I check their accounts methodically, and I was so touched by Ilyas's transparent pride in having me read what he had written that I had no heart to deny him the pleasure.

But one afternoon Gul Baz, who always listened to the financial discussions, came to me privately and told me that Ilyas had been kiting the accounts, that he had remonstrated with him about it, had been ignored, and had concluded that I must discharge Ilyas or at the very least reprimand him. The idea appalled me. I found it difficult enough to give orders to a man old enough to be my father: our conversations always turned into awkward exchanges of deference. Moreover, there was something broken in Ilyas, some spring of pride and purpose that had been snapped in him, which made his anxiety to please somehow embarrassing. He had spent most of his life as the bearer for a very important British official in India. For thirty years he had managed the affairs of that large household, superintending a numerous staff, seeing his employer rise to the governorship of a province, submerging his own life in the life of that family. Then British rule came to its end, and India was partitioned. Ilyas's employer had him flown home to safety from the bloody horrors of the Delhi riots, but there was little else he could do; like other officials, he was leaving for England. And so, when he was nearly sixty, Mohammed Ilyas had had his world and the focus of his life swept away from him, and was left with a new world in which he had no part. He had cracked then, into a hundred pieces, and it was Gul Baz Khan who had helped him to pull himself together, and had found a place for him.

He was indeed lucky to have found a job as a cook. Many other bearers in the same circumstances remained unemployed, or had to take menial jobs; a new arrival at Dean's Hotel would be besieged by them—sad, proud, defeated men, offering a handful of letters of reference half hopelessly. But Ilyas was no longer the master of a household, leader of a corps. And there were no more balls, no vast formal dinner parties and elaborate soirees to be managed to perfection. His world had shrunk, and even in that diminished realm he was not supreme. He was too old to look to the future, and so he continued to shrink and die within.

He tried to keep up the appearance of his more splendid days, and I helped him as much as I could. His eyes would light up for a moment when he heard that there would be dinner guests, and he would consult me elaborately about the details of the menu. Often he put forth great effort for even a most ordinary family meal. He served up puddings of pale lavender and green in stripy layers, or surprised me with a bowl of hot toasted pistachios and a fine cake at teatime. One bitter midnight in December I arrived home after the long weariness of the journey from Peshawar, to find a cheerful fire crackling in the living-room fireplace and an enormous Christmas fruitcake set out for me on the coffee table. On the top of the cake, spelled out in raisins, were the words "MERY XMS," and as usual, Ilyas was hovering anxiously in a doorway.

"Is spelled right, madame?" he asked softly.

"Perfectly, Ilyas," I told him. His faded face shone with pleasure. Then he touched his cap shyly and disappeared.

I simply could not face the task of humiliating the man. To accuse him was utterly beyond me, and firing him would be impossible. Even if Gul Baz was right, it could only involve a few cents a day. I much preferred to ignore the whole thing. I explained my feelings to Gul Baz Khan and suggested that we quietly overlook the problem.

"After all," I pointed out, "he is a good cook, he tries to please me. And he has had hard luck. And he is not a young man."

Gul Baz said no more about it to me, but he was clearly dissatisfied. Kind as he was, where his professional standards—and most particularly honesty—were concerned, he was utterly uncompromising and inflexible. Every day I heard the two men arguing in Pushto in the kitchen, and I could guess what it was about. So I was not surprised when Ilyas came to me one day and explained that family matters required his presence at home. I was sorry, after all, to see him go, but I was relieved to have the issue resolved without me and I knew that Gul Baz had felt dishonored by his friend's lack of pride.

Where duty and his honor were involved, Gul Baz was completely intolerant, but in a long career as a skilled administrator—for actually, that is what he was—he often was forced to suffer fools. He never learned or really tried to learn to do it gladly, but while dishonesty in the slightest degree was intolerable to him, stupidity was merely infuriating and he bore it with what patience he could muster. It was an inescapable part of his daily existence, for the houseboys were an unending trial, their ineptitude a torment to a man of his precision skill. From time to time his patience would give way and he would come storming into the living room. "That damn boy!" he would cry. "I'll kill that damn boy!" And off he would rush to set some mangled task to proper order.

It was not really intolerance on his part. The batchas were almost invariably slow and clumsy: someone who was quick and skillful was unlikely to take a job that consisted largely of chopping wood, pumping water, sweeping floors, and running errands. Gul Baz always hoped to find a young man who would look on the job as an apprenticeship, as he had done twenty-five years before—someone who would be anxious to learn the routines in order to step up to stewardship himself. But (like the hired girls of small-town America a generation or two ago) most batchas were village boys who came into town with no higher goal than getting a heady taste of city life and accumulating a bit of cash with which they could go home in style. In fact, this pattern was so commonplace that once when a very clever young man took the job, Gul Baz found himself disturbed and suspicious at the phenomenon, and he was quite correct. When we all went off to the wedding of Gul Baz's son Sher and left the household in the hands of that shrewd young man, he moved his wife in and turned the place into a bordello during our absence. This resulted in his prompt discharge. Nevertheless, a bemused policeman was stationed on our corner for several months.

After that, Gul Baz contented himself with less ambitious youths. They seldom stayed more than a few months, and invariably left just when he was beginning to hope that they were learning the job. Sometimes they would return months later, when they had spent their savings, so that we had less a series of houseboys than an erratic rotation. For Gul Baz, this had some of the nerve-straining aspects of Russian roulette.

Kalim, who left shortly after my arrival, never reappeared, but he was memorable because his departure solved the problem of Jimmy. Jimmy was a weight on everyone's conscience. He had been a perfectly normal, friendly dog (or so I was told) until a house guest who obsessively disliked dogs whacked him heavily over the head one day with a dictionary. Upon his recovery, Jimmy developed a thorough and un-selective dislike for humanity and thereupon began his career of biting people. He had bitten everyone he could reach, including our host, several cooks, houseboys and gardeners, numerous guests, and on several occasions Gul Baz, whom he nevertheless seemed to dislike less than he disliked everyone else. Putting his food before him was a difficult daily maneuver. Obviously something had to be done.

We consulted, and searched our souls. We considered Jimmy's essential victimization. We considered ours. Finally we decided that the poor dog had best be put out of the way and so, with heavy consciences, arranged for our physician to give him a painless hypodermic. Kalim dug a grave in one corner of the yard. Gul Baz and the other bitees—in short, the whole household—moped about, waiting for the doctor to arrive. Instead, his servant came with a note saying that he would have to postpone the job till another day. In the general relief, Kalim hastily filled in the grave and volunteered to take Jimmy home with him to his village in the valley of Panjsher.

"But, Kalim," I pointed out, "he bites people. He'll bite your family."

Kalim, always shy, spoke up for the only time in my experience.

"I know that," he said softly to the wall above my head. "I don't like my father-in-law."

And so Kalim left, taking Jimmy and his rope-strung bed, with our blessings. To Gul Baz's chagrin, however, he also took a bottle of ink, a bottle of shoe polish, and a bright-red, oversized Santa Claus suit which had been stored away from Christmas to Christmas; it was designed to be worn with several pillows stuffed inside, and could have held three of him. Unlike Gul Baz Khan, I did not object to the larceny, but the choice of items gave me pause, for Kalim was illiterate, he wore only wooden clogs, and I could not imagine him going about his village in red flannelette and white cotton batting.

Although he never returned to Kabul, I did see him a year or so after his departure, during a visit to Panjsher. I was riding on a very tiny donkey at the time and feeling ridiculous and extremely inhumane, when Kalim came walking down the road and greeted me. I asked him about Jimmy, and he assured me that Jimmy was well and happy. I asked him about his father-in-law, and he smiled shyly. Seated as I was on the sad-faced little burro with my heels almost touching the ground, I felt that I was in no position to start being self-righteous about the ink or the shoe polish or the Santa Claus suit, so their ultimate ends remained forever mysterious.

In spite of repeated disappointments with houseboys, laundrymen, and other functionaries essential to his ideas of a household, Gul Baz never gave up his efforts to build a proper staff. He found an excellent gardener from the village of Bimaru, which lay a mile or two north of Kabul, just beyond the low mountains which hemmed in the municipal airport. Ahmed-jan preferred to keep his home in Bimaru rather than move into the compound, so Gul Baz arranged for him to bring in each morning the household supplies of butter, vegetables, and chickens, which were available in better quality in the village than in the city bazaars.

The gardener was a small, nondescript-looking man with pale eyes and a snub nose, whose dress always seemed to be made up of a number of loose turban ends and flopping shirt tails jumbled together, from which his thin arms and legs and timid face projected as from a bundle of rumpled laundry. He was kind, he was eager to please, and very skillful.

In a desert land every blossom is precious. Afghans respond with acute sensibility to green and flowering things, and they cherish their gardens with delight. It is a commonplace to see a tall, tough, rifle-bearing countryman striding along the road with a flower cupped gently in his hand or tucked over his ear. In the springtime the ordinary smoke-and-dust smells of Kabul were overhung with the rich sweetness of acacias in bloom behind all those walls. Tall ragged clumps of sunflowers stood nodding and blinking brightly at odd corners in the bazaars; and on Friday, the Sabbath holiday, the public gardens were filled with strollers enjoying the colorful formal beds of marigolds and petunias and the flashing scarlet cannas which I, for their spikiness, could never like.

From April, when the rainy season ended, through the cloudless powder-dry months of summer and autumn, Ahmed-jan sedulously pumped and carried water to irrigate his plantings, weeded and hoed and nursed each leaf and tendril. As each flower in its season faded away, he carefully shook the seeds from the withered blooms into little packets made of torn newspaper, which he folded away against the coming spring. He set up shades to protect the young plants from the blasting sun in hot weather, and covered them with straw when the frosts came, pulling it aside for an hour or so of sunlight at the warmest hours. When the first snows were already white across the valley, he would lift away the straw packing to bring nasturtiums and asters to my table in December.

Once he invited us all to a wedding party in Bimaru, where we sat about for hours in a courtyard lit by the unearthly white glare of propane lamps, while musicians sang endlessly of love and dancers moved in and out of the shadows. He smiled constantly with shy pride, and showed us about his home, the walls of which were painted with a garden as brightly florid as any he drew from the earth.

So, with what he brought and what he bred, Ahmed-jan unobtrusively provided food for both body and soul, and in the end he even provided the houseboy Gul Baz Khan had been searching for: the teachable one, who would listen and learn and take pride in his work. But that did not happen until Gul Baz had repeatedly endured the conscientious ineptitude of Maullahdad, a dismally dull youth who worked for us spasmodically, perhaps six months or so of each year altogether. He disappeared whenever he had eight or ten dollars saved and reappeared whenever it was spent. Maullahdad was uniquely and eccentrically unteachable, and Gul Baz Khan could hardly bear him; but he was honest and amiable and he had, moreover, a knack for turning up, smiling his vacuous knuckle-headed smile, just when he was needed—which is to say, just when someone else had been fired—so he was always rehired.

"That damn boy!" That cry, the consummation of days of frustration and fury, rang out to heaven most often when Maullahdad was among us.

One afternoon, after we had acquired a yardful of dogs, Gul Baz burst into the living room with more than his usual fury; he looked driven.

"That damn boy!" he shouted. "He's eat my curry!"

All the servants had food allowances, with which they bought bread and rice; in addition, they were free to use the kitchen supplies of tea, sugar, and such staples, and to ask for anything else they wanted, so they usually dined according to their own rather undemanding tastes. Gul Baz, however, was something of a gourmet and regularly prepared one or another delicious curry for his evening meals, which the others declined as being too spicy. He ordinarily made enough for the next day's breakfast as well, and left it in the icebox over night.

For some days past, the breakfast portion had been disappearing between the dusk and the daylight. Finally he had taken the matter up with Maullahdad, who denied any knowledge whatsoever of the vanishing act.

"What shall I do?" he cried. "He's eat my curry every night! I know it!"

"Well," I asked, "how did he explain it? How did your curry disappear if he didn't take it?"

"He's say the dogs eat it up."

That appeared to leave an opening for logic. "Why don't you tell him that the kitchen door is locked and the icebox is hooked shut. How could a dog open it?"

"I tell him that, khanum." This, with anguish.

"And?"

"He's say he's is smart dogs."

I sat silent, trying to look profoundly thoughtful. But Gul Baz had not been so easily nonplused.

"I asked him, khanum," he went on, in a furious plea for logic, "how can a dog wash the pan and put it away in the cupboard afterwards?"

I hardly dared contemplate what the boy's answer had been, but I asked softly, "And what did he say?"

"He's say he's is *very* smart dogs!"

Frenzy and despair mingled in his voice. "He's think I'm a foolish mans! Khanum-sahib, I tell you now, if that boys eat my curry again I'm going to kill him!"

Everyone was inadequate in the face of Maullahdad's logic. It was hard on all of us. But for Gul Baz, it was martyrdom.

6

Gul Baz allowed himself two major self-indulgences: one was clothing, the other was radios.

He was more than fastidious; in truth, he was a good bit of a dandy. For ordinary daily work he wore blue jeans, a sleeveless pullover, and a white or gray shirt open at the throat. These outfits were as trimly neat as his dress uniforms (which were carefully tailored to his own taste, and elegant). Indeed, his most ordinary workaday dress was so natty that the absence of a necktie was quite noticeable. It occurred to me that the poor quality of the neckties available in the bazaar might explain his avoiding them, so I once offered to order some for him from abroad. He courteously declined the offer, remarking that he would never wear anything so dangerous. This struck me as a somewhat unusual explanation, but, as always, he had sound reasoning and experience behind it. In his youth he had been a wearer of neckties, until one day he got into a fist-fight with an unscrupulous opponent who grabbed his tie and nearly strangled him. Since then, as a matter of common prudence, he had relieved himself of the danger of strangulation by declining ever again to wear a tie. He had begun with a taboo on four-in-hands and extended it to bow ties for simplicity's sake. Aside from neckwear, he was perfectly turned out at all times.

His formal wear was chosen with discriminating good taste. He had several *achkans*, the high-collared, fitted North Indian coats, which were tailored to measure in carefully chosen fabrics, his favorite being a fine pale canary-yellow English flannel. He also owned several Western-style sack suits, but for important occasions he preferred the elegant achkans, with which he always wore his newest karakul hat.

Soon after our employment agreement had been tacitly arrived at, I was informed, by a process as discreet and indefinable as telepathy, that Gul Baz expected a new brown karakul hat as his annual holiday gift. The *karakuli*, a handsome, dashing sort of headgear, is the mark of the khan, the man of substance, the urban sophisticate, as the turban usually marks the small farmer, the laborer, the villager or peasant. But in addition to this basic distinction, there was a gradation of rank by color as well as by the quality of the individual skin used for each hat. Black was standard wear: a good black karakul skin is the easiest to come by. Next, a man might rise to gray. Natural brown karakul is the rarest of colors, and consequently the fur of the elite; it is easy to find skins which have been bleached from black to brown, but these are bought by social climbers, and Gul Baz would have scorned one. There were few men indeed who wore nothing but the true brown karakul. In fact, I myself knew of only two, and one of them was by hearsay: one was Gul Baz Khan, the other His Majesty the King.

Gul Baz was a proud man, but he justified his vanity. When he was dressed for a formal occasion, he presented a strikingly handsome figure, and he knew it.

His other weakness, radios, was less justifiable, and he made very few attempts to excuse it. Theoretically, his radios were his own business because he bought them for himself. Actually, this was true only of the first one. He never requested a replacement but he always got one, for he could not afford to buy it himself and it seemed somehow unkind to make him suffer just because he was constantly burning out his set. His problem was the result of the uneven power supply of the city. New generators were to be installed at Sarobi when the dam was completed, but meanwhile the equipment still in use had been installed more than thirty years before, and the voltage varied widely throughout the day according to the demand. In the early evening, when every home was lit, the current dropped to a minute flow; but at midday, when it was least used, the power would suddenly, sharply, swing up as high as three hundred volts—far above the maximum for which appliances were made.

He had frequently been warned not to risk using his radio then, but the middle of the afternoon was his time for relaxation and socializing. His friends would begin to arrive shortly after lunch, bearers and chauffeurs from various embassies and diplomatic households, many of them old friends from Nevekali. The street outside our gate would gradually fill with an impressive array of diplomatic limousines as the cronies gathered over tea in his room. Inevitably, the radio would go on in an ear-splitting burst of music. Almost as inevitably, the radio would go off again, and some hours later he would sheepishly report that there seemed to be something wrong with it. Sometimes it needed no more than substitutes for the burnt-out tubes, but once or twice a year the damage would turn out to be irreparable, and we would journey to the bazaar to find a replacement.

Among the upper echelon of bearers in Kabul—what one might call the career men—Gul Baz was the acknowledged doyen. One of his closest friends and frequent visitors was the British ambassador's chauffeur, Ilyas's hearty, handsome younger brother, who had a gay smile and a gallant manner and often saw to it that we had a ride to a party on a stormy night, which accounted for our invariably arriving half an hour after His Excellency did, and leaving half an hour before him. Others were men of similar rank and responsibility. Almost every day the downstairs hall was filled with the lively stream of their conversation and deep bursts of laughter. But, friends and equals though they were, there was always a slight aura of deference to Gul Baz—not to age, or to position (for they were all khans), but to his personal authority.

He had had very little formal education, and of that little, he retained only the ability to print his name, slowly and carefully, in the block letters of the English alphabet; his own language had not been taught to him in any school. He spoke English fluently, but with peculiarities which seemed often to be translated from Pushto but as often seemed purely his own. He used only one pronoun—"he's"—for the third person, both singular and plural; it was completely adequate except in some of the more complicated gossip he retailed, in which case one sometimes lost strict track of who had done what to quite whom. When things went well, they "went ups by ups"; but when they went ill, they did not go downs-by-downs, they "went to mash." Sometimes, in fact, he *made* them go to mash. All in all, his conversation was vivid and in no way limited by its singularities, and his complete comprehension of a wide-ranging vocabulary forced us occasionally into pig Latin in the vain hope of keeping any secret from him.

Like many intelligent illiterates, he had a prodigious memory which he kept honed to perfection. After Ilyas's departure, Gul Baz insisted on dictating the household accounts to me daily, despite my protests. If perchance he had forgotten even the tiniest expenditure— two or three cents' worth, perhaps—he would worry himself about it for days until he could come to me and say, "You remember that fifty pul I forgot about, khanum? Last Thursday week?" I would rack my mind, or the account book, until I discovered the item. "I took the bus that day," he would explain. "That's where he's go." Then, and only then, he would be satisfied.

He had great hopes for his three sons and was very anxious that they should have a good education. He must have been well aware of what he might have accomplished if he had had schooling, but he rarely allowed himself to dwell on it; and such thoughts in no way diminished his pride in his work or in himself. Still, some months before I left Kabul, he began to study with me, although I could not teach him in his own language but only in mine; and his delight in learning to read was offset only by his painful awareness that he had come to it too late.

He had, however, had a thorough professional education, beginning when, as a boy of fourteen or so, he had taken his first job, chasing tennis balls and waiting table at the Peshawar Club. He was as firmly grounded and trained as a Swiss *hotelier*, with a similar esteem for his position. In his chosen field he would be second to none; his peers acknowledged his primacy, and so did he.

Perhaps the lack of formal education accounted for a residue of credulity and superstition in certain areas, usually dealing with *things*, which contrasted strangely with his general sophistication. There were pockets of ignorance, so to speak, where wonderment still held sway untouched, and experience could not explain or enlighten. This was neither gullibility nor half-knowledge, nor the cynicism of the partly educated. Just as most of us accept many scientific claims on faith (unless we are scientists), so he accepted tradition on similar faith. So there were simply areas where one had to tread carefully, because, for all his worldliness, he had no skepticism about the universe outside of man and was capable of complete faith and wonder.

I once thoroughly alarmed him by joking thoughtlessly about jinns, those mysterious and often dangerous spirits whose frightening powers haunt the East. It was a winter evening, early dark, early still. I was puttering about in the dimly lit kitchen, and as we worked together, he had been telling me about different kinds of jinns and how to identify the wicked ones: their feet are turned backward, like those of the Devil in Montenegro. Stupidly, in a careless attempt at a joke, I remarked that I knew several people in America who possessed those qualifications. I said it completely thoughtlessly, without even realizing that I was mocking him. Then I heard the paring knife clatter to the table and looked up to see him staring at me, his face drawn and pale.

"Is that true, khanum?" he asked quietly. "Then I think I better leave this place. I better go Peshawar-side."

For once he meant it. With a shock I realized my error and my cruelty, and tried to apologize. Over and over again I told him that I had been joking; I swore that it was not true, that I had never known, never seen, anyone with the mark of the jinn upon him. It was a trembling hour: he wanted to believe me and stay, but he truly doubted, and it was, for him, a dangerous gamble. In the end he chose to trust me, and eventually it all passed away, but for some days I could see him looking at me sidelong, speculatively, from time to time, and I knew what was in his mind.

For in his childhood he had had experiences of jinns. He told me of them, and I could find no better explanations than he. I am glad, thinking back now, that I could not, for if I could have explained them away, I am sure I would have rushed smugly to do it. He had no need of such an access of rationalism into his imagination. What would it have given him? There are times when to explain everything is to leave it all diminished. It is not always wise to tamper with other people's dreams—nor, sometimes, with their nightmares either. So I never again allowed myself to intrude on those portions of his mind where I could not honestly follow. As for myself, I am a rational child of the West, and if you ask me whether I believe in jinns, I must say that I do not; but I remember certain stories.

The same credulity that could make reality out of nightmares could make fairy tales out of the stuff of reality, and Gul Baz delighted in motion pictures and descriptions of New York or other cities where I had lived. His imagination turned their concrete and asphalt into visions of glamour and he would picture himself someday in their midst, wringing every thrill from the dream. We often spoke of a time when he would visit America, and we argued earnestly over whether he should be a guest or should manage my household there. He had traveled all over India and knew all its cities; he had been through the great Quetta earthquake, had hunted in the jungly places, killed a cobra, and done a thousand things astonishing to me, but they were all part of his own landscape and for him, my side of the world had the monopoly on adventure. It was pointless to bring his visions down to earth. He wanted only the magic dream, so together we would spin it out, for hours on end.

If Gul Baz retained a judicious awe of nature and the world of forces and things, he was astute and knowledgeable and profoundly sophisticated in the ways of man. He was beyond surprise, which gave him an advantage in any situation. He unblushingly used his shrewd, practical psychology to rule the household, depending primarily upon the techniques of silence, anticipation, and surprise. As much as possible he managed affairs on his own, consulting me for my formal approval when a matter was a *fait accompli*. His foresight was occasionally unnerving when, for example, it would occur to me that I wanted to paint a room or have a new gate put up, and asked him to call in the necessary workman, only to be told politely that he had already made arrangements.

I knew that I was in for a struggle, however, if the answer to such a request was simply, "Yes, khanum," without comment, accompanied by an immediate increase of ostentatious silent efficiency. Ordinarily any household matter—and personal matter, too—was subjected to extended, entertaining informal discussion unless, of course, guests were present. His relapse into silent formality was invariably an indication of disapproval, which meant a tug of war as I tried to discover his objections and he withdrew into adamant hauteur. If he absolutely declined to interfere, I knew that I was making a major error.

"Is not my business, khanum," he would say. "I am just your bearer. You like that carpenter? Is not for me to say anythings. Is your house, not my house." (That was not true, and he knew it, but no matter.)

Still, the carpenter, or the painter, or the bicycle desired, would not arrive; the errand would not be run; the efficiency mechanism would be politely stuck; and every day we would exchange the same dialogue until I indicated despair and he reluctantly condescended to offer his opinion. First he would launch into a series of ritual protestations about the impropriety of his meddling in our affairs, about my rights, his duties, the humble quality of his judgment, the exaltation of mine. Then suddenly he came to the point: the woodseller we had chosen was dishonest, the carpenter used unseasoned wood, the bicycle was bound to fall apart (which it did). Occasionally I argued with him. A few times I insisted and he yielded. And invariably he was right, and I was the penitent victim of my own waywardness.

Sometimes his dictum was much simpler and more encompassing: "I don't like that man." When this was the case he would not elaborate or explain, but in time I learned never to argue with that judgment. If Gul Baz Khan did not like a man, that man was to be avoided. We overruled him only once, and we all regretted it bitterly afterward.

Ordinarily he avoided the obvious exercise of power and took considerable amusement in exerting his tyranny with such deftness and seeming innocence that there was no point on which one could counterattack. Awakening us in the morning was such a case: obviously we had to get up every day, and, equally obviously, it was a necessity we never ceased to resent. Gul Baz promptly recognized that I was easily awakened and then devoted myself to a passionate attempt to pretend that I was still sleeping. It was therefore merely for him to call my bluff as skillfully as possible.

He once confided to me that waking his employers was a delicate and even dangerous problem. For instance, a young British officer who had employed him years before could be awakened only by a glass of cold water flung in his face. Gul Baz was under orders to do it, but every morning, in a convulsive reaction, the man would leap out of bed, grab his baton, and chase him about the room, whacking at him wildly. He always apologized afterward, but nevertheless Gul Baz had had to develop both a sprinting technique and a high degree of tolerance.

He found us far less dangerous and more vulnerable, and worked out an irreproachable method. He used his shoes. They squeaked.

Each morning he would rap discreetly on the door, then enter the room, carrying a tray of steaming tea; he would take up his stance at the foot of the bed and gently begin to clear his throat with increasing volume. Within moments I was awake with my eyes tightly shut, hating him. Now he would begin to rock gently back and forth on his heels, his shoes squeaking with each movement. As he got me trained my endurance wore away, and eventually he could shred my nerves with the first leathery creak. As soon as I opened a baleful eye and started to demand silence, he would thrust a cup of hot tea into my hand and swiftly step back, leaving me to juggle it as best I could. By the time I was sitting up, furious, he was standing at the door again, looking blandly innocent, respectfully attentive, and intolerably smug.

"Breakfast in five minutes," he would say, and, smiling pleasantly, turn and leave the room. The remarkable thing was that he left silently, and at all other times his steps about the house were equally unobtrusive.

In Gul Baz Khan the man and the culture were truly met. The Pushtunwali—the ancient code of honor which has cast its influence across this part of the world—is like a steel armature around which the character of each man or woman born to it is molded. In his case, if it had not been his birthright, I think he would have had to devise it for himself.

The basis of the code is honor and all that touches upon honor: pride, courage, loyalty, faith, vengeance and a fighting spirit and, on the other side of the coin, profound friendship, hospitality, deep humor, and personal respect. It offers a tough, demanding way of life, bred from an unyielding land which offers no quarter to those who dwell thereon, while at the same time it develops great warmth and kindness in reaction to that very austerity.

Traditionally it measures a man by his courage, and it measures his courage in battle. The day of invasion and counterthrust may be passing, but the blood feud still remains, in which a man may have to prove himself. This seems hard to believe, on the macadam of a modern highway where the telephone lines swing along from pole to pole and the farmers plow their fields on either side behind placid bullocks. But it is there, and from the Indus north through Afghanistan, each village is a small fortress, walled and slotted. When Gul Baz's son Sher was married, the festivities which began at the bridegroom's home were shifted, in midday, to the bride's village, a mile or more across the fields. I walked from one village to the other accompanied by a pleasant, courteous man, very alert and somewhat grim about the mouth, whose left arm was in a sling. On his right, he carried a rifle, for a vendetta was in process. He had been struck down the week before, his brother killed; and we might be ambushed as we walked the furrowed wheat fields.

But in our household in Kabul there was little occasion for Gul Baz to offer such proof of his hardihood. It never occurred to him that he was displaying courage when he stubbornly ignored a malarial attack, or silently suffered the anguish of having two or three teeth brutally drawn by a clumsy knacker in the bazaar. That was the least he would expect of himself.

On the other hand, the daily life of our rather light-hearted household gave full play to his warmth and kindness and humor. So he frequently seemed concerned that he might appear to be soft, insufficiently tough, even sentimental, and set out to stiffen himself under circumstances which offered him no scope at all. This conflict accounted for his assumption of rigid severity at incongruous moments, and for a sort of dreadful verbal ferocity with which he tried to conceal his good nature. He succeeded in fooling no one (except, perhaps, an occasional stranger) but we all played along with him, except for children and animals, who outraged him by immediately displaying complete trust in him.

Still, there were times when his standards of propriety and his pursuit of austerity could freeze him unexpectedly and leave me standing confused amid burnt-out expectations. I was taken completely by surprise when I brought home the first of our many dogs.

After Jimmy's departure, a German physician who was leaving Kabul promised to give us his cocker spaniel, but to everyone's disappointment, the dog was stolen from him. One cold gray morning soon afterward, in the last worn barren dregs of December, I saw a half-starved street dog and her litter of scrawny puppies wandering in a gutter. The week had been as drab as the heavy skies; I made a quick decision; and in a moment I was clutching a trembling little black-and-white creature that screamed shrilly in miserable terror, drawing a crowd of passers-by curious to see what form of torture I might be applying.

By the time I got home, the howling had subsided and the poor creature lay sobbing and gasping limply in my arms. I pounded on the gate, and when the batcha opened it, I sent him for Gul Baz. A moment later he appeared.

"Look," I said, holding out the puppy, "I have a surprise for you."

He glanced at the dirty little dog distastefully. "Put it back in the street, khanum," he said coldly. "Is not a good dog. I'll get you a good one."

I was taken aback and disappointed. "But I can't do that," I told him. "Look at the poor little thing!"

"Is your house, khanum," he answered stonily, drawing back to let me pass through the gate. "I can say nothings."

He ushered me into the house without further comment and, at my request, barked an order to the boy to heat water for the bathroom. While I washed the filth of the gutter off the dog he remained icily aloof. He stood a good way behind me. If I asked for a towel, he stepped quickly up to hand it to me, and promptly stepped back again. Having expressed his disapproval and being overruled, he was obviously disassociating himself completely from the affair. There was no point in discussing it. He had thoroughly withdrawn.

The puppy—a female—was too frightened to cry any more. Her body was rigid and trembling, she was pitiful. I wrapped her in an old towel, took her into the living room, and tucked her into a box set next to the heating stove. As I knelt there trying to soothe her, I heard footsteps and looked up. Gul Baz was standing behind me, severity and embarrassment mingled painfully in his expression, a thick slice of chicken in his hand.

"The little dog looks hungry, khanum," he said stiffly. Then he squatted down and fed the ecstatic puppy. She stopped sobbing, and very slowly his face relaxed, in spite of himself, into a smile.

It seemed like a good idea to get a male companion for her, and I asked Gul Baz to help me catch one. He had still not formally renounced his disapproval, but he put on his coat and came along. We captured another clumsy ball of dirty fur and were starting home with our prize when suddenly Gul Baz was not there. He was walking slowly, very slowly, increasingly slowly, yards behind. I stopped. He stopped.

"What's the matter, Gul Baz?"

He looked away at some distant point in space and cleared his throat. "I was thinking," he said, "maybe I could get one little dog for myself."

So we set up our kennel with three.

Naming them was easy. Strauss's opera *Der Rosenkavalier* was a great favorite of mine, so I chose to name them for the characters Sophie, Octavian, and Ochs. It was a handsome selection, if one ignored the problem of ever actually calling the dogs, and I was quite pleased with myself when I announced it.

"Peggy," said Gul Baz, "is a good name for a dog, I think."

"Oh no, Gul Baz, not Peggy! Sophie."

"Here, Peggy," he said, and all three dogs pricked up their ears. "He's know his name, khanum."

Which is how Jenny was named. It was quite simple: she was named Peggy because Gul Baz said she was Peggy, but once he had won his point, not even he could remember to call her Peggy. No one could. We all somehow got it into our heads that her name was Jenny, and since she answered to that just as agreeably, Jenny she became.

My trio was irremediably demolished, but Gul Baz had the situation in hand. Looking at the puppy he had chosen, he explained that its name was Blackie. Then he allowed me to name the last one, and I chose Tossy, for an earlier pet. So much for pretension.

The dogs were a great source of amusement. Gul Baz obviously enjoyed their antics, but he was not affectionate with them and he flatly refused to pick them up or even pet them much.

'No," he explained, "I cannot take a dog in my arms, against my clothing. Then I cannot pray. A dog is not clean for a Mussulman to hold."

This is true: a dog is ritually unclean for an orthodox Muslim. I was surprised only because I had never noted any particular signs of devoutness on Gul Baz's part. In this he was unlike Ilyas, who regularly made his devotions on a square of rug which he set out in the yard before the door of his room. But I had no wish to argue about religious matters, so I stifled my curiosity and dropped the subject.

One evening, however, I heard a peculiar murmuring sound in the kitchen. Dinner was long since over and the servants had retired to their rooms. I slipped across the hall and peered surreptitiously around the corner of the door. Gul Baz was sitting cross-legged on the kitchen floor, his back to me. The three puppies were cradled in his lap and he rocked gently back and forth with them, crooning softly as he swayed, "Sleep, babies . . . sleep, little dogs . . . sleep, sleep . . ."

He thundered and lightened so violently that the house resounded at times as with an electrical storm; meanwhile he poured out kindness upon the young, the small, upon all he loved, and, in sum, upon all who needed it and many who didn't. Sometimes it seemed to depress him that he could not conquer this weakness, and he would make excuses for it.

As the Kayeums became increasingly regular visitors, they often brought along their two-year-old daughter Rona. She would march straight off to the kitchen and take up a seat on the steps there. Gul Baz would greet her with grave dignity and squat down on his heels until they were eye to eye, and the two of them would have long earnest conversations during which he fed her bread-and-butter and raisins and delightful stories. But, as he explained gruffly, it was only his duty. *Somebody* had to take the child off our hands while we visited with her parents.

One evening he found a tiny puppy being stoned by boys in the street, and rescued it and brought it inside, tucked under his jacket. He spent some minutes fretfully considering a properly hard-boiled way to tell me, until the puppy began to wriggle and gave him away before he had found an excuse.

When we had acquired a number of dogs, he thundered at them constantly and seemed to be very put out when they refused to be terrorized. Every day at dinnertime they would station themselves in a row at the kitchen door. He would roar at them, brandishing a nasty-looking carving knife and threatening to make them a terrible mash, while they gazed at him tolerantly, thumping their tails in unison on the floor. This simultaneously tickled his funnybone and injured his pride, so that the kitchen was alternately filled with imprecations and laughter.

His verbal fireworks were truly bloodthirsty. Theoretically he was appalling. But for actual cruelty, he had the coldest contempt. I have no doubt that in fury, of necessity, or by way of duty, Gul Baz Khan could kill a man; but I am equally certain that he was incapable of being unkind to one.

Once, and only once, did I know Gul Baz Khan to make a real error of judgment, and that mistake concerned himself. It was after I had begun to give him reading lessons, and only a few months before I was to leave.

One day as we sat working over his lessons, he fell into a melancholy mood. It was the quiet of midafternoon; everyone had gone off somewhere or other; the dogs were sleeping in the yard, nothing stirred in the street, and the house was still. He had stumbled over a line or two, and he pushed the book aside sadly, saying that it was no use, he would never be able to go on reading after I left.

"Is too late," he said. "Is all right for my sons, but too late for me."

"But it isn't," I told him, and I tried to cheer him up with that dream we pretended to believe in and halfway did believe: he would write letters to me in America, and I would write to him. One day I would write to tell him that I was coming back, and he would get ready to greet me. Then he would come back with me to visit America, and read all the signs on every street.

But he looked at me and shook his head slowly.

"No, khanum-sahib," he said. "You will go away, and you will forget me." I protested, but he hardly heard me; his thoughts were far away and his voice was very quiet.

"All my life," he said, "since I was a little-little boy, I come into people's houses. I live with them, I make them my family. And then, always, they go away and I must start over again, find a new house, make a new family. Always. Always.

"They say, 'Gul Baz Khan, we will remember you,' but they never do, khanum. I don't forget them ever, but they go far, far away and they forget about me. Only I don't forget. Only me."

His voice drifted off, and when he spoke again his voice was rising. "I think when you go, is best if I jump under the train at Peshawar Station and not try to start all over again!" Despite the edge of melodrama, he was speaking from deep within himself.

"Gul Baz," I cried, "don't think such things! I won't forget you," I promised him. "I won't forget!"

"Everybody's forget, khanum-sahib," he said, quiet again, and then he seemed to shake himself inwardly and stood up. "I think is time for tea now," he said, and went toward the kitchen.

But Gul Baz Khan, of Nevekali Village, near Peshawar, is, among the denizens of this earth, unique, and unforgettable.

7

Kabul is an old city and has the look of unutterable antiquity. When, in the dim recesses of prehistory, the Aryans swept by on their way to envelop India, it was standing here. And when, two thousand years later, the great-cities-to-be, founded by Alexander, had dwindled away, Kabul rose to dominate the approaches to the Hindu Kush along the old Silk Route. The adobe construction of its buildings makes all but the very newest of them appear to be crumbling with age, and one would think, seeing their walls and cornices runneled by winter storms, the eaves wrinkled like an elephant's hide, that they were about to melt away in the rains of the next spring. Along the mountain ridges which poke this way and that into the valley floor, dividing and channeling the spread of the city, layer upon layer of flat-topped houses rose like some hastily -built Babylonian ziggurat, earth-colored and tottering; but the look was deceptive, and they stood, the solid tenements of the city's life.

It was not beautiful as one usually thinks of beautiful cities. There were no graceful plazas, no fine façades, and in those days, as one went about the streets the gardens were hidden from view. But Kabul is wrapped in a cloak of splendor by its surroundings. Mountains rise up at the end of every vista and over them stretches the clear blue sky.

On the escarpment called the Sher Darwaza—the Lion Gate— which cuts off the valley proper from the approach to the Lataband, the ancient fortress of Ba'ala Hissar broods upon the mountainside, overhanging the city which once was huddled at its feet, protected and overseen; and which now spreads out in garden compounds and glistening rice fields as green as young leaves in April, into the raw desert of the valley floor and the foothills of the Paghman range towering in the west. It has seen much, the Ba'ala Hissar. It was the boyhood refuge of the Moghul emperor Akbar four hundred years ago, and the home of the Afghan emirs for centuries. In 1842 it was briefly the headquarters of an invading British army, and from its grim walls the Emir Shah Shuja watched them retreat from the city to a snow-swept death. The weary old crenellated towers seem about to collapse into exhausted dust, but still they stand, and still it is a citadel.

Seen from these slopes, the new sections of Carta Char and Shahr-i-nau spread out like formal gardens, each green plot carefully boxed by the rim of its brown walls. Shahr-i-nau took its prestige from the royal palace which had been built there, drawing the embassies, some of the ministries, and the homes of the wealthy to that part of town. On the other side of the walled ridge sporting its chain of lights, Carta Char was only beginning to develop. It pushed out toward the university section and various school grounds, and then turned onto a line of luxurious houses along a poplar-fringed road which led to Dar-al-Aman, the fragment of a new capital city which was planned and begun by King Amanullah before he was deposed in 1929. Amanullah was a gifted, energetic man who visited Europe and returned determined to haul his country into the modern world—by the ears, if necessary. Swept away by his own enthusiasm, he tried to do too much too fast. The immediate result was revolution and chaos, and the wreckage of a hundred hopes left strewn about the country behind him. His parliament building had been completed before the upheaval and was in use, although it was remote from the other government centers. But on an isolated hilltop his palace stood unfinished, left just as it had been when rebellion broke out: a solid, handsome shell, its windows unglazed and open to the winds, forgotten fixtures and unopened crates scattered about the silent rooms. It was still sturdy despite the ravages of many winters, but the royal residence only of the birds of the air who nested among the marble cornices and the butterflies that waltzed about the carefully tended gardens. Amanullah was no vainglorious Ozymandias, and he indeed left a heritage: he broke a path, and Afghanistan eventually turned to the modern world along the more cautious route of his successors. But that heritage was elsewhere, and less tangible: the palace at Dar-al-Aman stood like a monument to heartbreak.

Once I went with friends to picnic there, and explored the building and its gardens. Amanullah had planned to build a tramway from the old city to the new, and in a shed at the foot of the hill there was a donkey engine rotten with rust, a few yards of track running aimlessly out before it—the only rail line in the country.

An old man who served as caretaker invited us to tea. While his son blew up a little fire in a charcoal stove, he disappeared into his dark hut, and through the doorway we saw him reach up to a shelf and shake the last tea from a tin canister into his soot-blackened kettle; he took down a single round of bread lying there; and brought them out to us. As the tea brewed, a shepherd came up, surrounded by his flock of silly goats and fat-tailed sheep. He was carrying a small melon. He exchanged a few words with the old man, then, smiling, sliced into the melon and portioned it out to us.

It was almost sunset and the evening wind was blowing across the hills. The tea was weak: there had been just a few crushed leaves to brew with. Our hosts had none for themselves. They were offering us all that they had, smiling with exquisite courtesy; to our worried inquiries, they described an enormous meal that was momentarily waiting for them in some vague somewhere. Two things were clear: that they would go hungry, and that they would not allow us to refuse. It was my first real experience of what an Afghan means by hospitality: the first time I heard the words, "You are a guest in my country."

In a bewilderment of admiration and embarrassment, we struggled to find some way to avoid taking their all, but there was no way to do it without paining or even insulting them. At last we decided to explain how much we desired to make a proper expression of our appreciation by an appropriate gift in return; but we might not pass that way again. Therefore we begged them to spare us the humiliation of showing ingratitude, by accepting the few coins we happened to have with us and using them to purchase a gift for themselves which could, in effect, be our offering to them. Then we waited in painful suspense, afraid that we had wounded their pride. There were some long difficult moments. The old man's face fell and he turned to his son, consulting him as to whether or not we meant to pay them for their hospitality. At last, after many awkward pleas and dramatic explanations of our shame if they rejected our most inadequate gift, they accepted it with gracious gravity.

We ate their bread and melon; we drank their tea. They took our gift and eased our consciences, though it was truly enough poor return for their kindness—for the bazaars were closed, and they went hungry that night, smiling with pleasure to be able to do so.

If the new quarters of the city expanded in gardens and Dar-al-Aman stood beyond like an unawakened dream, the secret pulse of the city lay in the old bazaars which rooted themselves at the bases of the hills and ridges, and reached out to one another in tenuous linkage across broad paved modern avenues which had already been carved out along the river's edge and deep into the heart of those crowded tangled mazes of alleys and byways and ceaseless life. The new streets were spacious and quite handsome, and they surely presaged the eventual end of the old crabbed medieval quarters, but those ancient rookeries had their own beauty: the grace which age gives freely to the plainest face, and does not withhold even from an old mud wall. This was indeed the aged lined face of the city, wrinkled and riddled with the accretions of life.

Beneath the forbidding walls of the old citadel lay the great convoluted expanse of the Shor Bazaar. Here a labyrinth of crooked lanes twisted in and out, branched and turned and bent back upon themselves like a Greek key drawn higgledy-piggledy. They tumbled into cul-de-sacs and wrenched about through tiny passageways between unpainted mud-brick buildings two or three stories high— some of them lined with cubbyhole shops crammed with goods, others offering the blank backsides of serais and tenements which turned their faces inward onto balcony-lined courtyards. One could sometimes catch a glimpse of the life within through a great half-open iron-studded wooden door where a child stood peeping out, twisting her skirt shyly between her fingers, her beautiful dark eyes ringed with smudges of kohl, owlishly silent and observant.

The narrow alleyways were mere channels cut between the dun-colored walls which locked them in all-but-perpetual shadow. In the dim cavernous shops on either side, cobblers, bakers, tinsmiths and ironsmiths, capmakers, sweetsellers, wood dealers—the whole busy population of the hive—hammered and clanged and sewed and bought and sold and argued and drank tea from dawn till darkness, while an endless stream of traffic edged and shoved and wound its way along before their doorways. Coolies plodded along, bent over double under huge bundles of carpets, which were wrapped in jute sacking and tied with heavy cord; and the dusty cotton swaddling of their clothing, and the ropes with which they balanced their loads, so melted and blended into their burdens that one could hardly tell where man left off and bundle began. Patient little donkeys, their double panniers laden with onions or fruit or kindling wood, picked their way delicately in and out of the stream of pedestrians. Shoppers lounged on the wooden steps before the shops, chatting with the merchants, or moved slowly from doorway to doorway, fingering bolts of cloth and comparing prices. Street dogs, scavenging for scraps outside the food shops, slunk along the gutters among the endless moving feet. From burdened coolies and impatient donkey drivers a constant high-pitched cry rang out: *"Kharbardar, kharbardar!"* "Make way, make way!"

From time to time a student or clerk would appear (his dark suit, the badge of his status, protected with bicycle clips), stubbornly pushing his bicycle through the throng or even trying to ride, ringing the tinny bell with imperious insistence until he bumped into a donkey or an oblivious coolie and he and his cycle were unceremoniously tumbled in the dust. Then there would be a noisy argument, and a crowd blocking the thread of passageway, and cries and curses from before and behind until eventually, brushing his knees and nursing his wounded dignity, the cyclist would stiffly move off to be lost in the crowd once more, his bell still tinkling as he disappeared; and the river of traffic would thaw into motion again. *Kharbardar, kharbardar!* Sometimes a gawdi driver would force his carriage through the winding alleys, urged on by an insistent passenger or by God knows what whim, and the throngs of men and animals flattened themselves against the walls or leaped into shops and doorways until he had passed, his carriage bell clanging melodiously over the hubbub. In winter the lanes were churned into a rutted tide of mud; in the dry seasons they were beaten hard and stony by thousands of feet, hoofs, camel pads, and wheels.

Steam rose in little white puffs from samovars in the tea shops, and smoke and delicious aromas of roasting lamb floated across the bazaar from the kabob shops and the bakeries, to mingle with the smell of leather and hot metal, of dung and dust and cloth and sweat, of burning wood and tobacco and animals and whiffs of the sweet mountain air, to form a matrix for the shouts and cries and arguments and footsteps and laughter and the sounds of work which studded the life of the Shor Bazaar.

Aside from the children—the watchful little girls with their hands still hennaed from some wedding party, the bright-capped noisy street urchins, the schoolboys dodging in and out to buy a quick handful of walnuts—aside from these, who always seemed in danger of being trampled but never were, it was a completely masculine world. The few women to be seen passed silently, shrouded in their chadris: disembodied phantoms stopping here or there for a purchase, then moving on to disappear behind the massive gates.

The Shor Bazaar was the wholesale district and the artisans' quarter: to the Shor Bazaar one went to have something made or repaired or done. In one section, shipments of used clothing imported from America were sorted out and hung up, to be purchased by the poor. In the caravanserais on its outer fringes, trains of camels unloaded coal and wood for the city, and quantities of fruits and vegetables.

Within its twisted maze was the street of the shoemakers, where one bought the excellent sturdy sandals called *chupplees*, and supple black Turkoman boots high enough to top the deepest snowdrifts, or the heavy peasant shoes with turned-up toes which looked and felt as though they had been carved out of wood, and were anguish to break in, but then turned into comfortable things which wore forever. In another lane were the sellers of turban caps and cloths. The cloths were usually gray or brown, but the caps around which they were wound appeared in brilliant colors in every style, silk and gold thread embroidered on velvet: peaked Pushtun caps, round Tajik caps, the heavy wool geometric designs of the Turkomans and Uzbeks in purple and black and orange. In the streets of smithies one could get a solid-brass cooking pot, or a wrought-tin water jug elaborately chased—or have an axle welded. There were teapot and chinaware shops by the dozens, and repairmen who could take a shattered piece and, using only iron staples without any sort of cement, put a hundred fragments patiently together again into a teapot which would last forever without leaking a drop.

Shor Bazaar was also the center of the carpet serais, vast courtyards insulated from the noise outside, so that when you stepped inside, the sudden silence made it seem as though your ears were popping. The court was lined with rickety verandas and behind them dark cubbyholes from whose black depths a merchant would haul one after another of the glowing crimson mowri carpets from the north, rolled in tight bundles; and, with a sudden practiced gesture, fling them out on the earth in the full sunlight to blaze up suddenly red and black. Were none of them to your taste? He would plumb the depths of every storeroom until the rugs were heaped in gorgeous luxury on all sides. Amid the dull clay walls, in the brilliant light, one's mind was gorged and sated, drowned in color.

The life of Shor Bazaar streamed through its twisting channels from sunrise till darkness, until one by one the gates were closed and the shutters before the shops were slammed down. Then life withdrew within the blank walls for the night, with only a lonely little shop here or there, left behind by the ebbing tide, where a single tailor stitched on into the evening in the glare of an unshaded bulb, or a cigarette dealer waited hopefully for a few latecomers.

Along one of its edges a part of the bazaar had been shorn away to create the Jadi Maiwand, a wide straight boulevard which was one of the first steps in a plan to remodel and modernize the heart of the city. The street was lined with smartly painted new buildings several stories high; they held in the murky bazaars at their backs as sternly as a concrete border walling in some wildly overgrown thicket of abandoned garden. When one emerged there suddenly from the dim hubbub of the Shor Bazaar, the avenue seemed a vast gulf of unaccustomed light and air. Its planned order looked antiseptic compared to the jumble of life around it, accumulated by centuries of random whim: one could imagine that the tangle of the Gordian Knot must have looked much like that when Alexander's sword had slashed it through.

Perhaps because it was still unfinished, the Jadi Maiwand had not yet been absorbed into the life of the city. Although it began importantly among big government buildings, it ended abruptly at the parade grounds, which were usually empty except during the week of Jeshin, the Afghan independence celebration. Then for a few summer days the street was crammed with holiday crowds surging to the fair, but throughout the rest of the year it was little used. Because they could not go easily through the narrow bazaar streets, the big caravans of the merchants and nomads went that way en route to the Lataband road; heavy lines of shaggy Bokhara camels plodded stolidly along among work gangs surfacing the street. But it had not really accumulated the detritus of daily affairs: it was too new and big and impressive for everyday use. Nevertheless, little clumps of business were beginning to sprout up along the curbs and at corners, busy seedlings wafted that way from the bustling old alleys. Woodsellers and fruit vendors sold from the packs on their donkeys' backs to clusters of shoppers who were learning to look for them there, and one felt that ordinary life would root itself when the newness had comfortably rubbed off.

Where the Jadi Maiwand ended in the parade ground it was flanked on either side by a handsome new government mosque and a row of shops. All but one of these were empty except at Jeshin time. The exception, smack in the middle of the silent arcade, was the curio shop of Pir Ahmad, which always stood open, waiting for the carriage trade which found its way there.

Pir Ahmad was an engaging rascal who had been one of the first merchants in town to discover the tastes of the foreign colony and profit by catering to them. His shop was stuffed with a great many lovely objects, some very fine, even rare; and a lot of well-chosen dross was tastefully mingled in, upon the benign hope that the dim light, the proximity of excellence, and the customer's eagerness for a bargain would allow the stuff to be palmed off. Some of his customers in turn cherished the naïve hope of doing him out of a rare piece which, in his ignorance, he would let go at a comparative pittance. He encouraged these fantasies.

He did have a tempting collection. Here I first saw and coveted the elegant creamy-gold carpets woven in Herat. There was always a selection of fine antique damascened swords and daggers to choose from, some of them inlaid with gold or gems. A glass case was filled with polished lapis lazuli (the finest is dug in Afghanistan), some unset stones and others mounted in gold jewelry, and there was a large array of carved boxes of onyx and marble. You might also find fine work drawn from every part of Asia: beautiful Chinese bowls, bits of Indian brass.

Pir Ahmad himself was a skinny little man of indeterminate old age who fancied that a smile of bland innocence successfully masked his closed, calculating merchant's face. A shopper was free to move from table to table in the quiet of the shop, undisturbed, while the Pir discreetly estimated your taste and your pocketbook from his desk in a far corner. Then, once you had been hooked by the selection of some choice object at a merely exorbitant price, he pounced. All sorts of unprecious items materialized in his hands, were thrust under your nose, were hastily fetched in large numbers by his nimble clerks. These he was gallantly prepared to sacrifice for a really scandalous sum.

He knew his clientele; long experience had taught him the foreigner's Achilles' heel. Pushing a dreadful teapot into your unwilling hands, he would pour out a stream of rapturous praise in rapid Persian: it was a rare piece of Chinoiserie or a prize possession sacrificed by an ancient household, it was incomparable and irreplaceable and he would part with it only to one of your own obviously fine taste. From this mellifluous murmur two words of English invariably popped out, loud and clear, like a jack-in-the-box.

"Verry antique-y!" he would cry triumphantly. *"Verry antique-y!"*

"But, look here," you might say, turning the thing over and pointing at the bottom, "right there it says 'Made in Japan.'" "Nay, nay," he would protest, "verry antique-y ast!" And seizing the teapot, he would turn it right side up again to conceal the distracting inscription, while a reproachful look said that there were rules to this game, and if you please, there was no need to get unnecessarily involved in facts.

On Fridays I liked to go down to the center of town to see what might be happening out of the ordinary. Besides, it was a good day to ramble idly about in the bazaars, with Gul Baz along in case there was serious haggling to be done.

On a playing field behind the town theater a group of musicians often sat against the wall playing for hours. One of them produced incredibly agile arpeggios on a thick-reeded *sernai*—a sort of oboe—while his companions beat out the rhythm on deep-voiced drums slung from their shoulders or set between their knees. They were barbers the rest of the week but virtuosi on Friday for their own pleasure (they collected no money from the crowds which hung around them to listen).

Nearby on the field, youngsters ran back and forth playing tag. An undersized boy with a wasted leg used to hobble eagerly along behind the rest, using a crude wooden crutch. Watching, I was stung by the thoughtless cruelty of the other children. They never slowed down or watched out for him but let him hop along, alone, always behind, tripping sometimes over his crutch or tumbled in a melee, crying, "Hi! hi!" after them in his excitement. And yet one day I recognized something else, too, something which the conventions of my own world had hidden from me: by treating him as if he were no different from them, the boys were giving him freedom and that was the light in his eyes. I saw him on other days, limping down the street, and then he was a cripple; but on Fridays he was a boy playing games, and he was free.

Around the corner one sometimes found a group of Pushtuns—countrymen, not townsmen—dancing the rhythmic tribal dances, occasionally with swinging swords, to drums but to no music. Round and round in a circle they went, bending their heads forward and then flinging them back, so that their long black hair flew wildly across their eyes; round and round, hour after hour, with consuming intensity, while crowds streaming by to a cinema paused to watch for a moment and then hurried on, lured by the bright colored posters and the popular Indian film music pouring from loudspeakers on the marquee.

Although the bazaars were for the most part open, along the river the big stores were shut and the karakul dealers had no skins out bleaching in the sunlight on Fridays. Far along a spur of the Sher Darwaza, picnicking families strolled under the plane trees in the Babur Gardens.

When Babur, the founder of the Moghul dynasty, came down from the Oxus to rule in this valley, he built a garden here on the mountainside. He spent twenty years in Kabul and he said this was the most beautiful of all his lands. When at last he marched south to win the hot jewel of India upon the battlefield of Panipat, he wept for these hills; and dying on the southern plains, he begged to rest at last among them. He is buried in his garden beneath a simple sarcophagus, in a small white marble pavilion shaded by tall mulberry and plane trees, where his spirit can look out across the valley he loved above all others from the Oxus to the Jumna.

In the bazaars on Friday one might find something unusual, for villagers came into the city that day bringing their local wares. There might be a potter down from the hill town of Istalif, squatting on a curbstone surrounded by an array of bowls and plates. These were simple, cheaply sold, and largely ignored by the crowds passing by. But the glaze was the magnificent intense cerulean blue that one finds on ancient Persian ware in museums, and Istalif may be the only place on the Iranian plateau where it is still created. From a village near Charikar, on the road to the north, came smooth heavy-lidded crocks carved out of soapstone and incised with geometric patterns; ordinarily one could not find them in the shops. And once, as I was riding through the bazaars in a gawdi, I suddenly saw a tall Pushtun walking along with an elaborately embroidered shirt of full tribal dress draped over his arm. I had been searching for such a shirt for a long time, but they were made to order in distant provincial villages and I could never find one. I had no reason to think this one was for sale, but before the bewildered man knew what was happening, I had jumped down, seized the shirt, thrust a wad of afghanis into his hand and was riding off, waving cheerfully at him as I went. He looked satisfied, if still somewhat confused.

The best part of town for finding such things was the Da Afghanan Bazaar.

Across the river from the Shor Bazaar, near Shahr-i-nau, the Da Afghanan stretched out expansively, its back up against the light-strung ridge. Above the shopping streets, houses and tenements climbed halfway up the rocky slopes in haphazard pyramids. This was a more leisurely shopping section, nearer the new residential districts and the diplomatic quarter. Unlike the tortuous mare's nest that was Shor Bazaar, the unpaved streets here turned easily and lay open to the sun between low buildings. Many were wide enough to allow two gawdis to pass. They were filled with the same bustle of the market place, and the throngs were here, but unconstricted, diluted with space. There were more women—still shrouded but more purposeful, busy with their daily marketing; so they seemed more rooted, less phantasmal.

This was the householder's market. There were shops filled with pens, copybooks, ink, the supplies of the schoolboy and the clerk; others were piled with bolts of imported woolens, bright cotton cloth, and heavy local silks, with flashlights, radios, household utensils of every sort. Along the central alleys were the hatters, who would make a karakuli to measure overnight. On another street a row of stores sold great warm overcoats from every part of the country: white felt *chipons* from the Eastern Province, their long dangling sleeves embroidered with brown wool; thick quilted silk *chipons* from the north, lined with flowered cotton; and sheepskin *posteens* and weskits with the shaggy white fur turned inside, the outer skin sueded and dyed yellow, and embroidered with silk flowers in scarlet or gold or a rainbow of colors. Many of the stores carried imported goods: sweaters and watches, bicycles and pharmaceuticals were for sale in this district. As the foreign colony had grown, a few of the shops had begun to put up signs in French or English, occasionally more enthusiastic than they were accurate: one beguiling establishment which regularly repaired or replaced Gul Baz's burnt-out radio sets announced itself as "Electric Raper."

A large section of the Da Afghanan was devoted to food shops of all sorts. There were bakeries, and candy shops whose boiling kettles of honey syrup poured out a steamy sweetness to entice flies and eager children. In front of the butcher shops iron hooks displayed torn haunches of mutton, lamb or kid, marbled an ugly red and white. Along the bend of a dogleg street there was a colorful cluster of fruit shops, where wooden stands jutting out into the street were crowded with shallow baskets piled high with the sumptuous riches of Afghan orchards and gardens. Within the shops were neat stacks of cigarette tins and towers of match boxes; cones of sugar wrapped in green or fuchsia-colored paper; tins and jars and canisters filled with tea, sugar, salt, dozens of spices, English toffees; boxes crammed with papers of pins and needles, with spools of thread, penny whistles, hairpins, cheap toys, penknives from Charikar. Wire baskets of fresh eggs hung from the ceiling, and rows and rows of shelves were filled with grimy unlabeled bottles and jars whose contents were mysterious and unknowable.

There was usually a platter mounded with *roghan*—clarified butter, which keeps without refrigeration and was used for most cooking. (When it is pure it is delicious, but all too often the shopkeepers cut it with sheep fat, and from the food shops and every kitchen in the city the thick, stale smell of old mutton fat floated into the streets, overlaying and permeating all the other smells and leaving an indelible impression.) A pair of scales hung in a corner with an assortment of small stones beneath it, to be used as weights.

The shopkeepers sat cross-legged behind rows of bright pink or white sugar-beet root, complacently switching away the flies with a horsetail whisk.

One went, then, to this hub of the Da Afghanan for a new battery or a tin of cheese, a cap or some curtain material or a bag of candy. Where its streets began to meander off into a backwater of gullies and run-down houses, however, that was the place to wander in search of—anything: anything you had always wanted but never found, anything you had never wanted, never thought of, never imagined to exist. It was an Old Curiosity Shop of the world. Into the jumbledy cubbyholes along the back alleys some magnet had drawn the flotsam of ten thousand thousand needs and thoughts and wants and wishes. Most of it was utilitarian: used clothing, old bicycle pumps, chipped cups, the cheapest cottons, crank shafts, worn-out tires, a saw, a bundle of wire.

But these heaps of battered necessities were crowned with wild gaudy jewels: a gilded French telephone or a sheaf of lacquered Uzbek spoons; a volume of Sir Walter Scott, an exquisitely molded Greek coin turned up by some plow, the brilliant scarlet tunic of a royal regiment long since debased to khaki. Once I found a mortarboard cap from Oxford University and could only wonder what disillusion had banished it to lie amid a scattering of old crockery in a dark corner. It seemed as though, from the Universe of Objects, the crippled, the lame, the halt and the blind had all found their way here to await the day when someone might possibly look upon them again and find them good.

As dusk came and the shutters in the bazaars were clapped down and bolted to, life sprang up in the teahouses all across the city. Along one of the main streets between the Da Afghanan and some government offices there was a row of them where we sometimes went. At sunset they began to fill with clerks and men from the shops, reviving themselves for an hour or two with strong black tea and music. The wailing notes of a singer and the thrum of tambour and harmonium sounded faintly far down the quieting streets, and the windows threw cheerful squares of yellow light across the darkness.

Many Westerners did not bother to listen to Afghan music, so different from ours and so hard to tune one's ear to at first. It is a sort of bridge between the subtle classical music of India and the vivid erotic rhythms of the Middle East: less sweet, less sensuous, more melancholy than either, with a harsher, more astringent quality of sound. The voice is projected from the throat, not from the diaphragm, eliminating the chest tones we admire. One must do a lot of listening in order to learn to hear this music, and it was easy to decide not to, because usually one heard it first as a raucous noise blaring from shrill public loudspeakers mounted around the city.

Of the foreigners who listened, few were women; and of those, none came to the *chaikhanas* to hear it. So my arrival in a teahouse always caused a small sensation. When my husband and I stepped through the door into the close, smoke-filled room there would be a pause: at first, things used to come to a dead stop; later, as I became familiar, the pause was almost imperceptible. But it was always there, a sort of holding of breath while I threaded my way among the close-set tablets and benches and found a place. And then the singer started up again. The men in the bare crowded room watched me while they listened, with that plain unself-conscious stare which followed me wherever I went in public. There was nothing personal about it. I was simply a woman and unveiled, and therefore an object of curiosity. In the close quarters of the teahouse it was hard to avoid staring back. I would look down at the cracked marble of the tabletop, or watch the musicians sitting cross-legged on a cushioned dais in one corner.

The singer, his head thrown back, his eyes half closed, a cigarette held loosely between his fingers, lost himself in a long fluid melody. I could pick out a few words here and there—*bulbul*, the nightingale; *gul*, the rose—ah, it was a love song, a sad love song, of passion unrequited and defeated. But then, it was always a love song, and it was always sad.

Pot after pot of tea would appear on the table before me, and fresh cups, half filled with grainy sugar. The tea was drunk without stirring: the first cupful was cloyingly sweet, but with each succeeding cup the sugar dissolved away until in the end the brew was dark, rough on the palate, and cleansingly bitter.

There was almost no talk. Clouds of cigarette smoke drifted about the stuffy room. The swarthy throat of the singer, bent backward, was a quivering arc against the whitewashed wall. His voice rose and fell hypnotically. The tambour player strummed his drone absent-mindedly, his eyes wandering idly about the room, and the harmonium player bent over his instrument. The men stared unwaveringly. The tea was sweet, then bitter, then sweet again.

And then the spell would break for a moment. The singer, his soulfulness vanished, would stand up, smoke, chatter with friends. The plain wooden benches scraped on the worn brick floor as men rose to leave. The opening door flung a wave of fresh cold air into the room, and the departing customers took a last look over their shoulders at the strange foreign woman in their midst. Then the door shut, the harmonium player tested a few notes on his instrument, the singer resumed his exaltation, and the music went on forever.

8

*W*ith so much time at my service, I could explore the archipelago which was social life in Kabul, and for a foreigner social life could be very lively indeed. Within the small international colony there was an endless circuit of cocktail parties, dinner parties, and dancing parties in addition to official functions—enough to fill almost every evening, if one chose.

This was a quite self-sufficient territory to which Afghans were peripheral, being merely the waves that washed against its secure shores. Insofar as foreigners knew it—which was usually not much—the Afghan community consisted of Officials (major); Officials (minor); Non-officials (prominent); Servants; and Others. One had close contact with servants of course, and many people felt that they offered a sufficiently authorized text to enable one to close the book on Afghans.

Duty brought one into contact with officialdom and sometimes with the prominent. One also met them at various large social functions, and was obliged to invite them in proportion to their usefulness in connection with one's work. One made a point of liking them and was, indeed, politely deferential; because it was, after all, their country which one was there to deal with, to instruct, or to improve. In sum, one did everything short of meeting them as individuals. It was on the whole as unexpected to really like an Afghan personally as it was improper to dislike him personally. In theory Afghans were fine people, and in practice they were of little or no interest.

Most of the colony thought it surprising and even a bit peculiar if a foreigner and an Afghan became close friends. That they might simply like each other was scarcely considered. Such a friendship was subject to general speculation until at last some other, self-interested and therefore real motive was assigned to one party or the other to satisfactorily explain the eccentricity. Perhaps this was because friendship is a matter of both giving and receiving; and many visitors in Kabul were so sure of what they had to bestow that they failed to perceive anything they very much wished to receive.

Even the crudest classification of circles within the community itself must of necessity overlook many of those delicate but decisive elements which registered significantly on the social antennae of a hostess planning a dinner party. Any attempt at a Social Register staggers under a welter of divisions and stratifications and subliminally evaluated qualifications which located everyone in the proper niche. But at least, simply by being a foreigner, one was by self-definition in the upper crust. This was very convenient for everyone within the magic circle, and if it offered a smug temptation to overweening self-esteem, one must admit that it also gave a sort of democratic flavor within the foreign colony itself.

Since anyone who had been born Somewhere Else was automatically among the elite, this egalitarianism helped to lighten various otherwise stuffy occasions. For example, one American wife was a vivacious, likable young woman who had grown up without many inhibitions in the scrub-pine backwoods of Georgia. Few who were present forgot the soiree during which she candidly explained to her dinner partner—a particularly starchy ambassador—that her first marriage had broken up when she was fourteen because her bridegroom, an escaped convict, had been picked up and hustled back to the penitentiary from the cave in which they were honeymooning.

But the brotherhood of exiles had its limits, and as always, some foreigners were more equal than others. A sketchy map of the territory might have located enclaves of diplomats; United Nations personnel; non-diplomatic embassy staffs (honor by association); teachers (subdivided into teetotalers and the socially acceptable); and individuals without official connections who had come to Kabul on their own, which in some circles automatically made them suspect as possible eccentrics.

There was a pyramid based on national prestige as well. The French could afford to be cordial to everyone, for by their own acknowledgment they were indisputably at the summit. This was definitively demonstrated each year on Bastille Day, when they laid the embassy tables with champagne and a banquet of Parisian delicacies and invited only themselves. It was the most exclusive event of the year and, since invitations could be wangled only by proper arrangements at birth, the party most longingly eyed by the widest social range of the uninvited. There was of course no international club but there was of course a French Club. On Thursdays it was thrown open to their fellow-but-non-Gallic exiles, and the fancy-dress parties which were periodically held there stimulated the entire colony for days before and after. There, too, a gallant last-ditch battle was being fought to keep Franca the *lingua franca* of the community.

Next in rank, perhaps, came the British diplomatic colony, who lived beyond the edge of the city in an enormous garden compound. There they dwelt in quaint half-timbered Elizabethan cottages surrounded by hollyhocks and sweet william: the total aura absolutely cried out for a swinging sign before the gate to announce Ye Olde British Embassy. It is perhaps helpful in comprehending the subtle distinctions of rank if one notes that the British had to move out of town to preserve their superiority, while the French could move among the general herd without spilling a drop.

As for the remaining nations, status varied according to constantly shifting circumstance. At one time, there was an Indian ambassador whose wife possessed magnificent jewels and savoir faire, while simultaneously the Indian military attaché and his wife played a sharp hand of bridge. *Up.* The Turks usually gave the most lavish parties, but they were inclined to be more gregarious and jovial than soigné, and they invited the children. *Up and down*, depending on their party calendar. And the Russians, while *up* in terms of international importance—a factor never entirely overlooked—were in practice rather *down*—were definitely *down*, because they were so leadenly gay, never entertained unless they had to, eavesdropped openly at parties, and ruined social chitchat by falling into sudden significant silences.

And on the outer edge, smiling and appreciative and infinitely adjustable, hovered the little German colony. Due to temporary international circumstances, they had at that moment no status whatsoever and were rarely invited unless everyone was being invited. They spoke faultless English, were extraordinarily courteous, accepted their pariahhood with wistful stoicism, and were endlessly grateful for a polite word. Each of them in turn would take one off into a corner to confide his profound anti-Nazi sentiments and denounce his fellows, or to commiserate about what pigs the Afghans were, unless there were Afghans present, in which case they bowed and said, "Your Excellency." They were amazing.

All in all, the social life of a foreigner in Kabul had some of the overtones of the Second Empire, with its parties and position and supercharged gossip, while certain aspects of the late lamented colonial era were unmistakably visible in the structural hierarchy. But there was a distinctively Afghan quality in the institution of the informal call, where everything and everyone met and all distinctions were pleasantly muddled. Since there were few private telephones in the city, such visits were usually unannounced and one might expect to be dropped in on at any time from ten or eleven o'clock in the morning until quite late in the evening, although the most usual hour was around tea time in midafternoon. Anyone might come, and often did—even total strangers, who were friends of friends or at least acquaintances of acquaintances. Even when one made a business call, tea was usually served and a social bond established before taking up the matter at hand. This might interfere with efficiency, but it was quite a good way to get to meet people and of course a delightful way to see friends.

Status accounted for some of the teatime traffic.

I suppose it has never been much of a secret about Americans dearly loving a lord. If King George V had ever visited Chicago, and Big Bill Thompson had actually carried out his threat to punch him in the nose, it seems to me likely that the entire city from Mrs. Potter Palmer to Al Capone would have been united for once by anguish. Whatever the reason for this enthusiasm, there certainly seem to be few enticements for a solid Yankee citizen which can compare with a title, and in Kabul there were a great many men who could very legitimately be called "Prince." The royal family is a great joint-family, in effect a clan. Moreover, the Emir Habibullah, who ruled until 1919, had been the last king to indulge in polygamy, and he had left many children who by now had grown children of their own. Afghans, as it happens, are not terribly impressed by titles and do not use them much, being more inclined to attach prestige to education and individual accomplishment. But royalty was in great demand among the American colony, both as guests and as hosts, and fortunately there were more than enough princes to go around.

Meanwhile, many Afghans, stimulated by an urgent desire to see their country take its place in the modern world, had a vivid admiration for the American ideals and achievements which the Second World War had brought to world attention. They seemed inclined to give credit generally to all of the citizenry, singly as well as collectively, and to assume that our national virtues were somehow dispensed by our individual presences. There was therefore—for minor officials, at any rate—a certain cachet to be had by knowing and visiting Westerners, particularly the prestige-laden Americans. *Any* prestige-laden Americans.

These two enthusiasms combined to produce a peculiar two-way social stampede, rather like two herds of buffalo blindly streaming past one another on some international prairie: Americans rushing breathlessly off to chalk up another tea with a His Highness while Afghans hurried by obliviously in search of the democrats.

You might murmur a polite hope to meet again to a bank clerk who had been helpful, and find him on the doorstep the next afternoon, radiating friendly good cheer. Somehow it seemed unkind to decline a visit from someone just because he was a total stranger, or perhaps a bore, or because he thought of you simply as some sort of embodiment of national virtues; especially since Afghans were so unfailingly hospitable themselves, even though *you* might be a bore. So you invited him in and did your best to be an embodiment. I imagine that some of the titled Afghans must have felt much the same with the foreign lion-hunters.

Our landlord, Sharif, was such a visitor. Once a month, of course, he came to collect the rent, but often he would stop by without any ascertainable reason, just to chat.

In Afghanistan, landlords are considered as something of a race apart; only woodsellers are presumed to equal them for guile and greed. A man may be devoted to his family, honored in his profession, and in his total person one of nature's noblemen; but let him acquire a rentable property and it is simply assumed that in his character as landlord he is villainous. As landlords go, or at least as they are said to go, Sharif was really not bad at all.

He was a slight, ferrety man of rather ordinary mind and ability who seemed vaguely ill at ease with himself, although he should not have been. Nature had intended him to be somebody's younger brother and Fate had kindly seen to it that he achieved his niche: his brother was an official of some prominence and consequently he himself had attained a position of modest importance where he was likely to do no harm and on the whole be useful. He was, in short, the sort of man to congratulate himself on catching a flounder while the whales are swimming by.

Whenever he stopped in for tea he appeared so unhappily happy, and fidgeted so on the edge of his chair, that I somehow had the impression that he had been looking forward to the visit with unattainable expectation. It was as if he had rehearsed in advance what someone would say, and then what someone else would say, and then the *mot* which he would produce on cue to cap the conversation, at which point everyone would admire his effect as we sank into easy camaraderie. But then, somehow, no one ever said what he had planned for them to say, and he never got a chance to uncork his *bon mot*; and it wandered about in his head looking for a chance to get out, while the conversation ran to matters he did not want to discuss at all, such as smoky fireplaces and pump repairs.

At any rate, he always sat with a disappointed air, crossing and uncrossing his knees. Whatever it was that he wanted to say, it may have been connected with a topic which he always brought up, so to speak, casually.

Apparently, his great desire was to attend an American university. This was his favorite subject. He always sidled into it and then enlarged upon it with hesitant fervor. He knew that there were scholarships, both private and governmental, and it seemed to him possible that we might at some time be able to recommend him or help him attain his dream.

At first glance there was something rather touching about his ambition. He was not a particularly gifted man. He had fallen into his work more or less by family connection. He had only a journeyman approach to it, and yet, it appeared, he yearned to do greater things. But bit by bit the dream emerged in more concrete detail which shifted its focus slightly. In his dream there was a sunlit campus. This campus was filled with impressive buildings, within which scholars offered their nuggets of wisdom. Between those buildings were green lawns and shady trees; and beneath one of those trees sat Sharif, his textbook idle in his lap, watching the coeds go by. And every single one of them was wearing a sweater.

A knock on the gate might as easily mark the arrival of a good friend. Then Gul Baz would glance in to identify and count the guests and, without a word, send the boy out to the bazaar for additional provisions. Then teatime might pass into dinnertime, and dinnertime move on toward midnight unnoticed. There was time enough to explore the possibilities of one another's mind and spirit, time to savor good company, throughout those long, quiet, delightful evenings. Fruits and nuts and cake were reduced to a rubble on the coffee table, teacups were filled and emptied and refilled again and again until they were forgotten. I never had a fireplace that drew properly, so we could never enjoy the grace of an open fire, but in the cold weather the sawdust stoves, ugly though they were, gave out a steady comforting heat; and when, as the evening grew late, they slowly cooled, we tucked our feet up beneath us on the sofas and, ignoring the creeping chill, went on with that most human of explorations, conversation.

Our physician, who had first been summoned to deal with a case of dysentery brought on by ignoring Gul Baz's warning about the ambassador's cook, returned frequently to share phonograph records and musical tastes. There was a tall young Swiss travel agent who reveled in the dust of Kabul: he said he had spent his childhood and youth being scrubbed into intolerable Swiss cleanliness, and he proposed to spend his adult years being grubby.

An American couple, Walt and Clara Stockwell, lived in the compound next door. Clara was small and sprightly and kind, while Walt was a stocky, good-natured man with a thick mop of black hair, who had been a die-sinker in the automotive industry before he came to Kabul to teach machining at the new technical school. He was from the bayou country of Louisiana and had an incredible drawl which concealed a shrewd wit, a cheerfully independent mind, and a very low tolerance for humbug. His manner was linsey-woolsey homespun, and he read Herodotus because he liked Herodotus.

We had met casually in the street, but we did not know one another until one evening when there was a loud unexpected thumping on the gate in the wall between our two compounds. The puppies flung themselves into a frenzied clamor: they had been teaching themselves to guard the front gate and were outraged at the unexpected flank attack. The batcha hurried to unlatch the gate, and amid this Lilliputian uproar Walt and Clara came through, bearing a fresh chocolate cake which she had baked for us. From that evening on, the side gate was often used and seldom locked, and instead of having only a home, we had a neighborhood.

Shaban too came often, ostensibly for lessons but actually to escape his loneliness. At first I tried to put him through the formalities of vocabulary and drill, but the role of middle-aged schoolboy ill fitted him and made him feel much abashed. So instead I taught him to play gin rummy, which he liked, and he broke through the barrier of his reserve. He could not help being dignified if left to himself, but he loved to be made to unbend and laugh, and playing cards *en famille* opened the way for him. He began to come several times a week, staying for dinner and playing cards far into the night, and bit by bit he began to learn English, and to try it out on us.

He missed his family terribly and kept promising himself that he would join them by this or that deadline—which was always perforce extended, month by month. In the meantime, he presented them to us in words, as though talking about them brought them all together again for a few hours. He would bring over every snapshot he received of his wife and three young children, and eagerly recount each newly arrived scrap of news. He spoke of his wife until she almost seemed to materialize in the room with us. He told me about each child and his plans for them, and asked advice about their American future, until, at the end of an evening, the phantoms with which he had peopled the room vanished and he left reluctantly to return to that lonely house.

Meanwhile he had adopted a surrogate family: he appointed himself as fatherly guardian of our household. With Gul Baz Khan fiercely manning the inner defenses against woodmen, laundrymen, and similar domestic menaces, and with Shaban on guard against any storms that might blow in from the outer world (such as a temporary shortage of cash), we appeared to be very well protected.

There was no question, of course, of taking payment for his "lessons"; he did endless unobtrusive kindnesses for us. Once, after

I had politely thanked him for one of the searing Russian cigarettes his firm imported, he brought over fifty packages of them. When he noticed that they went unsmoked, he switched his own smoking to the sort that we did like so that he could always be ready to offer one.

He consulted me anxiously about gifts for his wife. He brought over a beautiful matched set of the finest lapis lazuli and asked me to design settings for them that she would like. I made scale drawings of a bracelet and ring for the goldsmith to work from; and on his next visit Shaban pressed a small packet into my hand. It contained a large amethyst of lovely deep color as his thanks. When he had learned enough English to take pride in using it, he gave me a wrought-silver cigarette case with an inscription I treasured because he had worked it out himself with the help of his dictionary: "Memorial to Rosanne from Shaban."

As a student he progressed well, if unevenly. He became a demon at gin rummy and was not doing badly in English, either, but in English he had no self-confidence. I tried to encourage him to use what he knew, but he would not do it when there was anyone else around; he retreated into stubborn silence and for a long time would not be budged. But I bullied him relentlessly over every hand of rummy until at last he promised me that he would plunge in at the very next opportunity. Of course Walt was the first visitor to appear after I had sworn Shaban to the attempt. In fact, he had just committed himself when we heard a knock at the gate, and I prodded him onward. He smiled unhappily and nodded. Then Walt ambled in and launched amiably into some topic or other rendered arcane by that sorghum drawl.

I saw bewilderment pass over Shaban's face and then, as his painfully mustered self-confidence drained away, a look of vague anguish. Before I could make contact with Walt, Shaban had leaned over and managed to ask me if this man was talking English. When I answered yes, he sank back into his chair in utter hopelessness. I interrupted Walt to explain the situation, and Walt kindly directed his full attention to Shaban and tried to be comprehensible with—I should say—some success. But Shaban had already given up, and the full blaze of our unified concern sent him into numb retreat. Weeks passed before I brought him round to venture more than a mumbled "hello," but this had no ill effects on his card game.

Meanwhile I continued my pilgrimages to the Ministry of Education about a job. A post at the university still appeared to be a good possibility, but the long winter vacation had begun and various officials had gone off on holidays, so there was no definite answer yet. I reminded myself that no news was good news; and waiting was becoming almost a way of life.

The Kayeums often came to visit. During the autumn Joan had been busy during the day, teaching at one of the girls' schools, while Abdul had of course been preoccupied with the administration of Darul Mo'Allamein. With the beginning of vacation they had more time: they frequently stopped by to spend an hour at midday and stayed to talk the night almost through. When they arrived, Gul Baz would automatically send the batcha out for an enlarged supply of cigarettes and *jalroza*, little paper-shelled pine nuts which served very well to occupy the fingers during the heat of argument. Then he would bring in tea and offer his own formal welcome. He liked to greet Kayeum as one khan to another, in Pushto.

"Please don't bother about us," Kayeum would tell him. "We'll only be staying a little while. I told Kalandar to wait."

"Yes, raïs-sahib," Gul Baz would respond politely, and then he would go out to their gawdi-driver Kalandar, waiting in the street, and persuade him to lead his horse into the garage, unhitch it, feed and water it, and come into the kitchen. Unlike Kalandar, he attached no importance to instructions that were obviously at odds with common sense, and when, hours later, we all awoke with a start to the realization that poor Kalandar was still waiting out in the cold, Gul Baz would smile his smuggest smile as he revealed the driver sitting in comfort in the kitchen.

So we talked the hours away. In the course of an evening we were likely to find ourselves jockeyed around until each of us was hotly maintaining a position directly opposed to the one he began with. No matter. We started anywhere and ended anywhere and covered anything that seemed to lie in between. We could argue the merits of piano concerti and of Chinese restaurants on Chicago's South Side. We talked philosophy and nonsense and the destinies of the world—and our own. We swapped books and quotations. One evening Kayeum found himself launched on a long and accurate recitation of most of one act from *Antony and Cleopatra:* he explained afterward that when he read it as a schoolboy he had no idea that he would ever be able to own a copy, so he memorized the whole play in order to be able to keep it forever.

We planned trips for the coming summer. They were determined that we should see the whole of Afghanistan, and they wanted to do it themselves, too.

"Doggone it!" Kayeum would burst out. (He exercised a conscientious control of expletives which he had imposed on himself, apparently in response to fatherhood; he could explode the most ferocious non-profanity imaginable.) "Doggone it, I've been in practically every state of the Union and I haven't seen all of my own country yet!" But, above all, he assured us that we must see Laghman province, his boyhood home, which was unquestionably the nearest thing to Eden in our time.

If one were designing ideal guides for a new life in a strange new world, how could one hope for more than this? Abdul, who was so profoundly Afghan, knew America deeply and well; Joan was an American woman who had found her place in Afghan life. Both stood on the bridge between the life I had come from and the one I was trying to understand, and both had a sense of poetry and vision. It was one of those rare moments when a group of people came together and the foundations of friendship strike suddenly, deep into bedrock.

The conversations often turned to Darul Mo'Allamein. Kayeum had completed his first full year as the raïs of the school, and he was simmering with plans for its future. He saw it as a microcosm of the nation: the students, chosen on merit, came from the farthest villages of every province. He saw them meeting here, learning to put aside communal and social differences, to feel themselves, above all their vivid individuality, one people, one nation. Those students were the future; and they could do anything, those boys. He knew them; they were the finest, the best; they would be—they were—the strength of the country.

Abdul, fired by his dreams, always managed to generate that same electric atmosphere of great possibilities which had stirred me the first evening in Kabul. Sometimes, as he spoke of the school and the students, it seemed as though all the visions of the future could be projected on its walls as on a screen, and as though anyone with the will to see could see there what might flower now in this remote and desert land.

The most important thing was to teach them, for they in turn would teach. He seemed almost to ache with the longing to open their minds to the whole world and all that it could offer them. They would go out to the villages, to the mountainsides, to every fold and cranny of the farthest provinces, carrying as much knowledge as he could put within their reach. And not just knowledge. Understanding, too.

They were the key to all the good dreams and the great dreams, not only his but their own. Everything would be possible for those boys and everything was possible with them; you had only to know them to know their eagerness and their strength.

And then one day somehow that word "everything" included the possibility that I might teach them.

I do not recall when—or whether—Kayeum ever suggested in so many words that I might teach at Darul Mo'Allamein. I was still "at liberty," of course, and with every passing week I was growing more discouraged about the possibility of finding a place. There had been an opening on Kayeum's staff since our friend left. But no woman had ever taught at the school, or at any school for provincial boys.

Perhaps he asked me if I would want to, but it seems to me more likely that as we all shared in the sketching out of his visions, the need to ask slipped away and the idea emerged almost unnoticed until it was just there. And truly there was no need for him to ask, for who could resist a chance to put one's hand to a dream and try to move it onward?

Of course, the officials at the Ministry of Education saw things somewhat differently and rather more practically. They had never even considered the school as a possible post for me. From their point of view, Darul Mo'Allamein had just recently been one of the toughest disciplinary problems they had to administer. It was true that in the past year and a half, under Kayeum's direction, it had quieted down, but so far as they knew, there was no guarantee that it could not errupt as a trouble spot again at any time. The boys came from the provinces, where there was little or no contact with foreigners and where conservative orthodoxy was strongest. No one had forgotten that in 1929 the rebellion that overthrew King Amanullah began with provincial rioting, ignited by protests over his attempt to force the unveiling of women. They were not at all certain what would happen if a woman appeared at the school.

So the Ministry shook its collective head discouragingly. Of course, Dr. Kayeum's optimism was understandable. He had been away in America for many years, had been home and at the school for a relatively short time. He was naturally full of enthusiasm for many new ideas and it was not surprising that he wanted to try them out and minimized some of the problems involved. But, after all, the students were not children. They were young men, some of them well into their twenties. On the whole, the idea seemed unwise, perhaps even dangerous—did I realize that there might be serious difficulties?

It was put to me as politely and mildly as possible, for they were really in an uncomfortable position. Since the dean at the university had declined by now to take on the administrative problem of adding a woman to his faculty, they had no other position to offer; and they were unhappy about the circumstances surrounding my unemployment. But they were convinced that Darul Mo'Allamein would be a mistake.

Shaban, fatherly and conservative, was inclined to agree with the Ministry. The American Embassy thought—speaking informally, of course—that the scheme might be imprudent.

To Kayeum, both friends and officials put it more bluntly: why did he want to risk setting off new problems when the old ones had just quieted down? Was he willing to risk a riot? How could he guarantee to protect me? It would be bad enough if I were subjected to verbal mischief, but what if—who knows?—I should be set upon physically?

To all of which his answer was, "I know my boys. I'll vouch for them. There won't be any trouble."

For myself, I was willing to try it. However, there was another side to the problem which Kayeum tactfully did not bring up but I did: if my presence at the school created trouble—any trouble—it would boomerang against him. There were his family and his own future to consider: Joan was expecting their second child. He gave me the same answer, and Joan quietly nodded her agreement. So we were decided.

The Ministry officials were once again on a spot because of me. There was no rule against hiring me for Darul Mo'Allamein, and technically Kayeum had the authority to request my employment. Moreover, they hesitated to suggest that Afghan students might behave badly: badly enough, indeed, for them to worry about my safety.

On the other hand, I was a foreigner—a guest in their country— and they felt a responsibility for my welfare. And beyond their personal concern, there was always the possibility that if something went wrong it might turn into a minor diplomatic incident. They would have been even more worried, no doubt, if they had been reminded that although I had the proper diplomas and certification, I had never taught a day in my life; Kayeum knew it, and I have often wondered at his confidence—and at my own.

The Ministry avoided giving any definite answer and continued to worry about the matter for weeks. But the winter was wearing away. Already the snow was melting in rivulets in the gutters. Kayeum pointed out to the Ministry officials that he had only a few weeks in which to work out his schedules for the school year, which would begin in March. He needed an answer, and he needed a teacher.

One dreary afternoon in late February he stopped briefly at the house. "The Minister says he'll give me an answer tomorrow," he said. "He wants to mention it at the Cabinet meeting today and see what they think."

That took me aback. I tried to imagine the Cabinet ministers turning from, say, problems of the national budget to the miniscule question of my well-being, which had never been other than my own worry till now. I felt like a pest, and rather wished that I could vanish into thin air. And then, too, it struck me that the problems ahead might be a little more serious than I had really been willing to admit.

It was almost dusk the next day when the Kayeums finally knocked on the gate. Joan seemed as calmly cheerful as usual; Abdul appeared tired and rather tense, but he was smiling.

"The Cabinet thinks it isn't a very good idea to hire you for Darul Mo'Allamein," he said. "Informally, they recommended against it, and the Ministry advised me again not to try it. However," he went on emphatically, "they feel that they should not interfere with my autonomy as director of the school, so the decision is up to me."

"Abdul," I said, "you can still say no. If you go ahead you'll be held completely responsible. If anything goes wrong, I mean," I added in a hasty mumble. "Are you sure you want to do this?"

Abdul pushed his karakuli to the back of his head. "I know my boys," he said. "There won't be any trouble. If you want to, you can get your contract at the Ministry tomorrow."

So I did.

9

*T*here was no time left to worry any more about my reception at the school. However I might be met, I was going to be standing in a classroom with work to do. Dreams and possibilities had been adequate enough until now, but every one of them had been swathed in that gauzy attenuation with which one builds castles in the air. Bricks and mortar were what was needed now, bricks and mortar. There was not much time to lay hold of them, and there was little straw.

For years the Afghan government had poured all the funds it could muster into education, but the needs always ran ahead of the available money, like the mechanical rabbit in front of racing dogs. So people were always working on shoestrings, and frayed shoestrings at that. I had already had a glimpse of the meager facilities. Long before I thought of teaching there I had spent a few minutes visiting the school. That was on a late November afternoon, during the final examination period: schools closed during the winter to conserve fuel. The bleak unheated rooms held the bone-touching chill of an icehouse in summer; teachers and students had moved out onto the grounds, where the waning sunlight offered some slight warmth.

Kayeum showed me through a few of the empty classrooms. They were all alike: bare whitewashed walls and worn, uneven brick floors; a desk for the teacher, set on a low wooden dais, with a small scarred blackboard nailed to the wall behind it; rows of unpainted wooden tables and benches, their surfaces scarred into random bas relief by a succession of sharp pen nibs. A line of windows on one side let in the only light: there was no electricity. Here was the structure of education stripped to its skeletal essentials: a place for a teacher, places for students, little else. The equipment would be the teacher's mind and the students' minds.

We sat down to do some planning. The school had two divisions: one prepared teachers for the primary schools, the other for the secondary schools. Only the students in the secondary section studied English. Kayeum decided to assign me to four of the younger classes—one eighth grade, two ninth, and one tenth. Afgan students often begin their schooling late. In a poor family a boy may have to wait until an older brother has finished school, or until someone else is available to help with the farm work, before he is free to study. So my students might be as young as thirteen or fourteen—but they might as easily be twenty. One or two were married and had children of their own. Still, comparatively speaking, these were the younger groups and prudence seemed to dictate my being assigned to them. Since they had already had a year or more of English, I would be spared having to start from scratch with the alphabet.

With a rueful look, Kayeum handed me copies of the worn, dog-eared textbooks that were on hand. I thumbed through them and was appalled at what I saw: "Little Red Coat" was one selection, "The Babies in the Woods" another. I looked hastily at the title pages: the books were part of a series which had been created many years before by a complacent Edwardian pedagogue for use in the primary schools of British India. One could imagine generations of small scholars there bending their heads studiously over these nursery tales—the dark-eyed little girls with their long braids, the boys wriggling their toes impatiently in their sandals as the Indian sun shone outside. Eventually they would have graduated to a conditioned appreciation of Lord Macaulay and Lord Tennyson, and learned to con Shakespeare and Milton; and meanwhile there would be enough of the living language beating about their ears in the classrooms and in the shops and the post office for them to pick up a practical knowledge of English and perhaps even an enjoyment of it.

But for my students the classroom would be all. Kindergarten stories seemed hardly appropriate for young men without time to waste. Besides English, they would be taking three other languages—Persian, Pushto, and Arabic. At the same time they would be studying algebra and geometry, trigonometry, biology, chemistry, two courses in history, geography, theology, and more, with athletics to occupy their presumed spare time. With all this on their shoulders, English had no purpose unless it could serve as a key to the knowledge locked in the typeframes of presses throughout the world . . . knowledge they had not yet had a chance to study, which they would someday have to ferret out for themselves as they needed it. If English was to be of any use to them and not just another burden of classwork, it had to be a key their hands could turn to unlock that knowledge, and it had to be put into their hands as quickly, as directly, and as practically as possible.

Yet these purveyors of pabulum were the only textbooks on hand, and even if better ones were available, there was no money for new books. I felt guilty for not wanting them, when they had been bought and paid for and preserved over so many years as carefully as possible. I was actually glad that they were frayed and grubby and falling apart; it was the only excusable excuse for rejecting them out of hand. They would not be thrown away, of course; the storeroom keeper who was responsible for them would have been horrified by that. But I decided to return them to his care and try to work without them. Now all I needed was a complete new plan, pulled, presumably, out of thin air, and a way to make it work.

We stumbled by chance and necessity onto a method when a helpful outline of the Basic English system turned up. I eventually learned that many specialists in teaching English look upon this method with some horror, but luckily I did not find that out until long after it had turned out to work admirably; so I was free to try it. With this much to go on, I began to fill up notebooks with hopeful teaching plans, and spent my idle moments trying to calculate how I could get hold of some books. Unfortunately, there appeared to be no way and none to be gotten.

But one day when Shaban stopped in, he showed me a little paper-bound teach-yourself-English book based on the very same methods we had planned to use. He said that it had been given to him the day before at the American Embassy library. I threw on my coat and headed for the embassy.

The librarian was a quiet young man of both sense and sensibility, and great good breeding—one of those rare people who win not only affection but respect from everyone who knows them. He was kind, he was practical, and he was interested in making books and information available to all who wanted them. He had, moreover, a useful ability to keep his human eyes open and his official eyes shut when the situation called for it. I wanted to persuade him that this situation did. I wanted some of those books, a lot of them, enough to supply the school. I was determined not to let them escape me; and while I might never have hoped to master the art of the rapier, I would have excelled with the mace.

But there were several excellent reasons why David Nalle simply could not give me any books. The best (and the only one I was willing to accept) was that he had none left. And in the second place, he explained, even if he had had any, he was not authorized to give them to an institution. They were to be handed out to visitors to the library. Books in quantity came under the heading of educational aid, and that was in the bailiwick of Somebody Else. So even when the next shipment came in . . . .

The next shipment?

Well, there might be one. But even when another shipment came in, *if* it came in, he could not give me more than a very few books. To get more I would have to see Somebody Else.

But that involved Policy. That meant Red Tape, because Darul Mo'Allamein was not a part of Policy at the time, nor was it scheduled to be. Therefore any request for assistance would have to be considered in the light of a Change of Policy, and generations of students might live and die before that process came to a conclusion.

He could see that, he sympathized, but what could he do? He might perhaps siphon off a dozen copies or so . . .

It was not for nothing that both of us had learned to haggle in the bazaars. "When the next shipment comes in," I told him flatly, "I want five hundred copies." Claiming to be staggered by this, he countered by reminding me that he really could not give me any, but that *if* he could, two hundred would be the maximum. Two hundred was just about what I needed, so I promptly seized on that. As a matter of form we spent a few more minutes discussing policy versus practicality until he said at last, "All right . . . I'll see what

I can do. Of course, I'll have to keep a few copies to hand out here"—I begrudged him those few—"and I don't know how many I'll get, or when, or even if I'll get any at all. And I can't make any promises. But if they do come in I'll see what I can do."

Meanwhile, of course, there was still nothing in hand but plans and of course a certain determination. Once a foreign aid administrator, conferring with several Afghan officials about an important project, told them, "Don't start to build yet. I've sent for an architectural adviser." One of the Afghans, who was himself an expert in the field and had been much beset by advisers—who often came for three-week visits, submitted reports, and went home—leaned across the conference table.

"Don't send us another adviser," he said quietly. "Send us three bags of cement. That's something we can use."

That seemed to me an excellent definition of my own task: I was there to be a bag of cement.

The first bright March days came and the term opened, but I did not go out to the school at once. Kayeum wanted a few days to pave the way for me. Just what these preparations were to be, he left vague, saying only that he wanted to speak to the faculty and the students before I made my appearance. It would be some days before all of the students were there, anyhow. Those who lived in the nearer provinces or on the main roads would arrive in good time, but others lived in mountain districts, in distant provinces, or in villages far from the high roads. They had to set out on horseback—or perhaps even on foot—to the nearest town where they could get a ride to the highway, then transfer to a bus or hitch a ride on a truck, and so make their way to Kabul. Late snows and muddy roads, washed-out bridges and weather and luck would determine their arrival.

Since I had no idea of what to expect from the students, I was at a loss to prepare any attitude in advance. Between the cross-currents of high visions and ugly forewarnings, I found myself at a still point of utterly blank expectation, feeling nothing but that sort of detached curiosity with which one looks through a microscope at an unidentified slide. I was bound to be surprised and I knew it, so nothing could surprise me. I could not even be nervous.

My debut was set at last for the first day of the following week, that is, for a Saturday. On Friday evening Kayeum stopped in for a moment or two, to say that he was going out to the school to speak to the students about me. He was in a hurry. He only had time to suggest that we come out by gawdi, instead of on the teachers' bus, until I had been formally introduced to the staff. With this advice and an air of unconcern, he left.

The next morning I put on my soberest, most sensible and schoolmarmish manner and, clutching a briefcase, climbed into the back seat of a gawdi, which set off at once, with Gul Baz calling good wishes after us in Pushto.

The morning was bright with cold sunlight, the air clear and damp as though it had been washed. The shops were just opening, the buses were crammed with men on their way to work and children going to school, and the bazaars were stirring into life. In sunless corners and alleyways patches of dirty snow still lay unmelted here and there, and elsewhere a thin layer of mud, liquid as slip clay, covered the frozen ground. The gawdi clattered through the center of the city, along the river road and around the light-bedizened mountain, then turned off the pavement onto the long rough road which led to the school, and beyond it ran straight to the foothills of Paghman. Against the bright blue sky the frosty peaks of the ranges stood out like a rimy hedge. Along the side road that led to Amanullah's deserted palace city, tall pale rows of poplars lifted their bare yellow branches like fragile arms, showing no sign of sap or bud.

Darul Mo'Allamein stood on the far edge of the city among empty lots where, one day, it was expected that the city would expand. Near the suburban village of Deh Mazang we passed the grim prison, that walled secretive relic of medievalism of which one heard fantastic, ridiculous tragic stories which were sometimes true and terrible and therefore pitifully comic: I never passed it without wondering what forgotten souls lingered in the wretched confusion behind its eyeless walls. We came into the half-built-up Carta Char section, where houses were bunched among vacant lots. There was a public telephone alongside the road, then a final group of neighborhood shops: a butcher, a cigarette stall. Then the last bus-stop and beyond it, more empty fields. And finally, there was the school, sprawled along one side of the road. An administrative building and a laboratory building, identical boxes two stories high, faced each other across a narrow side road sparsely lined with skimpy young trees. On either side of these two blocks, long low wings of classrooms and dormitories, their yellowish paint streaked by the weather, were flung out. Behind these lay the barren playing fields.

The faculty bus was already parked, empty, in front of the low steps leading into the administrative building. A few groups of students were standing about, and they turned to stare silently as the gawdi drew up before the steps and I went into the bare entry hall of the building.

The raïs's office was upstairs, a long room lined with low sofas and chairs which were now filled with the members of the staff, apparently waiting to meet me. When I appeared in the doorway, Kayeum jumped to his feet; I saw in his hand the orange beads of his *tasbeh*—the beads that are designed for use by a Muslim telling his prayers, but used as commonly to keep the fingers busy; like chain-smoking.

He led me first to one end of the room, where a white-bearded, turbaned man of patriarchal look and great dignity was sitting: Behtab-sahib, the poet laureate of Afghanistan. The poet nodded, murmuring a few words which I did not catch, his voice grave and polite. Having paid deference to age and art, we turned to rank. The *mudir*—the principal—of my section of the school was a square-faced man of middle age who wore a trim mustache and goatee. His severe look was compounded of pride and discipline: he was called the Hazrat-sahib, for he was a member of an influential family of conservative religious leaders, one of whom had led the reaction against Amanullah's abortive attempt at unveiling women twenty-five years before. My appearance at the school could hardly have been unexceptionable to the Hazrat-sahib, but he welcomed me with grave if reserved courtesy. Then around the room I went, meeting one man after another in a confusion of names and faces as they rose, bowed, shook hands. Several who knew a bit of English tried to put me at ease by using it; others offered the elaborate Persian greetings. Twenty or thirty names and faces—I tried desperately to memorize them at once, and failed; and then it was time to meet the students.

Kayeum escorted me downstairs and across the road, through the laboratory building, and into the long classroom wing. I barely had time to ask him about his meeting with the students.

"What happened last night?"

He answered almost absent-mindedly. "Last night? Oh, I told the boys you were coming and I said I wanted them to do their best."

"That was all? Was there any reaction?"

"No," he said. "That was all."

A wizened old man perched on the steps bobbed and beamed and chuckled at us as we went into the building. Kayeum waved him a greeting. "That's Baba Ghulam," he explained. "He hits the gong outside when it's time to change classes. Don't forget to listen for it. Of course," he added as we walked down the corridor that ran the length of the building, "he doesn't have a watch, so he isn't always exactly precise. You'll get used to that, though. Well, here we are."

We were at the door of a tenth-year classroom where my first students were waiting. We stepped inside.

Twenty-seven young men leaped to their feet in a clatter of scraping tables and benches. Then there was absolute silence. Kayeum suggested I step up to the desk on the dais. I then stood, mechanically, at a loss as to what to do with my hands. He motioned to the students to sit down. There was another scraping of benches, then silence again: they sat stiffly at their double desks, all faces turned to him, all eyes fixed on him. He spoke to them briefly. I did not follow much of what he was saying—it was an introduction, of course—but I gathered from his tone and gestures that he was being eloquent. Then he was done. He turned, nodded to me formally, excused himself, and disappeared. The twenty-seven pairs of eyes swiveled to fix themselves on me: twenty-seven pairs of eyes in twenty-seven strong, unsmiling, and absolutely unrevealing faces.

I heard my own voice speaking. I reintroduced myself. I stood up to write my name on the blackboard and found no chalk. A young man detached himself impassively from a front seat, set some chalk on the desk in front of me, and returned silently to his place. No one else stirred. The blackboard, I found, was just that: wooden boards fastened to the wall and painted black. The chalk squeaked roughly across the grain, piercing in the silence.

Somewhere in the back of my mind an automatic prompter was reminding me to speak slowly and distinctly, and I was enunciating every word as though my fate depended on getting each consonant out precisely. I seemed to be talking about the year ahead, about the new methods we would use, the work we would accomplish. I paused now and then and asked for questions. There were none. There was no visible or audible reaction of any sort at all. Just stillness, utter silence.

My words were coming out by themselves while my mind was trying to burrow behind those closed faces, the eyes so completely impenetrable, so veiled and inexpressive. Baffled, I tried to decipher something from those faces. The students were, I guessed, roughly between sixteen and twenty years old. Under their uniform stolid reserve there were signs of individual qualities which would be revealed in other times and other places: a laughter line, a glint in the eye, an added intensity, it seemed, here or there. Some of them were scowling slightly. Was it concentration? or animosity? or perhaps just near-sightedness?

My nerve-ends were responding to so many sensations at once that I was unable to formulate their impact with conscious thought; but intuition, that faculty of unaware observation and conclusion, was already eliminating the idea of animosity. Belligerence, anger, these are vibrantly active qualities: they will animate the most complete stillness and make their concentrated force felt through the sternest armor. They are unmistakable; and they were not there. I felt instead a high tension, as of long-held breath, and a complete vacuum which I was at a loss to fill except, for the moment, with the sound of my own voice.

"Do you understand me? Do you have any questions?"

Silence.

Into the vacuum again, into the void. I smiled a great deal. I informed them of my confident enthusiasm for our future work. I smiled a great deal. I remembered suddenly to send a paper around for their names. I smiled a great deal. Then outside the window there was a sudden noisy bonging and reverberation: Baba Ghulam at his gong, the end of the class. I smiled again desperately and took up my brief case. The students, still mute and inscrutable, still utterly, impersonally courteous, rose to their feet. I was out in the hallway again, where Kayeum was waiting to take me to the next class. There was no interval between classes, so I had no chance to consult him.

The sequence repeated itself each hour. There was again the uproarious clatter of rising; again the brief eloquence; and then again my mechanical introduction while I scrutinized a room full of stony unreadable faces. Again I was silently handed pieces of chalk, once by an intimidatingly large and severe-looking young man with an unsettling scowl. I smiled and I smiled into silence. I wondered and I wondered. The faces of the younger students were not quite so sternly set, but still they were solemn and intense: young, but terribly grave and silent. I was unaccustomed to that. There was no response at all anywhere. I might have been talking to the walls, except for those eyes which never wandered from my face.

Then the morning was over. They had sat and listened to me. They had been perfectly polite and disciplined. And they had given me no indication at all of what they were thinking—not one of them.

The next day was the same. Suddenly all concern about their conduct toward me became unnecessary and irrelevant. Obviously Kayeum had been right. What was in their minds I did not know: they might think me a brazen hussy. But I need expect nothing but the utmost courtesy from them. Riots indeed! Their manner would have satisfied Jonathan Edwards on a Sunday. What was important now was to find a way to reach them, to shake their mass into individuals, to get some sort of response. I couldn't go on talking *at* them forever.

With the lists of their names in hand I began to call on various students, asking them commonplace questions which, I hoped, would break the ice. Where are you from? What is your home like? At once I discovered the source of their unremitting silence: they stumbled, they staggered, they did their best, but Little Red Coat had done her worst. In two or three years of study they had acquired quite large vocabularies of words like "ogre" and "hut" and "fairy godmother," but few of them could put commonplace English words together well enough to answer such simple questions. They had hardly understood a word I had been saying for the past two days, it seemed. I asked the class leaders—for such, I learned, were the boys who supplied me with chalk: the top-ranking students in each class, who served informally as liaison between class and teacher. Reluctantly they had to acknowledge, embarrassed and stumbling themselves, that the classes had not understood.

"But why?" I wailed to Kayeum. "Why didn't anyone tell me? I kept asking if they understood! I must have seemed like an idiot, talking and talking when they couldn't follow it at all. Here I thought I had explained all about how we were going to work. Why didn't a single one of them stop me?"

"I should imagine," he said thoughtfully, "that they didn't want to seem discourteous. I'm sorry ... I never speak English to them, you know, and I didn't realize myself that they were so far behind."

Discourteous! The next day I stopped smiling for a while and glowered at each class with all the ferocity I could muster.

"If-you-do-not-understand-what-I-say," I told them frigidly, "you-must-tell-me. If-you-do-not-tell-me-I-will-be-very-angry. Do-you-understand?" I asked the leaders.

"Yes, sir."

"Then make sure that they understand!"

"Yes, sir."

"And please do not say 'Yes, sir.' When you speak to a woman you say, '*Yes, ma'am.*'"

"Yes, sir."

Now I knew where I had to begin, which was far back beyond where I had started off. But how to reach the students, how to achieve something more than acquiescent obedience, how to get behind those masks of deep reserve which turned every face, no matter what its features, into a blankly inexpressive likeness of every other face—that I still did not know. During the recess periods, when my husband and I sat in the sunshine chatting with other teachers, the students gathered in little groups and watched me covertly from a distance, but except in the classroom none of them ever spoke to me, and even there, only when I called on them. What were they thinking?

After several days, an idea struck me; it seemed absurd, but it prodded at my mind and would not go away. Could it be possible that the *students* were afraid of *me*? I hardly dared to ask anyone about this, because the word "afraid" is anathema in the Afghan vocabulary. Suggest it even idiomatically—as, for example, "Aren't you afraid you'll be late"—and the chin goes up, the nostrils flare slightly, and the answer is: an Afghan is *never* afraid! This is of course not true, since only fools are never afraid and Afghans are no more fools than anyone else. But it is true that they have a tradition of courage to maintain. And just as an American will admit to almost any sin except the lack of a sense of humor, so one element of the Afghan tradition is a refusal to even refer to fear. This was a delicate issue to raise and to phrase, but the more I thought of it, the more likely it seemed. There was perhaps some charm in the irony of the idea that these students, whom I had been warned to fear for life and limb, might be every bit as uneasy about the unknown quantity that was me.

Ghulam Ali Ayeen, a tall, owlish science teacher universally known as "Marshall" (for uncertain reasons), who was quite popular with the students, seemed to me a likely source of reliable judgment. Besides, he spoke fluent English of a delightfully singular sort: he was largely self-taught, through omniverous and catholic reading, and he talked like a grammar book. He used an enormous vocabulary in the most ordinary conversation, he never made an elision, never left a sentence incomplete, and rather gave the impression of an encyclopedia conversing.

Because of the narrow corridor, the students remained in their assigned rooms while the teachers moved from class to class. One morning I had almost bumped into "Marshall" as I arrived and he left a room simultaneously. He had bowed slightly, beaming at me amiably through his glasses. "I make my egress," he said, "so that you may make your ingress." I was transfixed and enchanted. I decided to turn to him for advice.

After giving my hypothesis some consideration, Marshall was inclined to agree with it. Of course, he pointed out, the students would not be afraid of me, that is, not in the precise sense of the word; but it seemed to him very likely that one might accurately suggest that they were ill at ease with me and possibly in some degree uncertain about how they should conduct themselves. After all, I walked about the world unveiled—although he hastened to assure me that no one thought the less of me for that, quite the contrary. But my very presence in the classroom was clear evidence that I lived by different rules of conduct than those the students were accustomed to. What, then, were the proprieties which I was accustomed to? They were at a loss to know, and rather than risk offending me they remained immobilized, behind the protection of their frozen courtesy. Marshall counseled patience.

I was amused, while at the same time I was somehow awed to think of myself as being awe-inspiring to anyone. I had no clue as to how I could resolve the problem. So finally I smiled as much as possible and plowed on with the classwork, hoping for a revelation.

Meanwhile, the other teachers and staff members had gone out of their way to make me feel welcome. Whatever his private opinion of my being at the school, everyone extended himself to be nice. Every morning when I got into the school bus, each man in turn managed to get to his feet between the close-packed seats and to greet me with the elaborately complicated forms of courtesy. Since most of the teachers sat squeezed in three to a seat, a place for me was a problem, but invariably someone offered me a window seat and himself perched precariously next to the aisle while my husband provided a safe barrier between us. I was greeted again each time I passed a teacher in the halls; my questions, however naïve, were answered seriously; I was very grateful, and even began to feel a little bit at home.

There were only four men who refused to accept my presence: the *mullahs*—the religious teachers. Two of them obviously avoided me. A third, a slight, nervous young man with a wispy beard, passed hurriedly with an uneasy look, as though he wished to say hello like the other teachers but was somehow deterred. This was probably the case, for the leader of the group was a great handsome man with a craggy face, a full black beard, and the flashing eyes of an evangelical spellbinder, whose contempt for me was absolutely clear. He did not ignore me, much less avoid me; he made no acknowledgment of my presence so positive as that. To ignore is to see and overlook, and he simply did not see me at all. He looked through me; I was dissolved, I ceased to exist. He was an awesome figure, striding fiercely down the corridor in his dramatic black hieratic robes and black-and-white turban. When he looked through me and saw me not, I felt for a moment that indeed I was not there.

One day, two or three weeks after I had begun teaching, I almost bumped into him as he came out of the tenth-year classroom. I hurriedly stepped back, although it seemed almost unnecessary. His piercing gaze went through and past my invisibility, and for a moment I could almost imagine that if I had not stepped out of the way he would have walked straight through my nonexistence. I felt terribly embarrassed. He had been talking with a knot of students who were standing near the door, and I wondered if they had thought me rude.

One of the boys leaned across the desk toward me. He hesitated a moment, as though weighing whether or not to speak. Then, "You know, sir," he said confidentially, nodding in the direction of the departing mullah, "we call him Bluebeard!"

I was astonished, and then I laughed. And then he laughed. And a ripple of laughter spread through the cluster of boys and washed like a wave across the room; and for one brief moment we all laughed together. Suddenly the invisible barrier which had stood between us like a wall of glass shattered into a thousand pieces, every splinter of it dissolving in that moment, and we were laughing not at a student joke but with the delighted discovery that we could meet.

A minute later I was at my desk and the students were at theirs, silent as ever and ready for work, their faces serious again. But the masks were gone forever. Through that morning I exulted. Jubilation sang in my head like Cavaradossi's "Vittoria! Vittoria!" in "Tosca."

And somehow from one class to another the invisible walls of constraint melted away, and smiles sprang up like the little red wild tulips that were beginning to shine in the cold fields of earliest spring.

10

*T*he end of March brought Nauroz, New Year's Day, and the city paused to receive the turning of the year.

Calendars are made by men, but the seasons make their own patterns in each part of the world. Therefore a calendar is at best and at worst a bed of Procrustes, a mathematical universal into which we try to squeeze the uncontrollable rhythms of growth and decay, which are the reality we instinctively recognize. The rhythm of the year is bred into each one of us, as into all other organisms, according to the seasons we are born to.

An event of passionate significance may succeed in superimposing itself upon this reality: the Islamic calendar, for example, is pinned to the date of Mohammed's flight from Mecca, the Jewish calendar to that of the creation of the world—both, events of inescapable importance. But even then the private pulse remains true to the natural rhythm and not to the imposed system; at heart we respond to the evidence of the world as we see it around us.

Now, the Gregorian calendar, by which the world commonly does its business, was created around the Mediterranean, where the vineyards come early into bud and the shepherds are carrying the new lambs to shelter before February is out. But northward in the temperate zone one feels instinctively that whatever ceremony may prevail on January first, it is a sham; for the year truly begins with the melting of the snows and the return of light and warmth and growing things: the rebirth of Adonis comes with the spring equinox.

The Afghans are pragmatists; they use three calendars. Affairs involving the world at large are conducted according to the Gregorian calendar of the West, that solid fixture by which airplane schedules and banking hours are everywhere regulated. Religious matters are scheduled by the Islamic calendar, which is lunar and shifting. But for daily life they use their own reckoning, which accords with the realities of land and sky and sowing and reaping as they know them. This is a solar calendar which has been used on the Iranian plateau for thousands of years, since the time of Zoroaster or perhaps even before, and it is attuned to the seasons there. When the country was converted to Islam, the years were renumbered to date from the Hegira, but Afghanistan continues to begin each year on March twenty-first, when the fields are being plowed and the trees are shining with their first budding leaves, and around the city of Mazar-i-Sharif in the north, the plains are in flower.

On New Year's Day in Kabul, though the skies were gray with the approaching spring rains and the air was still damp and unwarmed, there were festivals in the gardens throughout the city. Families strolled placidly under the ancient trees of the Babur Gardens, and along rivulets in the grassy parks near Dar-al-Aman. On the rocky mountainside overlooking Deh Mazang, not far from the school, perches a small mosque painted bright blue; it is the shrine of a holy man whose visions, so they say, led to the miraculous discovery of the tomb of the Fourth Caliph, the Prophet's son-in-law Ali, at Mazar-i-Sharif, many centuries ago. Crowds flocked to the little mosque, toiling up a muddy path to a terrace where booths had been set up to sell oranges from Jalalabad and sweets, and bright toys for the children: papier-mâché horsemen and dolls painted violent pinks and greens. There were games, and a hand-powered whirligig in which the very smallest children were twirled round and round rather slowly, to their terrified delight. There was an aura of sedate satisfaction, of dignified pleasure in the holiday. Some of my students were there and seemed surprised to see me—off the pedestal, as it were. We nodded and passed, reluctant to intrude formality on each other's enjoyment . . .

By Nauroz the wild tulips were everywhere glittering red against the fallow earth: tiny, shaped like rose hips, with bulbous cups and pointed petals, like the tulips in a sixteenth-century botanical plate. It seems at first surprising that the Afghans, who so love flowers, do not cultivate the tulip in their gardens. There it is, springing up willy-nilly in the fields and on the hillsides, ready to hand; yet one sees none of the many carefully bred varieties we know in the West. Perhaps because it grows so profusely by itself, there seems no need to cultivate it. Or perhaps there is simply greater pleasure in leaving it to appear, unplanned and random, spontaneous beauty.

In the north, around Mazar, the fields are absolutely covered with wild tulips, a sheet of glossy red spread out in every direction. The city rises from the broad fertile Oxus plains, and the tiled turquoise domes of the Mosque of Ali rise above the brown city into the deeper blue sky. The tulips are massed so thick in the earth of

Mazar that the very clay of which the houses are built is embedded
with them. When the fields are a crimson carpet around the city
walls, the rooftops burst into bloom like a new Troy burning with
springtime, and Mazar-i-Sharif is a dazzling vision seen from afar:
scarlet fields, and stretched above them the dun-colored walls; then
the scarlet flowering rooftops; and hovering above them all float the
glistening blue domes and minarets of the mosque.

From Nauroz, the city holds festival through forty days of tulips.
From every part of the country thousands of people come to camp
about the walls. They make a pilgrimage to the shrine of the Caliph
Ali (who is greatly revered, especially by Shi'ite Muslims), which
nurtures their souls; and to the vision of flowers, which feeds their
spirits. Numbers of musicians come too, and hold forth night after
night, as long as the world is a garden.

Before the tulips have faded in the north, the foothills of the
Hindu Kush are covered with flowering Judas trees in the Koh-i-
Daman valley, just north of Kabul: a veil of purple flung across
the craggy face of the mountains. At Istalif the blossoming trees
cover the mountainsides with their delicate violet haze, which rises
like smoke from the deep-cut gorges to meet the heavy gray of the
clouded April skies.

Shaban once arranged a picnic there when the trees were in full
bloom. He borrowed a car—he was always borrowing cars and
drivers to take us places—and we drove north through a light rain,
across the valley floor and then along the roots of the mountains, to
where the town clung precariously to the sides of a wooded ravine.
Leaving the car, we climbed up to a high grassy terrace from which
we could look out over the cascade of blossoms and beyond, to
where the valley below spread out in a patchwork of spring fields
until, far away, mountains bounded it in a thin shell.

Shaban had sent his servants on ahead of us. They had already pitched a large tent, paved it with carpets, and filled it with cushions. Over a nearby wood fire the cook was roasting spicy kabobs on long skewers. He served them to us with hot fresh bread and fruit and bowls of rich clotted cream. For some hours we stayed there in rapt languor, playing cards from time to time, or simply watching the pale light shift across the lustrous treetops below us, where each delicate branch was sheathed in blossom, sleeved in violet-colored lace.

We walked about the terrace to observe a changing view and met other picnickers, a family from Kabul. The husband was a friend of Shaban's, and we stopped to talk. The wife had hurriedly pulled her veil down: it had been thrown back so that she could enjoy the view. Now her husband encouraged her, and she shyly drew it back again to smile at me while her young daughters looked curiously from their mother to me, and I wondered what they were thinking.

Before the afternoon waned we left the servants to break camp while we drove north again, this time to the village of Gul Bahar, which is poised beautifully alongside a wedge of rock where two rivers meet. These are the Ghorband, which cuts a pathway down from the central massif of the Hazarajat, and the Panjsher, which spills in foaming torrents through the green fertile Panjsher valley. *Panj* means "five" and *sher* means "lions." It is said that the river is named for five great men, perhaps saints, who lived there once, long ago in the forgotten time before Islam came to the country. No one remembers now who they were, or what they did, or even if they ever really existed, nor anything at all about them except that they were very holy; but they gave their name to the valley, and their presence is still invoked by village women when troubles come.

After Alexander the Great had conquered Bactria, he marched south along the valley of the Ghorband River; and when he reached this confluence he wisely decided to build a city nearby. There was already a city there, Kapisa; although it is now only the little town of Bagram, it was a great center then. But Alexander did not want somebody else's city; he wished to build one of his own, which he could then call Alexandria. He founded so many Alexandrias that one loses track of them all; and one would think that his imagination, which must have been very great, would have triumphed over his vast egotism, and that he would have simply wearied of them all— all the same, Alexandria, Alexandria, and Alexandria—and thought of something different. But no, he was content to have them go on and on like reflections of himself in an endless series of mirrors, one after another, distinguishable only by a place name attached to each of them. In Afghanistan alone he founded two or three Alexandrias, and he did not stay there for long.

Alexandria-in-Arachosia has survived as Kandahar to carry on his name, which is S'Kandar in Pushto. But Alexandria-under-the-Caucasus, which he founded in this place near the rivers, faded away after his death, leaving only a treasure house for archaeologists. Kapisa, although he scorned it, outlived Alexander's city; still, it had its ups and downs, and eventually it too dwindled away. But beautiful carved ivory plaques have been found, and fine vases, and the remains of temples, a multitude of objects made by one people and another, which testify to the grace with which men once crowned this lovely spot.

These valleys are places to make anyone wish to found a city and to stay. The rivers do not flow gently into one another. They are mountain torrents, creatures of the rocks; they meet at an acute angle and rush headlong at one another, flinging themselves together and tumbling over boulders and shoals in a churning tumult of spumy waters. Where they meet, the people of Gul Bahar have made a park and planted it with a grove of tall mulberry trees so they can walk in the shade and watch the play of waters. On the misty spring day when I saw it first, swordlike blades of iris had sprung up among the grass, and there was no sound at all except the rush of the rivers and the faint hissing fall of the rain.

That hovering veil of rain was only a prelude. With April, the spring rains began in earnest and then there were no excursions. The rainy season is called the *haftah-ba'arish*, the Week-long Rain; it lasts nearly a month.

Day after day the sun rises in a clear bright sky only to be shrouded in black clouds before noon. Then the downpour begins, and goes on into the night. Until dawn you can hear it drumming relentlessly on the flat roofs, pouring down, pouring down, as though heaven had decreed that the earth must be washed clean all the way to bedrock, and scoured. At night the lightning lights up the landscape in garish flashes, and thunder cracks among the hills until the walls vibrate; then day dawns bright again; and then it rains.

Roadside gutters and irrigation ditches run brimful, the trees burst out in sudden leaf. Unpaved streets become channels of mud, sucking at every footstep. Gawdis churn their way through it—the horses struggling, the carriages rocking crazily back and forth— and men slog heavily through the streets if they must, heads down against the pelting rain. Only the donkeys pick their way along with dainty unconcern, but their lives are hard and they seem to take every trouble for granted.

By the second day of rain the roof of our house was beginning to leak. It was then that I learned that an adobe roof must be reclayed every summer in time to harden so it can withstand the melting snow and spring rains. Once the rains begin, it is too late for any repairs. Our landlord, knowing a greenhorn when he saw one, had economized by omitting to repair the roof the season before, and we had neglected Gul Baz's warnings.

At first, Gul Baz Khan set pots and pans around the house to catch the drips, but soon there were not enough pots for any but the very worst leaks. Water began to drip in along every joint of the elaborate wooden ceilings. All day long there was a monotonous plink! plink! plink! as the drops landed with irritating irregularity in the multitude of odd receptacles which formed an obstacle course on the floor of every room. In the kitchen, a faint hissing could be heard as drops landed on the hot stove and rose in miniscule geysers of steam. The other rooms were clammy . . . I expected to find lichens growing on the north side of the furniture any day.

Gul Baz found a worn shower curtain and contrived a canopy over the bed. It swung there like the draperies over some medieval throne, sagging slightly as it slowly filled with a puddle. Like a royal canopy it was richly fringed, but instead of golden tassels, it had threads running down into kettles on every side; instead of pearls, these were strung with beads of water which rolled slowly down the threads and trickled into the pots. But until the canvas became waterlogged, it offered one assuredly dry spot in the house, and we received guests there in somewhat cramped and graceless levees.

One Friday a student paid us a visit. For his weekly holiday he had visited his family, who lived in a suburban village. His father was a gawdi driver and they were poor, but they kept a cow and the boy had brought us the gift of a bottle of milk. We had nowhere to receive him except at a little table crammed under the edge of the tarpaulin. He seemed some-what surprised at the circumstances in which his teachers lived; we all perched cross-legged on the bed, Gul Baz brought tea, and we tried to achieve an air of welcoming nonchalance, while around us the endless irregular dripping sounded hollowly through the house, and rain drummed on the roof, and everything was damp and cold to the touch.

Eventually the tarpaulin began to leak, and then we did our best to sleep on the narrow couches in the living room. They were light and could easily be moved about during the night: leaks had a disconcerting way of traveling along the ceiling joints, so that a spot which was dry at one moment might be deluged the next. The dogs had been allowed to stay indoors and instructed to sleep under the couches to keep dry; they preferred to worm their damp furry way under the blankets.

It did not take many days of this to erode my patience: I determined that I would camp out in the streets before I would renew the lease on that house. I set Gul Baz Khan the job of house-hunting, and for days we spent almost every afternoon trudging through the muddy streets to inspect vacant houses he had located.

For me, the first—and at that moment, the absolute—qualification for any house was that its roof should not leak. One drop visible on a packed-earth floor—or even on a polished marble floor—and I dismissed the house out of hand, no matter what its other virtues. The owner might try to discuss the question reasonably, might promise thorough repairs, but at the sign of a leak I had permanently lost interest. Gul Baz would give the man a knowing look and shrug his shoulders, and we would leave, with the landlord remarking sadly, "But the roses are so beautiful!" as he showed us out the gate.

Even among leakless houses, few appealed to me. In the privacy of one's own home, one likes the comfort of familiarity; this is especially true in a far, foreign land. Most of the houses I was shown had been designed to meet the needs of Afghan family life, which of course included purdah. They were usually similar in plan and, to me, characterless: a long corridor running the length of the house would have a chain of boxlike rooms strung along either side. Doors opened in every wall to connect each room to its neighbors and to the corridor, so that women could easily pass about the house unobserved by visitors. The rooms were usually about the same size and with little differentiation for purpose, except for an occasional built-in buffet which defined a dining room. Houses differed in details, of course. Some had fine marble floors and baths. Older houses often had lovely gardens and lawns. Still, none of them engaged my own particular nesting instinct.

Since they were all so much alike, I had resigned myself to choosing more or less at random, and was trying to decide between a house which offered a multitude of roses and one which had a grape arbor, when one day Gul Baz cleared his throat noisily as he stood behind my chair at lunch. Following this conventional fanfare, he announced that there was yet one more house I might wish to see. He had apparently been weighing this suggestion for some time, for he seemed a bit uneasy about it.

"The house is a very good house, I think," he said. "Is a new house, khanum, not finished yet, no garden. But I think the landlord is not a very good mans."

"What landlord is a good man?" I asked bitterly, moving my coffee cup slightly out of the line of a new leak. "Is the one we have now a good man? If the house is good, let's see it."

Gul Baz sent the batcha off to notify the owner that we wanted to inspect the house. It was not far, and the boy returned quickly with a note saying that we would be expected at once. When we arrived, the landlord, a former police officer, was waiting at his gate, nattily attired in a tightly belted trench coat. He turned out to be a clever, unctuous man who showed all of his extremely white and abundant teeth when he smiled, which he did constantly. Having spent some years abroad, he spoke fluent English and pointed out unnecessarily the very apparent virtues of the house he was building. He had designed it expressly to rent it to members of the foreign colony, who generally paid higher rents than most local families. He had gotten the design from a magazine and had planned well. The house was compact and comfortable. Rather unusually for Kabul, it was built on two floors, with bedrooms over the garage and storerooms. A lower hall connecting the front and back yards had a room that would be suitable for Gul Baz. The building was almost finished, and there was not a leak to be seen. Of course, there was no garden at all—the yards, front and back, had been trampled into mire by the workmen and coolies—but from the upper windows one could see beyond the compound walls and neighboring roofs to the mountains, east and west. I liked the house at once.

The kitchen, however, was separate and outside, which is necessary if one cooks with wood or charcoal, as most Afghan families do. I wanted an attached kitchen. Brigadier Akbar bridled at the prospect, and spent half an hour trying to persuade me that I did not really want it; but I insisted that I would not consider the house without it. He looked increasingly unhappy behind his smile, and hinted that another room would bankrupt him. But just then the recent stream of foreigners arriving in Kabul had dried up, and since the house would not do for an Afghan family, he was also very much afraid that if we did not rent it, he might not be able to rent it at all. Torn between his reluctance to add a kitchen and his eagerness to get a lease signed, he was visibly thrashing about. At last, in consideration of an advance bonus, he conceded gallantly to a feminine whim.

I would have given him my word of agreement then and there, but Gul Baz Khan was nudging me; so I announced that I must go home to contemplate the decision and would give him my answer shortly, and, leaving him apprehensively eager, we withdrew.

Gul Baz, it turned out, was not entirely enthusiastic. The house, he agreed, was the nicest we had seen, and it certainly had a good roof. He liked the prospect of having his own room inside, instead of the usual outside quarters. But he seemed unimpressed by the concession of the kitchen. He argued this little drawback and that little drawback until each of his reservations had been dissolved in talk. Then he got down to his real objection: the landlord himself. He pointed out that Brigadier Akbar lived just a few doors away, close enough to be a nuisance.

"I don't like that mans, khanum," he said. "I think he's is not a good mans."

"Well, a good landlord just doesn't exist—everyone says so, everyone complains about them. Why is this one worse than the others? What could he do?"

"I don't know, khanum. I just don't like him."

I thought about this. There was no doubt that Akbar's manner was an annoying amalgam of pomposity and obsequiousness, but one cannot demand wholesome charm from everyone. There was no need for us to have anything to do with him socially. Since he was so frantically eager to rent the house, we should be able to arrange a lease that would eliminate any potential friction and give him no excuse to hang about. I had put up with Sharif and his scholarly ambitions often enough; surely I could endure the brigadier's incessant smiles. I didn't want his eternal friendship, only the rental of his house.

Anyhow, I liked the house. So in spite of Gul Baz's misgivings, the lease was drawn and signed. As soon as the rains stopped, work began on the kitchen; and a few weeks later we moved in.

When the rainy season was over, the clouds vanished as though forever. Not another drop fell from the china-blue, china-hard skies until winter came gray and heavy again. Suddenly and at once, it was summer. Under the blazing sun the muddy roads dried up as hard as cement. The land was baked, the city was baked, and every drop of water became important again and was measured.

The nights were cool and beautiful, and when one looked at the skies one knew why astronomy began on this plateau. It was impossible not to look at them and, looking into their dark brilliance, not to be drawn to wonderment, to the wish to know, order, and catalog, and try to comprehend them. In the mountain air, the atmosphere was like a clear crystal window on the universe, and the dust of day had vanished.

It returned. The heat was not oppressive, but the dust was always there. By midday, when we returned from school, a fine haze hung over the streets, and little puffs of dust rose from under carriage wheels and horses' hoofs. Water carriers gathered at the public faucets to fill their goatskin bags. Some of them were employed by the city to pace slowly along the streets all through the hot quiet afternoons, their waterbags slung across their shoulders, swinging the necks of the goatskins back and forth in methodical arcs, sprinkling the streets to put down the dust.

The acacia trees in the walled gardens came into bloom and for a week or two their perfume filled the city, coming as a sudden delight on an unexpected wisp of breeze. Then the blossoms withered and turned brown, and presently the leaves of the acacias, and of the thick-trunked, twisted willows growing outside the walls of the Prime Minister's house, and of all the other trees which had glistened like green satin under the rains, were all brown with a fine film of dust. Gradually they assumed the same khaki color as the walls they shaded, and the streets, and the plain dull cotton clothing of the coolies and workmen and farmers who filled the streets. In the glare of noonday, everything gleamed pipe-clay white.

I spent my afternoons happily roaming through the bazaars with Gul Baz in tow, searching for household goods: a hand-woven fabric from Kandahar, a bit of pottery or an ancient bronze dug out of the hodge-podge in some shop. We designed some furniture and had it made quite cheaply of a light wood. It turned out rather handsome, although the wood was not properly seasoned, and for months, as it dried out, the long dining table would crack unexpectedly from time to time with a sound like a pistol shot.

Shaban lent us carpets for the new house. They warmed the rooms with their color. Shaban also gave me an Afghan hound, which I named Timur. Timur was an elegant creature with a delicate, powerful body, and very affectionate. He would slip into the house whenever he could, and if the doors were shut, he would leap in through the front windows, some six feet or more above the small patio floor. Guests sitting on the sofa beneath the window bay were often astonished by a dog soaring gracefully over their heads into the middle of the room.

The other dogs accepted him according to their individual natures: Tossy was clumsily friendly, Blackie implacably jealous, while Jenny fell passionately in love with him and followed him about everywhere with a silly moonstruck look on her face, as though he were Bottom and she Titania. All of them were big dogs, fast and muscular from racing constantly around the yard in their self-appointed guardianship of the premises. (Jenny, the smallest, could leap up ten feet against the walls when a neighbor's cat appeared on top.) They had burrowed a peephole under the front gate, where their noses were to be seen as they scanned the street outside for any approaching menace, and every visitor was announced uproariously. They embarrassed Shaban—who did not care much for dogs—by loving him. They also were very partial to a white-haired English gentleman, whom they welcomed by flinging themselves at him, all of them at once, the moment he came through the door in the gate. As they landed on his chest and sent him staggering back against the fence, he would beam at them benignly and a near observer might hear him murmuring, "Good chaps. Down, chaps."

As soon as we moved into the new house, Ahmed-jan set to work to create a garden from the mud. I received from America a packet of seeds for climbing nasturtiums which I gave to him, saying that I wanted them to cover the walls. He looked at the picture on the packet. He was too polite to contradict me, so he turned to Gul Baz and explained to him that nasturtiums do not climb.

Gul Baz, who agreed with him, explained to me that nasturtiums do not climb.

I explained to Gul Baz that while most nasturtiums do not climb, these nasturtiums did.

Gul Baz repeated this to Ahmed-jan.

Ahmed-jan politely replied to Gul Baz that with all due deference to the superior wisdom and learning of the khanum-sahib, nasturtiums do not climb.

Gul Baz agreed with him.

We finally compromised. Ahmed-jan planted the seeds along a wall and put up strings for them, but he did not attempt to train the sprouting tendrils onto the strings. When the long runners spread out across the ground, we all looked at them and agreed that it was indeed apparent that they could climb but equally apparent that they showed no natural impulse to do so. This satisfied everyone.

I also persuaded Ahmed-jan to plant moonflowers. I planned to enjoy them glamorously by moonlight, but it turned out that the only way to see them in bloom was to slip out with a flashlight in the middle of the night and catch them, unawares. After that I left the gardens completely in Ahmed-jan's hands, and he made them lovely.

As for the landlord, he did start to make a nuisance of himself almost at once, as Gul Baz had predicted. I escaped most of the annoyance myself. I ordinarily saw Brigadier Akbar only in the mornings, on the way to school. He was often standing before his own gate a few doors away, waiting for his government-provided gawdi, at his heels one of the little white Pomeranian dogs which he kept without affection because he considered them valuable. A short man in his early fifties, perhaps, he was rather glossily handsome, with graying hair and a dapper mustache. He preened himself on his military qualities and invariably appeared wearing his officer's tunic, a Sam Browne belt and holster, whipcord breeches, and riding boots polished to a high sheen. He often carried a riding crop, which he slapped smartly against his boot from time to time, although he never appeared to get nearer to a horse than when he climbed into the rear seat of his gawdi. He would call out a "good morning" and smile in his pearly fashion until we had passed by. Then sometimes he would go to our home and go in, and try to pry about among our things.

He found that he could neither bully nor condescend to Gul Baz Khan, who was forced to admit him but trailed him closely as he wandered from room to room. So he tried to win Gul Baz over by treating him confidentially—as a fellow Pushtun, a fellow fighting man, boasting a little; but Gul Baz snubbed him. The Brigadier, for all his panoply and airs, fooled no one: transparently, he could not have commanded enough loyalty to lead a lemming to the seashore. It was only certain family connections that had got him the minor post he held. Surely he must have known it; for popinjay he may have been, but he was not stupid. Everyone else certainly knew it, and that must have rankled with him, too. Perhaps it was this which distilled his particular venom; perhaps he could be nothing but what he was.

Whatever virtue is demanded by the world at any given time or place, it will be bred there. Where the sense of honor is powerful, and courage and strength are required to fulfill it, courage and strength will be bred, as they are in Afghanistan. But there will always be those who somehow lack whatever particular quality happens to be demanded by the world around them. Such people have no alternative to public shame except hypocrisy, and no hope for anything but the counterfeit of honor.

But the compelled hypocrite, aware of himself, can never be assured of his ability to convince others; and, besides, he suspects them too, even while he envies them; and then, since he sees around him the very virtue which he cannot attain to, his rewards for all his efforts must be bitterness and anger. He must hate and thereby distort the very virtue he apes: piety, as an example, will be warped into sanctimoniousness. The false mirror image of courage and strength is cheap cruelty. One could see it sometimes in Afghanistan. It cankered in this man.

Meanwhile, after Gul Baz's snub, the landlord came calling only when he was sure that the bearer was out, for he could bully the batcha or the gardener. Then he would poke about, picking up personal papers and reading them, commenting on the taste of the furnishings, and vanishing again before Gul Baz returned. When I complained, he only smiled blandly and changed the subject.

Gul Baz was outraged. So was I, but I was determined not to let it rub at me, so I simply tried to keep personal effects out of sight and to ignore the man. Fortunately, Maullahdad had just returned from one of his wanderings and rejoined the staff, and his misdirected energies absorbed much of Gul Baz's exasperated attention. Despite the Brigadier, it was a nice house, and a happy home.

Afghanistan was changing. For many of the older men on the staff, the innovation of my arrival must have been one more sign that the tradition they knew and represented was passing, that the ark of time was moving beyond them, leaving them to extinction on the sinking shores of the past. When they had come to their work years before, it was in schools where the students existed for the teachers. The teacher was absolute; to him all deference and concern were directed; he was the bearer of tradition, and his learned existence was almost all that was demanded of him. These men had taught by rote and the rod, as they had been taught, and their fathers, and their fathers' fathers; and they had thought that it must always be so, for so it always had been. Now their whole conception of themselves and their role was being set aside, and every day brought its graphic reminders that through the accident of their era they were bound to a past which would be severed from the future, and put aside. New thinking was coming into the school, into the Ministry, into the world around them. Their central place was being usurped by the students and by ideas themselves. They must adjust somehow to shifting circumstances in which they could only guess and grasp.

These were the men who had been accustomed to pass on to their students, word for word, what they had learned, word for word, from their teachers thirty years before. That had always been enough until now. Now it was not enough, and it would never be again.

Some of them were of the stern school which said—as, again, it had always been said, and never questioned—that knowledge must be beaten into young heads. Kayeum had forbidden all corporal punishment in the school, which must have seemed foolish and wrong-headed to such men, and which left them bewildered to grope for unfamiliar means of facing their classes and maintaining the awe-inspired dignity they expected as their due. It was not that they were vicious; they were simply traditional. Occasionally one of them would lapse into old habit and slap a student, or rap a ruler across his knuckles; but they knew that their right had been declared wrong, and that they and not the offending students would be subject to reprimand. To find one's thinking turned inside out— this is hard to live with; and as I was by my very existence at the school a dramatic sign of the times which were outmoding them, I thought that their kindness to me was a generous gift.

Then, too, although my salary was modest by my own standards, it was enormous by theirs, far more than any of the local teachers got, larger even than the director's. It was true, of course, that life in Kabul was more expensive for a foreigner, but that sounded like an excuse even to my own ears. I could not have lived on their salaries—but then they themselves barely could, and strained mightily to keep up their threadbare gentility. Each month when the paymaster counted out a stack of afghanis for me, I felt ashamed in front of my colleagues, who worked as hard as I for so much less. To make matters worse, the paymaster—a fussy, bumbling little man—always seemed to have nothing but small-denomination bills; so that as he sat in the main office and laboriously counted them out on the table, the pile of money appeared mountainous to me, and the time endless. I wished that my pay, or I, or both, were invisible, although it was usually very much needed. I felt as though I were somehow taking unfair advantage of just being me, and flaunting my unearned privilege before everyone. One afternoon I saw a Soviet film in vivid color in which plutocrats sat idly toying with their bars of gold, only pausing now and then to kick a ragged urchin. It sometimes seemed to me I was playing such a role myself. I could never solve the equation to my own peace of mind, and I dreaded paydays.

I might have crossed some of these chasms more easily if I had been able to join the other teachers in casual sociability, just to talk and get to know one another. But I saw them only on the bus in the morning or, briefly, between classes, in the office or the halls. Most of the teachers had classes scheduled throughout the day; during

free hours or over lunch, they relaxed together in the teachers'
dining hall. I rarely joined them, although I knew, and regretted,
that this appeared to be a snub. The breaking of bread together
is still and everywhere an important gesture of friendship. If this
seems old-fashioned, anyone need only imagine for a moment his
own feelings if someone refused to eat in his company, or to accept
his offered food.

However, my classes were all grouped together in the morning,
between eight o'clock and one, and when they were done I left
for home as quickly as possible. Except during the examination
periods, when it was necessary to work through the afternoon, I
almost always declined to stay for lunch. I did not mean to be aloof;
it was necessity, not snobbery, that hurried me home. If anyone
had asked me why I did not stay, I suppose I would have managed
to explain. But out of politeness no one pressed an inquiry, and
I was too shy to create the occasion to explain that there was no
woman's lavatory at the school; and I could hardly ask that one be
built exclusively for me.

So the only fact apparent to my colleagues was that I did not
choose to eat with them. I thought that perhaps I could overcome
the appearance of uncordiality and express my good will by inviting
them all into my home. I would ask them to tea.

Kayeum thought the party was a good idea. He gave me a
complete list of the staff, and volunteered the use of the school bus
to bring them to the house. I sat down to write out fifty-odd formal
invitations. Near the end of the list I hesitated, uncertain what to
do about the mullahs. On the one hand, they had made it very clear
that they wanted nothing at all to do with me, and in the face of
their blunt disapproval it might seem impudent to invite them. On
the other hand, it might seem rude to leave them out. I considered

the problem for a time, then decided to consult Kayeum. He agreed that it was a question of some nicety. "It's sort of 'damned if you do and damned if you don't,'" he said finally, "but I think it's probably better to invite them. Even though they won't accept, it would look worse to leave them out. They may not want the invitation, but I don't really think that they can take offense at being asked."

So I finished the list and left the invitations in the main office, to be handed out. The answers came promptly. Among them were notes from three of the mullahs, who said that they would be very happy to come. The fourth mullah was Bluebeard, the tall, fierce man who refused to acknowledge my existence. He was the only member of the faculty who did not accept. He sent a letter of regret, explaining that he was ill and confined to bed, which turned out to be true.

Astonished and nervous, I went back to Kayeum, who seemed as surprised as I was. "Now what?" I asked him. "The mullahs are coming. What if anything goes wrong? What if they decide not to eat the food?"

"If they refuse the food," he said, "just about nobody else will eat it. If they get offended, the party is busted. I don't know just what to expect—they've never been in a non-Muslim house before, and if anything goes wrong . . . well, now everything had better go right."

I reserved for myself the job of round-the-clock worrying and put the logistics of the occasion into Gul Baz's hands, joining him only to fret out decisions on the menu. For many of my guests besides the mullahs, this would be their first visit to a *kafir*—infidel—home, and the first time they would eat kafir food. While a few of the younger men were ostentatiously iconoclastic, most of them were devout; and while of course I knew that I would not serve them anything which broke Islamic dietary laws, they would have to accept the food on trust—and it was commonly thought that Westerners used pork and lard in all their cookery. As far as possible, I wanted the food to be visibly reliable. Fruit, nuts—those were no problem; but cakes, cookies, sandwiches were potentially dubious. I could only hope that they would trust me, and not doubt the food and reject it.

Gul Baz had begun to rally his forces as soon as he heard of the party. His circle of bearers had a smooth unofficial system of mutual assistance which was the underpinning of most of the major social events throughout the foreign colony. Outside of the important diplomatic establishments, few homes had enough china, glass, silverware, or servants for a really big party. Never mind. You might go out to, say, a dinner dance and find yourself eating from one of your own plates with one of your own forks, while your own bearer stood behind the buffet serving you. He would acknowledge your presence with a silent smile—or, in Gul Baz's case, with an elaborately solemn wink—but any sign of recognition on your part was not only uncalled for but bad form. For when it was your turn to be in need, some First Secretary's dishes would materialize in your home, and his bearer with them. Employers had no part in these arrangements except to avoid meddling and gumming up the machinery.

A bearer would accept such an extra job only if he was not needed at home, which of course greatly influenced the arrangement of the social calendar. When Gul Baz had such an outside engagement, before he vanished for the evening he would provide for our welfare as solicitously as a squirrel provisioning the nest against a hard winter. (Sometimes, if we too were going to the same party, he helped me on with my coat and then managed to whip around to the party in time to help me off with it again. I never knew how he did it, but I fancy it had something to do with his friend, the ambassador's chauffeur.)

Of course, bearers always returned home in fine condition, thanks to the bit of extra cash in their pockets. More remarkably, equipment was equally well taken care of. No piece of china ever appeared to suffer so much as a chip in these complicated transactions, no single spoon was lost; nor was there, among these experts, the slightest lapse in the efficient machinery of one's own household. When Gul Baz was making arrangements within the network on my behalf, my only task was to inquire, a day in advance, how much money he would need for extra help. I would hand it over to him and not even bother to ask what arrangements had been made, certain that they were designed for maximum efficiency.

In his usual style—with a display of virtuoso ease and a great deal of hard work—Gul Baz prepared for the teachers' party. Stacked sardine tins towered on a kitchen shelf, cigarettes were piled on the mantelpiece, enormous quantities of nuts and raisins and candy overflowed huge canisters on the pantry table: the visible signs of preparation. Dozens of slabs of *non*, the crisp flat bread, and eggs, fruit, everything else that would be needed, were on order in the bazaars. All day long the batcha and the gardener ran in and out on their assigned errands like the old couple on a Swiss weather clock.

I stuck to my worrying. With the mullahs coming—and the Hazrat-sahib, too, for he wielded similar religious authority—every aspect of the occasion appeared to offer some rock of orthodoxy on which the whole party might founder. Sometimes I worried clockwise that there would not be enough food, and sometimes I worried counterclockwise that the devout would refuse everything as suspect, and it would all be left uneaten. I worried that the dogs, ritually unclean, might get loose among the guests; I worried with conviction that they would certainly, at the very least, bark. I worried about entertainment: usually one can enliven an "office party" by inviting wives and outsiders, but here it was impossible. I would be not only the hostess but the only woman there, and I could hardly be everywhere at once. I was uncertain about showing films, which was the entertainment I had originally planned: some orthodox folk considered them graven images and refused to view them. I tried to think of an alternative, but there was none better; I decided to risk movies, and then I had that to worry about, too. After agonized consideration, we selected three films from the embassy library: a one-reel comedy about trained chimpanzees, a film of New York, and one showing the Prime Minister on his recent visit to the United States. I worried about the choice for a while after it was made, and then I began slowly to comprehend the concept of *kismet.*

Everything was checked and double-checked, planned and double-planned, to hang on the brink of readiness; for we had no refrigeration, and had to be set for a racing dash on the day of the party. A teachers' meeting was scheduled for the early part of the afternoon. Kayeum promised to delay the staff as long as possible, and I rushed home. By the time I arrived, hot and nervous, every chair in the house was lined up against the walls of the living room, which looked like a dancing academy. Ten dozen hard-boiled eggs were being inefficiently chopped by a bemused Maullahdad. An assembly line for sandwiches had been set up along one side of the kitchen. We had two hours.

By three o'clock the dining table, ten feet long, was hidden under platters of sandwiches and cake. Reserve supplies were being steadily manufactured in the kitchen, but no extra help had yet appeared. The guests might arrive at any moment now. I ran upstairs to dress, remembering suddenly and shouting back over my shoulder, "The dogs, Gul Baz! the dogs!" and heard the kitchen screen door slam a moment later. A few minutes, just enough, and then down the street there was the sound of the school bus.

Coolly poised and numb, I stood at the door, greeting my fifty or so guests as they crowded into the house behind Kayeum. I said hello to each of them. Each of them said hello to me. No one said anything more. They all just stood, woodenly, in a bunch just inside the door. Ill at ease, uncertain, they waited for a cue, as anxious to do the proper thing in my way as I was to do it in theirs. I moved back into the living room and the crowd followed docilely.

Top: *The Khyber Pass, wide enough for history's armies to march through.*
Above: *The border crossing at Torkhum in 1962.* [BILL WOODBURN]

The gorge of the Kabul River above Sarobi. [PAUL CONKLIN]

Above: *Afghan workmen carving the new road out of the Kabul Gorge by hand at Tang-i-Garu with spades, drills and dynamite.* Inset: *Rosanne and Bill on the way to Kabul.* Below: *Road workers amused at being photographed.*

Gul Baz Khan **. . .**

A reading lesson.

*. . . and his nemesis,
Maullahdad.*

*The assiduous gardener,
Ahmed-jan.*

Playing with the dogs in the back garden.

*Our shaky sleeping
porch in Panjsher.*

*Climbing the Great Buddha
at Bamian.*

Shaban Ibrahim.

Chevy.

Right: *Kayeum and Rona in Panjsher.*
Below: *The Kayeums: Abdul and Joan with their children.*

Amanullah's half-finished palace stood open to the winds, the remnant of a dream.

The author shopping. Every neighborhood had its own corner bazaar: a butcher shop, a bakery, a shop selling fruit, nuts, candy, cigarettes, and, in summer, blocks of frozen mountain snow for the kitchen icebox.

The rules of purdah closed in upon each girl as she reached puberty. Shrouded in the shapeless chadri, women moved like huddled shadows. In 1959, when enforcement of purdah ended, a young woman wrote to the author, "I have come out of a prison into the world of light. In my whole life I shall never ask for anything more…" [UNITED NATIONS]

The spring torrents of the Kabul River dwindled to a trickle through the long dry summer. Along the parapets on either side, crimson carpets and piles of quilts were laid out for sale and karakul skins bleached in the sun; workmen cleared silt and debris from the river bed in preparation for the springtime spate of the next year.

The Afghan people is a mingling of many peoples, its face is the face of the world . . .

Above: *Buzkashi being played at Kabul.* [BILL WOODBURN]

Right: *Buzkashi rider in our front yard.*

Buzkashi player and his mount. Holding his whip or reins in his mouth leaves his hands free to control the horse and grab for the carcass.

In cold weather, classes moved outside to catch the warmth of sunlight. A final examination: l. to r., a student, the author, an observer from the Ministry of Education, Dr. Kayeum.

Baba Ghulam hit the gong for classes.

The reading room, a major achievement.

A classroom. Some of these boys went on to take advanced degrees in Europe and the U.S.

...a magazine and a purple pencil to keep...

The pulse of the old city lay in the shops and adobe houses heaped along the narrow alleyways twisting up the rocky hills in the heart of Kabul. Beyond them, spacious new residential neighborhoods stretched out into the valley.

"Wouldn't you," I asked, gesturing vaguely toward the buffet table, "wouldn't you like something to eat?" I led the way, and stiffly, shyly, the men surged obediently into the dining room. Then they stopped again, and stood silently looking at the laden table. No one moved to take anything.

"There is nothing here you can't eat," I said, in what I hoped was a tone that inspired confidence. "There is no pork in anything, no wine." Kayeum repeated this for me in Persian and Pushto, adding reassurances of his own. Still they all hesitated, while all attention was obliquely focused on the few men who could be decisive. Then the Hazrat-sahib made his way through the crowd at one end of the table, picked up a sandwich, and bit into it, smiling. Suddenly I realized I had been holding my breath. In a rush of murmur and movement the tension broke, and all at once everyone was smiling and talking and reaching toward the table. I helped the mullahs to fill their plates; they were smiling too, and suddenly I found them delightful. Then I realized that the men were unaccustomed to buffet service: the front ranks were standing about, helping themselves, while the rest were pressing in from behind them futilely, so I began to explain, and to shepherd the crowd back to the living room with their overflowing plates.

There was no time to celebrate any hurdle passed; the next was at hand. There were enough seats for fewer than half of the guests. Since everyone was trying to do things my way, men were squeezing themselves down politely, two or three to a chair, wedged in acute discomfort. Then Kayeum, who had been standing in the middle of the room, disappeared from view. I felt a tug at my hand and looked down to see Abdul sitting cross-legged on the floor, calling out for companions. I promptly joined him. After a surprised moment in which we seemed likely to be stepped on, half a dozen of the younger teachers joined us in informal comfort on the floor, and the chairs and sofas were by common consent designated for the older men.

The mullahs sat together on the sofa beneath the front windows, eating heartily, eating everything, and with gusto. I had a brief horrid vision of Timur sailing in over their heads, and wondered where he was and prayed that wherever he was he would stay there. Everyone was laughing and talking now. Gul Baz, transformed from dungarees into formal elegance, appeared in command of his corps, which had of course materialized on time after all. They moved about the room offering an unending flow of trays and platters and pots of fresh tea, while the food vanished with delightful speed.

We set up the movie screen, and an exclamation from the end of the room confirmed that the three religious men had indeed never seen a moving picture before. But they waved us on: we must think nothing of it, we must proceed, this was after all a day of adventure. Everyone liked the films, but the mullahs liked them most of all and we ran through them twice while the three of them exclaimed in surprise and nudged one another, and laughed with wholehearted amusement at the comedy. Then one of the mullahs spoke up. He earnestly assured me that it was a pleasure to see our great city of New York, and a privilege to witness how the Prime Minister of their country had been welcomed in our country; and would we perhaps be good enough to show the funny picture once again? So we did, and they laughed just as heartily all over again.

Suddenly, through the heat and cigarette smoke and laughter, someone looked out the window and called out that the sun was setting. The mullahs rose at once: they must make their devotions. With all my worrying, this was one emergency I had not thought of; but Gul Baz of course had, and he was prepared. Stepping to the front door, he held it open with a reverent gesture and announced that a carpet had been laid on the terrace for those who wished to pray. A number of the men went outside. As a hush fell on those who remained in the room I had an awful premonition about the dogs: if they heard sounds outside they would surely bark. As Gul

Baz deftly side-stepped the remaining guests on his way back to the kitchen, he bent down to light a cigarette for someone near me and without a glance in my direction muttered, "Is all right, khanum—dogs locked up tight."

Conversation sank to a self-conscious murmur during the prayers, but when the men returned, laughter broke out again quickly. Then it was dusk, and the driver, who had been fed and entertained in the kitchen, was honking the horn of his bus outside the gate. I shook fifty hands and accepted fifty thanks and repeated fifty times the barest truth, which was how very glad I was that they had all come. My husband and I stood in the gateway waving and all the men hung out of the windows waving back as the bus rattled off in a cloud of dust.

One morning about two weeks later, I was walking down the long school corridor when I saw Bluebeard coming toward me on his way from a class. He had only just returned to the school after his long illness. As he approached, he seemed to hesitate, barely breaking his stride. Then he looked straight at me, and nodded stiffly, and as he passed me, ever so faintly he almost smiled.

12

*I*n the classroom, friendship by no means reduced respect; informality was a matter of degree. When I walked in, the boys still jumped to their feet and stood stiffly silent as I went to my desk. Sometimes I forgot to tell them to sit down again, and looked up to find them standing patiently, waiting for my permission. They were still very serious; it bothered me that they should be so very serious, and I struggled to make them laugh sometimes, or at least smile. This seemed to puzzle them at first and they carefully restrained themselves from any sign of improper levity, until they realized that I was trying to joke, that I did not consider it lese majesty. After their first surprise, their own humor at last began to flash out. But even when they remained solemn, they no longer shut themselves away, their eyes were no longer veiled. Each earnest face was individual, each boy intensely himself. One after another, I began to know each of them.

That boy there in a back seat in the tenth class, with the face of a courtier in a Timurid miniature, and a look of suppressed laughter—he is from Herat, as he had to be, for he has the worldliness of that worldly old city, achieved through centuries at the courts of princes, spent composing graceful couplets and turning the pages of exquisitely painted manuscripts. His name indicates that he is a Sayyid, a descendant of the Prophet. I should like to see him in the emerald-green turban which is the badge of his heritage, and in a robe of shot silk, instead of the plain black coat he habitually wears. While others struggle dutifully with English conjugations, he whisks up every new scrap of language and sets it to use at once in puns and verbal jokes, amusing himself to see how far he can go with them; since he is witty and good-natured and has a subtle mind, he can go far, which delights him. I am amused.

In the front seat of his class sits the top student, not nearly so clever, but industrious and sensible. He is older, he is married and has an infant daughter; and although she is only a girl, he is very proud of her, which he confides to me, since I am a woman and will not be surprised. He is anxious to learn about child care so that he can instruct his wife, in order that their daughter, and other children yet unborn, will grow up to be healthy and beautiful; he comes to me one day to tell me that his child has smallpox, and to anxiously ask my advice; and then I wish—how I wish!—I were a doctor. I tell him what little I can, and share his relief when the baby is well again.

That very tall, thin, gangling boy in the eighth year has emerged as Azizullah, who is growing so tall so suddenly that it is as though his limbs had no relationship to one another: they get in his way, feet and hands. He is extraordinarily gentle and soft-spoken; he writes beautifully and flushes with pride when I tell him so. And here in another class is a boy from Badakhshan who is so unhappy to learn that I have not seen Badakhshan that he forgets his uncertainty in English and stumbles over his lack of words to tell me how beautiful it is. His passion for his home is so great that through his fumbling words I catch a breath-taking vision of high green mountain valleys and foaming streams, and women in red headdresses walking, tall and proud, down to the river with their pitchers in their hands.

Another tall boy, in a strange cap, turns into Abdul Ghias. Abdul Ghias thinks. He wrestles with ideas and comes back to them, weeks after the other students have passed on to something new, asking another question and revealing a pondered, deepened insight. The shy Uzbek student who shares his desk is his chum Mansur Hashemi, whose wide solid cheekbones and round face give him a placid look, as though he had hold of some private joy. He speaks seldom, and then very softly, and admires his friend's ability to express his ideas.

These are the young men I was supposed to fear. And yet, those warnings were not completely phantasmal; they were rooted in long memory. There is not one of these boys who does not have behind him a lineage of conquest and fierce struggle and bloody action. Their heritages are great but they are frightful. There is no people in Afghanistan that has not won its way in battle, or fought hard to keep its foothold, whether by choice or by necessity: in this much-fought-over land, those who would not struggle for their place have been trampled down and have vanished into time. Each people in its day was a conqueror, each has been bound to the land by blood; it was not so long ago when that long day of battle ended, and its beginning is beyond the knowledge of time. The past is an ever-present face behind the mask of the present, so that now, when the reasons and the causes—the migrations and the famines and the princes and powers—have all been forgotten, there remains the shadowed memory of horrors lingering from ancient wars which we, who never knew them, may perhaps overlook in the miasmic horrors of our own time.

Yet in these faces I saw none of this. They were strong faces; one might guess that they had been born with the knowledge that life was not easy. But they were warm and full of light, intelligent, and not harsh. Strange! Not long ago, as history goes, the Uzbeks arrived here as the terrors of Central Asia—and there sits Mohammad Gul, shy, reddening with pleasure when he does his lesson well.

And here in the front row of another class sit two cousins who come from the irascible Eastern Province, which rises swiftly and rebelliously when its nerves are touched, that endless incubator of arms and anger. And they? Last winter they begged their fathers to let them come to Kabul to study, they bedeviled Kayeum to let them enter the school, although they would be far behind the rest of their class, and they are working eagerly to catch up. They are an engaging pair: Ismatullah, tall and straight and handsome, with a delightful boyish grin that flashes out again and again like the constant returning beam of a beacon light; and Mohammad-jan Safi, sensitive and withdrawn, holding himself in deep, thoughtful silence within himself, and in his face the light bone structure and the esthetic strength of a Donatello bronze.

As for that unnerving young man with the crushing look of a football tackle, whose scowling intensity had so depressed me on the first day—why, that is Mohammad Aman, whose whole will is concentrated on stretching his mind and filling it with knowledge which he expects to use in improving the world around him; his brooding is the turning over of dreams. He is completely unaware that he has the awe-inspiring air of a Roman proconsul—unsettling even to Kayeum at moments—and he would be shocked and horrified if he realized it; for he has a great sense of propriety, and although he seems about to thunder that Carthage must be destroyed, he has actually stepped forward only to ask a polite question.

And the questions!

"Sir, in America you have horses?"

"Yes."

"And sheep and goats?"

"Yes."

"And cows and ..." A boy hesitates before the name of the tainted animal of Islam, the unclean of the unclean; but truth must be acknowledged. "And pigs?"

"Yes."

"And camels?"

"No, no camels. We don't have camels in America, except, of course, in zoos and parks, just to look at."

"No camels, sir! But how do you take things from one place to another if you have no camels?"

How indeed?

They ask questions about the things they have read about or heard about and perhaps not quite believed: they will take my word for the truth of them. How do the high buildings stand up? What is the ocean like? How do people live their daily lives in my country? The answers that show differences interest them; the ones that they can recognize please them; for we all wish to be reassured that all men are indeed brothers. There are endless questions about myself, my family, and, above all, my education. Did I really go to a university? Did men and women both study there? How many books have I read? (I estimate. There is a gasp of awe. Is it possible to have had more than a thousand books in your hands?)

They had an insatiable appetite for new words: "Sir, what is the name in English . . ."

One merry-eyed boy was particularly persistent in bringing me objects to name for him. He fished in his pocket one morning and held out his hand.

"Sir, what is this in English?"

I looked: on his open palm a large white scorpion was stirring uneasily, its sinister stinger waving slowly back and forth.

"That's a scorpion! It's dangerous—get rid of it!"

"Yes, sir," he said, and thrust it back into his trousers pocket. "I will take it to biology class."

It was the same intrepid researcher who told me casually another day, "I know a new word in English—'black widow spider.' We are studying them in biology class."

"Do you have black widow spiders in Afghanistan?" I asked.

"Oh, yes," he said. "I have one right here," and he pulled a little matchbox out of that same rich pocket.

"It's dead, I hope," I said lightly.

"It wasn't when I put it in the box," he said, as he left for the laboratory.

Sometimes they asked questions the replies to which would answer the questions they could not ask. Did I like Afghanistan? which was to say, "This is our country: we are of it, it is of us: do you like us?" Or, was I homesick? which had to be answered both yes and no. Yes, because if I were not homesick there must be some heartlessness in me, some flaw in my land; no, because if I were too homesick I was saying that I was not happy in their land. A judiciously balanced answer brought an understanding nod of sympathy, and a smile.

One day a boy asked me about poetry. Did we have many poets in English? It was a searching question. Afghans, who are forbidden the use of wine and spirits, intoxicate themselves instead on words, on couplets and rubais, on lyrics and epics. Sometimes the words seem to sing in their heads until their very souls appear to vibrate with the music. In their harsh landscape, in their plain houses, in their impoverished villages, they luxuriate in the gorgeousness of poetry. Literate or not, they know it by the yard, by the mile, by the volume upon volume, the works of Hafiz, Saadi, Ferdausi, Omar, and dozens of others barely known to the West. Indeed, those who know the Koran by heart—and there are many, there were several among the students—learn it for its holiness but love it also for its literary beauty.

Some poets they consider particularly their own. The great epic poet Ferdausi was born in Persia, but he established himself at Ghazni, at the opulent court of Mahmud the Idol-breaker, where he completed his masterpiece the *Shah-namah—The Book of Kings*—which is as individual as the *Aeneid*, as limitless a well of imagination as the *Odyssey*. (When his royal host rewarded him penuriously, he added to his epic a sardonic description of that king and that court which should serve as a warning to the powerful: do not trifle with artists, for their revenge may just happen to prove immortal.) Then too there are Jalal-ud-din Rumi, the great mystic, one of the illustrious sons of Balkh, and Jami, whose tomb is a national shrine, and Khushal Khan Khattack, who used Pushto as if words were torches.

I once attended a program in honor of some date in the life of Saadi, the philosopher-poet—the eight-hundredth anniversary of his birth, perhaps, or of his death. It was one of those occasions of official appreciation when a large audience must expect to sit for hours on hard folding chairs and look attentive. Everyone arrived with his face prepared in an expression of polite interest, concealing the boredom with which one anticipates a long torpid afternoon spent listening to oratory of predictable nobility while the mind wanders idly off until even vacant thought dissolves in the syrup of ennui. The program was being held in the garden of the Iranian Embassy. The sun was hot, and the microphone of the loudspeaker system was already emitting uneasy crackles and growls of static, when the master of ceremonies unexpectedly announced that the main speaker was unfortunately indisposed, and called upon one of the guests to take his place. The substitute, a diplomat, apologized for his inadequacy. He was not a scholar, he explained, and he had had only a few minutes' notice that he was to speak. He was therefore quite unequipped to tell us anything about Saadi, so, with his audience's permission, he proposed instead to quote from the poet's great works. He begged our indulgence for any flaws in his memory.

There was a stir; people straightened up in their seats and leaned forward, listening now, while he launched without notes into forty-five minutes of quotation. He did indeed stumble from time to time; and each time, twenty voices cried out from the audience, correcting him and helping him along. No one seemed to think that this was in any way remarkable and it was, as everyone agreed afterward, a pleasant if conventional sort of afternoon.

So my student's question about English poetry was really an inquiry into a whole culture. I explained something of the history of our poetry on either side of the Atlantic. To amuse them, I quoted some of Fitzgerald's translations from Omar Khayyám, and, delighted, they answered me with the originals. I recited poetry and they listened to words they could not always understand, feeling the music. I named some names —Keats, Whitman, Shakespeare of course . . .

A hand went up. It was Sayyid Abdul Ali, a dark-eyed boy from Herat. "I have read a play by Shakespeare, sir," he said proudly. "My father brought it from Tehran, translated into Persian."

I wondered, What is Shakespeare like in Persian?

"What did you think of it, Ali?"

He thought for a moment and his face became grave as he turned his mind back to the play and searched for words to say what he meant. Then his eyes widened, and in a very low astonished voice he said, "He writes about *everything*"

On ceremonious occasions the students would send delegations to me at recess time. An important American politician died; his death was mentioned in the local newspapers. A little group of representatives came to me solemnly to offer their condolences, which I solemnly accepted.

Sometimes, when they were unsure of themselves, they delicately sounded me out. When the Kayeums' second daughter was born, Abdul rushed to our house with the news, pulled us along to the hospital to see the new baby, and spent that evening being as ridiculously fond as a new father is entitled to be. The next morning the delegates approached me warily.

"Dr. Kayeum's wife has a new baby," said one of them.

"Yes, I know."

"Is it a boy or a girl?" asked another.

"It's a girl, a second girl."

There was an uneasy silence. A new baby is of course a fine thing, but a girl is not such a fine thing as a boy; and especially since his first child was also a girl, perhaps the second had come as a grave disappointment to the raïs-sahib. Still, one could not very well suggest to a lady who had once been a baby girl herself that girls might in any way be less desirable than boys.

At last: "Dr. Kayeum is very pleased, I suppose," someone said.

"Oh, yes!" I said heartily. "He and his wife are very, *very* happy."

There was a faint sigh of relief as they discovered the appropriate attitude to take. "Yes," they agreed cheerfully, "it is a very good thing," and hurried away to offer their congratulations to the raïs-sahib.

Individually, however, the students hesitated for a long time to approach me outside of the classroom. At recess they would stand at the corners of the buildings watching me sidelong from a distance and nudging one another forward. If I happened to be chatting with another teacher, they would ask him to ask me their questions.

Amused, I answered them directly and added, "Why don't you ask me yourself?" Eventually they did.

One day I found a note from David Nalle in my mailbox at the embassy, asking me to stop in at the library office. The little office was filled with shipping cartons: the books had arrived. There were enough, just enough, and he gave me all of them.

After lunch I hired a gawdi, loaded it with the boxes, and set out for the school, the poor spavined horse hauling heavily at the unaccustomed load. When I got there I called old Baba Ghulam and sent him off to get a *chiprossie*, a messenger boy. Meanwhile, some of the students had seen me arrive and came running across the grounds to help. Their faces lit up when I told them what I had brought, and they lugged the boxes up to the English office, a small room next to the main office, where I unpacked them and spent the afternoon counting and numbering them so they could be handed out. When I left the office some of the boys were waiting for me.

"Did you really bring books for us?" they asked. "Will we get them tomorrow?"

I promised that they would, and asked one or two to be on hand the next morning to help me cart the books to the classrooms.

They were waiting for me when I arrived the next day, and the other boys were waiting in knots at the classroom doors. As I walked in, followed by my aides with their loads of books, the students rushed to their seats. I gestured to them to sit down, and they sat in rigid expectation. I took one of the books, glossy and bright with a red-and-yellow cover, and held it up to show them. They looked at the book as a dog looks at a bone, their eyes unwaveringly focused on it; the sightlines were almost visible, as in a diagram of perspective.

Since the books were not very sturdy, I had decided to give the boys a lecture on taking care of them. I was brief but I was emphatic. I warned them how slight the books were, how flimsily bound. I showed them how to open a book properly, how to press the pages to avoid breaking the spine. I spoke sharply about rough handling, reminding them that each student would be held responsible for his own book, and that there could be no replacements. When I had finished, I sat down at the desk and turned to the job of distribution. I had a class list before me from which I began to call the roll, methodically noting the book number beside each student's name and checking it off as, one by one, they came up to receive their new texts. I was concentrating on the list as I worked, my head bent over the desk: with one hand I wrote, with the other I picked up one of the cheap, bright little books and, pausing only to note the number, automatically handed it to whatever boy might be there. I was too preoccupied to look around, and for some time I noticed nothing unusual. Presently, however, I became aware that each time I held out a book, two hands, grimy at the wrists and knuckles, chapped and rough from dust and cold water, reached out to take it very carefully from my casual grasp. The room was peculiarly silent. I looked up. At my desk, a student was holding his new book gingerly in both hands. At their tables, the other boys were examining their books in much the way that a connoisseur might turn a piece of rare porcelain in his hands. Some had opened them, and were turning the pages carefully or gently pressing them down into place, examining the illustrations or studying the text. Others were looking at the books as objects, turning them about to see the bright glossy jackets, the red-edged paper: colorful blocks of knowledge to have for their own.

In most of their classes, year after year, they had no books. They took down the teacher's dictation in their flimsy copybooks and studied it later, or they listened to his lectures and tried to memorize the information as they listened. The few books they had were plain and worn and old. And I had told them to be careful! I, who had had a thousand books! What, after all, did I know of what a book is? But they knew, as we have forgotten since we lost the need and ceased to chain our books as treasures onto the shelves on which they lay, and ceased to encrust their pages with the illuminations of gold and azure which once marked them properly as the keys to the universe. We know books; but we have forgotten the book.

Now I remembered. In a moment I returned to my list; some of the boys were still waiting. But I was abashed, and gave no more sermons.

On a bright morning, as our faculty bus rattled its way into the school yard, we saw all of the students gathered in front of the administrative building. At that hour they should have been on their way to the classrooms. Although there was no sign of disorder, we were disturbed to see them there—somehow one always presumes disaster—and the bus had hardly pulled to a stop before several of the younger teachers had swung off the back steps and hurried into the crowd to find out what was happening.

The students were standing very quietly; the dormitory directors moved among them, marshaling them into class groups. The mullahs were all there, too, standing together on the steps of the building, in the shade. Kayeum must have heard the bus arrive, for he emerged at once from the office building with the two mudirs at his side, all of them looking worn, and he came over to speak to the teachers as we got off the bus.

During the night a student in the infirmary had died of dysentery. The boy came from a far province, too far to return his body home for burial, as custom would ordinarily require; at least now, in midsummer, too far. So the school had been gathered; we were going to a cemetery on the mountain spur a mile or so across the valley: we were going to bury him.

Kayeum took me aside to tell me that everyone would understand if I preferred to return home—the walk was a long one, the day was hot. But I waited with the rest. I did not know why we were waiting.

With the surface of my mind, of course, I could understand the news at once; but I could not comprehend it at once. I looked around at the students, bewildered by their calm. They looked serious, but then, they often looked serious. I saw no visible sign of sorrow and I wondered at that, until it slowly grew upon me that their restraint came from experience; and the meaning of that realization appalled me.

The dead boy had not been in my classes. He had been enrolled in the other section of the school, and I wondered whether I had known him. I spoke to one or two of my own students, trying to identify him, to place him in my mind and give him a face. Perhaps I had seen him, or talked with him one day? His friends spoke of him quietly. He had been eighteen or nineteen years old, he was an average sort of student, he was a good friend, he liked to play soccer. I could not learn whether or not I had known him: apparently I had not. That mattered only to me, and in a sad way it did not really matter to me, either. The numbing quality of his death was not focused in an individual: I could not picture a particular boy, the particular boy, the one who was dead. No, for me the dreadful fact was the fact of death itself—such pointless, needless death—at such an age; and more than that, it was in the acceptance of that fact by the boys standing around me, their familiarity with such a death, the absence of any protest against it, of resentment—yes, of outrage. For I was outraged. Death itself must be accepted; but I had thought it should come to the old, or be an offering of valor by the young, or else be resented. To these boys it was a reality so well known that they did not argue. I wanted to protest, I wanted to insist that it is wrong for a boy to die pointlessly before he is twenty, it is cruel, it is unfair. They knew it was unfair, but they had learned to accept it.

It was dreadful that death walked among boys; it was worse that they could endure its presence so stoically. It is wrong, it is wrong, for youth to know that life is so little and so vulnerable. Some of them were only twelve or thirteen: surely they should have had more time before they needed to learn that. I could not be quite sure of what I grieved for, with a strange abstract sadness—for the boy I had not known, for his family, who had yet to learn of his death, for his friends, for the existence of death itself? . . . but perhaps it was most of all for such knowledge known too soon. But it was not for me to say a word of this, for the lesson of acceptance was one I had not yet learned.

We waited a long time, almost till midmorning, and then a group of students emerged from the infirmary building. Four of the tallest were holding on their shoulders a rope-strung cot on which the body of their classmate lay wrapped in white grave clothes. The massed ranks of the students opened to admit the little group and then closed around them again, and we all began our march under the glaring eye of day. Kayeum walked with the students in the lead. Sweat ran down their faces. Some of the students and chiprossies were carrying spades. In the midst of the procession, the litter was carried high; from time to time there was a stir about it as one or another of the boys stepped forward in the throng to grasp a corner of the cot, and a previous pallbearer loosened his grip and moved aside. So, each in his turn, the dead boy's classmates put their hands to the task of carrying his body toward the hillside ahead.

We trudged for nearly an hour in slow unmarshaled procession, across the fields and then up a narrow footpath along the sun-baked flank of the mountain to the cemetery on an arid spur overlooking the hospital of Ali Abad. The earth was bare around us, littered with rock and almost white in the dazzling heat. Watered land, fruitful land, cannot be spared from the living, so cemeteries are in the barren places like this and they are very simple. A mound of stones, perhaps a slab for a headstone—that is all there is to mark a grave. The greatest princes are so simply buried here that it does not seem surprising that an ordinary man should be so little marked. But it is sad, sad enough for the old, but sadder still that the young should have no green thing springing up to mark that they were so young. As I walked I felt—more oppressive and palpable than the heat, beyond the sadness of this unreal death of a boy I had not known but who seemed one of mine—that furious helpless sadness that hundreds of other boys should be seeing youth to its grave without rebellion, come so early to acceptance: that they should be so very well prepared.

Several of the older students and chiprossies had gone ahead earlier to dig the grave. It was deep: wide at the top, and then shelved on either side, with a narrower trench down the center, as deep as the two young men who stood in it, smoothing the sides and packing them so that the earth would not fall in upon the body. We waited silently until their work was done and other boys standing at the edge of the grave helped them to climb out of the trench. Then the funeral began.

Several of the students and teachers gently lifted the body in its white cerements: such a thin bundle that it hardly seemed a body. Dysentery wastes away the substance and draws the skin close to the bone: he must have been tall, and anyhow slender, and he must have been ill for a very long time.

One of the students leaped down into the grave again as the others carefully lowered the body, with the outer winding sheet as a sling. Standing below, he helped to ease it into place, and turned it so that the dead boy lay with his face toward Mecca. The winding sheet was withdrawn and the body lay in its white shroud.

Then other boys pushed through the crowd, carrying thin slabs of shale they had collected across the mountainside, and the student standing in the grave put them carefully into place across the shelved earth, so that no earth would fall upon the dead when the grave was filled. At last he called out, and was helped up again. Others took up their spades and began to fill in the grave. The dry clods thudded on the stones. A mullah stepped forward, and recited verses from the Koran, and interpreted them in a sermon, and prayed. When he had finished, the crowd of students began to scatter up and down the mountainside, searching for stones and returning, silent and sweating, to heap them upon the mound of earth. I found some I could carry and struggled back with them to the grave. Boys came to help me, wordlessly taking the stones from my hands and putting them on the heap.

The sun stood straight overhead before the last stone was set down. We stood for a few minutes and looked at the grave, as people will after a funeral, united in the very isolation of their thoughts. Then, teachers, mullahs, students, we began to straggle back down the rocky path again and across the fields, in little groups, in two's or three's, and alone.

13

*T*he village of Paghman in the valley of Paghman was marked out to be transformed into splendor; or, failing that, at least elegance; or, failing *that*, at least some slight touch of monumentality. Its builders accomplished none of these. They achieved instead only a sort of wistful ponderosity which suggests that the original intentions must have been so vaguely grand in conception and so utterly uncertain in detail that nothing could possibly have turned out quite as it was supposed to. The town has absolutely no style, but it does have a cheerful aura of good intention. All the heavy-handed architecture which was meant to grace the summer court of kings, Tivoli to Kabul's Rome, is after all agreeable. The will is taken for the deed, and Paghman is much enjoyed. It is as though Michelangelo's hand had failed and he had never quite managed to carve out the David from that lopsided piece of marble, but everyone looked at his good try and amiably chose to imagine that they saw the David there anyhow.

Of course Paghman's redemption really lies in the overriding beauty of the valley itself, tucked high in the foothills of the ranges a few miles to the west of Kabul. Mountain streams cascade from the peaks above, lacing the fresh green valley with shining rivulets before they are channeled into underground aqueducts to Kabul. The air is cool and fresh, the sound of water is everywhere to be heard, tall stands of oaks and aspens and mulberry trees filter the brilliant summer sun. Since the end of the nineteenth century every king has had a summer palace in Paghman; many of the wealthier citizens have summer homes in the valley, while others rent cottages for the season or take an occasional holiday there among the gardens. For Paghman is its gardens, its gardens are Paghman, created with an absolute surety of touch.

On every side the valley was terraced into lawns and plantings which spread into every available cranny, reaching far up among the rocky heights wherever there was a trickle of water and a bit of soil. There were formal gardens of imposing dignity and modest little squares among the village streets, there were tangles of green wilderness left to itself, orchards, rockeries, enormous public gardens and walled sheltered private ones. All through the hot, dry summer the people of Kabul traveled to Paghman to soothe their sun-weary eyes, to flick the dust from their spirits.

We went too. On hot, quiet afternoons, when even the street cries seemed blotted up by the soft, dusty stillness of the heat, Shaban would often borrow a car and we would all drive across the sunburnt plain and up into the hills, to wander gratefully under the trees. If it was a Friday, Paghman would be thronged as a stream of buses discharged city folk in the center of the town, but, since everyone went his own way, enjoying the gardens with private relish and not intruding on anyone else, one felt no sense of crowding. Still, I myself preferred to go on a weekday when it could be managed, for then Paghman had a beautiful quietude, broken only by the trickling water and the winds brushing through the leaves overhead.

The royal public gardens were a great expanse of smooth immaculate lawns embroidered with formal flower beds in the elaborate geometrical patterns of Moghul and Persian tradition. Long pools set in the greensward mirrored the clear sky and dark clumps of cypress and evergreen. Terraces stretched to the very edge of the mountainside, where cliffs dropped away to the valley far below, its dry earth and pale fields shimmering in the dusty heat, the city a brown block heap in the distance, and beyond it, bounding the horizon, the narrow ribbon of the eastern mountains.

But we more often chose to visit the Court Minister's garden, which was usually open to the public: a grassy slope fitted into a niche of the valley where channeled streams bounded down the hillside and sprayed up here and there in little fountains. It had been laid out with studied informality; there was none of the rigid careful grooming which made me feel uncomfortable about walking on the lawns of the royal park. There were instead fruit trees and casual scatterings of flowers. Along narrow pebbled paths the grass sprouted in untrimmed tufts, and benches were set under the trees. There was a faint welcome smell of dampness and fresh leaves, of leaf mold and turned earth; and sometimes the breeze caught the fountain spray and blew it lightly in our faces. Everything seemed arranged to a very personal taste for relaxed pleasure, with the easy beauty of forests in fairytales or in *millefleurs* tapestries. In spring the fruit trees flowered. In earliest summer one could pick a few of the first strawberries. Then as the trees came into full leaf we strolled in their shade picking cherries and still later, purple-and-white mottled mulberries, very sweet, perhaps especially sweet because the trees were tall and the fruit was hard to reach.

Modern Paghman was largely the creation of three kings who drew the country over the threshold of the twentieth century, but it was the greenhouse of the Kabul Valley long, long before that. When Babur the Great conquered Kabul at the beginning of the fifteenth century he was delighted to find gardens and groves already in Paghman; he noted it happily in his diary among matters of state. Babur happened to have a passion for gardens. Wherever he went he built them, enlarged them, remodeled them to his own excellent taste. He set to work eagerly to improve the waterways and expand the plantings in this valley.

His imperial descendants inherited his tastes, so the gardens were kept up until, eventually, the Moghuls enwrapped themselves entirely in India, and Afghanistan became first a remote province of empire and then was lost to them entirely. Then the gardens of Paghman apparently lapsed into bramble and mountain grass and memory through two centuries and more of wars and dynastic struggles until, near the end of the nineteenth century, the Emir Abdur Rahman established his summer court in the valley, giving it social cachet once more.

But at first its renewed pleasures were designed only for the court. Whatever his virtues, Abdur Rahman was not the sort to throw flowers to his people.

He was a remarkable man, an astonishing man in his own way, and is still controversial today: revered and admired, reviled and hated. The frontispiece to his memoirs is a photograph taken of him during the years of his exile in Russia, when he was barely forty and had long been consigned —permanently, it seemed then—to obscurity. He looks straight out of the picture with a forceful, intelligent, but veiled gaze, leaning forward slightly in his seat. His full beard is already graying; he is somewhat too stout, too heavy-set to cut a truly handsome figure, but an arresting one, nonetheless. He has an air of readiness—the springiness, the inner tension one associates with the coiled-spring muscles of a cat when it is poised, ready to leap or, as suddenly, to relax. In his face there is the enigmatic reserve of a strong man who is waiting, who knows what he is waiting for and what he will do when his own time comes.

When it came at last in 1880, and he mounted the throne, he proved to be shrewd and ruthless, dedicated and tyrannical, cruel and generous and far-seeing. He knew that he would be judged for all of this, and judged harshly; but he also knew his goals, had estimated the price and was ready to pay it. The country had been nearly shattered by almost a century of British, Russian, and Persian meddling. He pulled it together again—by guile, skill, devotion, intelligence, by brute force. He even succeeded where for a thousand years everyone else had failed: he imposed Islam upon the idolaters of Kafiristan and brought the province under control.

But a dynamic tyrant is not necessarily unusual; there have been many of them everywhere. And Abdur Rahman was most unusual. The embedded traditionalism, the ancient guile and more ancient cruelty, the sheer innate intelligence, even the warmth and generosity of the man are no surprise to anyone who has glanced even lightly at the history of Central Asia. The surprise is elsewhere, visible through hints and oblique reflections in his actions and plainly set forth in his writings: it is his remarkable vision of the century to come, its changes, its needs, its demands. He had an astonishingly clear perception of the future and of the path his people would have to take. Dying in the same year as Queen Victoria, when much of the world was sentimentally eulogizing the end of an era without really understanding just what, and how much, had ended, Abdur Rahman in his remote kingdom had already astutely prefigured the sweep of much of what was to come.

His response was superficially quixotic. He could make use of the most medieval and brutal torture, yet he could—a small thing, perhaps, yet so surprising in his time and place—employ an

Englishwoman as court physician. His memoirs, dictated toward the end of his life, give some unity to his career. They suggest that in his own way—a hard, ancient way—he was trying to drive and manipulate the country he loved into position on the brink of that future he foresaw. Others would come after him to take the leap; he outlined the way for them.

Such a king offered his people hard bread and no circuses. When he built in Paghman, it was his, not theirs.

During the reign of his son, the Emir Habibullah, Paghman again reflected the era. Habibullah consolidated, held firm, and took the first careful steps along the path his father had counseled. He was a builder in many ways—he constructed the first hydroelectric station, built a factory, opened schools—but he kept the old framework intact. In Paghman the village grew, the valley was beautified, new palaces were built and new villas for the great who came to spend the summer with the court. But it remained essentially a courtly resort. The old kingdom was changing, but slowly, slowly.

Then in 1919 Habibullah went on a hunting expedition near his winter palace in Laghman, where his elephant corps contributed their lordly presence to such royal diversions. A faction which had been disgruntled by his steadfast refusal to assist—profitably—the Central Powers in World War I, seized this opportunity to assassinate him. Afghanistan had played no part in the Great War. Afghanistan was still walled off and alone. Yet, ironically, with the death of Habibullah the skyrocket of change burst upon this isolated land at the very same moment when, throughout the rest of the world as well, the twentieth century was revealing itself with shattering force in the aftermath of that war.

Habibullah's son Amanullah followed him to the throne, the last of that dynastic family. He changed his title from "Emir" to "Shah," and it was he who changed Paghman, too. He wanted to change almost everything.

How often one comes back to him: Amanullah, that gallantly mistaken man, that knight-errant out of his time, who came to the throne an era too soon—or too late. Or perhaps he was simply the one who had to come first, to try and to fail, so that the ground might be prepared for more prudent men to come after him and succeed. It was characteristic that Amanullah threw open Paghman and its gardens to the people—to *his* people, setting out to make it theirs and splendid. In this last he failed, as he failed in so much. Yet it is what he tried that comes back to mind so constantly and tantalizingly; one can hardly take a road that does not lead to something he tried.

He must have been a bundle of contradictions. One imagines him as forever a cocky young man, self-assured, impulsive, enthusiastic, mercurial, arbitrary. And politically naïve. Certainly he lacked the astuteness of his father and grandfather; but then he apparently did not wish to depend on their iron means. He won the hearts of his people in the beginning by fighting for the third and last time with Britain and breaking the last humiliating fetter on Afghanistan's pride, her enforced dependence on British India for the conduct of foreign affairs.

Amanullah stood before his people and said, Now we stand fully among the nations. They cheered him; and he must have thought then that they would always cheer him, wherever he led.

There was the blueprint for the future: his grandfather had set it down in detail, item by item, from foreign policy to tourism (it is still useful today). His father had moved methodically along that path. But Amanullah was too impatient, too incautious, too careless of where he led and, even more, of how. He wanted to create the future at once, and with a word.

Besides, one guesses that he was himself too uncritically entranced by the Fata Morgana of progress to distinguish always between its dazzling shadow and its substance—a chronic failing of our time and hardly his alone. He was too eager; he lacked sufficient salvation of doubt. So in the end they flung him out and sent the fragments of his hopes clattering after him, and it was left to others to pick up the pieces of the future and fit them back together again.

To compound the humiliation, Amanullah's place was snatched up by a tatterdemalion rogue, a brigand called Bacha-i-Saqao— Son of the Water-Carrier. The Bacha crowned himself, of all things, Habibullah the Second, and sat on the throne—it is impossible to say that he ruled—for a few wild chaotic months, until he was swept aside, and the present dynasty came to power. Well, there was your vagabond king, and a far cry from operetta he was, too.

But when it was all over, passions cooled and memories revived, and then, while Amanullah the man lived out his life in silent exile, the legend began to grow. For whatever else he lacked, Amanullah had the Harun al-Rashid touch, which kindles the imagination and is cherished forever while more solid, more prosaic achievements are all but forgotten. It is purely a gift of grace, and it was his.

In the bazaars more than twenty years later, one would still glimpse him now and then as though he had just passed by:

"Will you have a cup of tea, madame, while I wrap your goods? Even King Amanullah had tea with me once, though that was long ago, of course . . . Yes, he used to come to the bazaar, you know, like an ordinary man, and go into the shops and talk to the people and ask how things were with us. He was a good man, madame, and perhaps we did not understand him then . . . but that was long ago . . ."

Amanullah started a university, opened new schools, even began a literacy program for adults. Classes were held in the mosques at night; he taught one himself. Every evening he would go from his palace to the big white mosque by the river, where, in little wall niches, votive lamps flicker through the dusk: standing before a blackboard with chalk in his hand, going over the alphabet with his students. In 1927, on the night before he left for his glittering tour of Europe—the tour which led him to his most naïvely ambitious dreams and his most flamboyant follies, and with pathetic speed to abdication and exile—it is said that he went to his class and taught as usual, then returned to his palace and prepared for the coming visits of state.

A friend once told me of meeting Amanullah. This man was middle-aged now, and eminent, but then he was just an eager young schoolboy who had come up to Kabul from a province where the King had recently put down an armed rebellion against some of his policies; the boy's father had been among the leaders of the uprising.

One day Amanullah came to visit his school and went about the classrooms speaking informally to the students. The boy was pointed out to him as an outstanding scholar. The King came over to his desk, inspected his notebook, complimented him on his work, and then asked him where he came from and who his father was (for there were very few family names in use in those days).

"Ah," said the King when he heard the answer, "that is a coincidence. I know your father. He has been giving me a great deal of trouble lately." He reached into his pocket and pulled out an official-looking paper. "Do you know what this is?" he asked.

The boy shook his head.

"This is an order for your father's arrest and execution," the King said, showing it to him. "He is very troublesome, your father!"

Then, as the boy sat dumbstruck with fear, Amanullah smiled.

"But it seems to me," he went on, "that a good student deserves a reward for his work, so I shall give you this." He tore up the warrant, put the pieces on the boy's desk, patted him on the shoulder and told him to keep applying himself to his studies, and went away.

There are of course much better ways to rule a country . . . alas.

When I was leaving Afghanistan, a friend brought me as a farewell gift a rare surviving copy of a frayed paper-covered photo album entitled, in the scrolled gold-leaf lettering obligatory for such works, *Souvenir d'Afghanistan: Afghanistan Nouveau.* It was published in Paris during Amanullah's halcyon days, when the future seemed to be within a moment's reach. In its faded photographs one can see Paghman as it appeared to its builders then, through the eyes of their respectable pride and confident hope. In the light of our mid-century, the text has something of the touching assurance of a high-school valedictorian address: *We go forth now to meet the future . . .*

"By the artistic photographs which are presented following this note," the introduction concludes in precise anonymous textbook French, "the reader will be able to judge the beauty, the charm of this country, which join to the very appropriate pride in the possession of such natural riches and so many picturesque sites a very plain understanding of modern necessities, and which strides, under the enlightened direction of its King, toward a future of economic prosperity and intellectual culture." Paghman was obviously to be a herald and symbol of that new culture: more than half of the album is devoted to it. Amanullah had turned the town from a courtly resort into a popular one. When the national holidays were celebrated there each year, people flocked in from the towns and villages; hopefully, they were to be uplifted by its manifestation of the future.

Besides opening the royal gardens to the public and adding new ones, the King had already done much to build the little town into a center of the new cultivated modernity. Ministry buildings had been put up to make it a true summer capital, and a library, a hospital, schools. Broad drives were laid out for the newly introduced touring cars. In the gardens, fountains sprang upward from statuary groups set in the midst of reflecting pools: plunging horses, miniature Berninis. On the lawns there were marble statues of swans and playful children—modern Italian garden sculpture, the last ghostly bleat of a dead renaissance brought here in all innocence to herald one a-borning, and a startling innovation, for orthodox Islam forbids the making of images.

Pavilions and gazebos, Grecian temples and pillared statuary were set among groves of aspen and beds of hyacinth and petunias. An Arch of Triumph rose, a Tomb of the Unknown Soldier, a Monument to the War Dead, adorned with the same fluted columns and entablatures and Corinthian capitals that everyone else was busily using for similar structures all around the world, celebrating their own particular wars. One turns the pages of the album and there they are, gay with flower garlands and the new electric light bulbs, lighting up the holiday nights and *Afghanistan nouveau*.

There was an open-air theater in a terraced garden, and a regular theater which was still, when I saw it, much as it is in the album. From the outside it bore a strong structural resemblance to the nearby barracks buildings, except that it had decorative lintels and pilasters and fanlights and numbers of classic capitals crowned with acanthus leaves. Inside, it resembled a provincial opera house ingenuously decorated with a mixture of classical motifs and traditional Eastern floral intaglio designs. The acoustics were good: when we wandered into the dusty silence I climbed onto the stage and declaimed, using the limp excuse that I was testing them. The house had once been filled with hundreds of wooden chairs, shoulder to shoulder in expectant rows, but they were splintered and long gone by then. For alas, the theater had housed nothing more cultivated than a forlorn troupe of British vaudevillians when rebellion broke out and it was shut down and left empty; and later used for this and for that, or for nothing much.

Like most of the other buildings, it was at heart strong and stolid and unpretentious and rather dull. They were not even ugly. There can be, after all, a virtue to real and extreme ugliness, a point at which wholehearted ugliness carried out enthusiastically enough perversely triumphs into delight. In the state of Ohio, for example, in one county seat after another there are courthouses unsurpassed in dreadfulness, perfectly awful bricky heaps of jumbled false Gothic, Byzantine, Romanesque, and crenellated gingerbread. Once the shock wears off they are a joy: in the little town of Van Wert the courthouse is so ludicrous that it is completely enchanting; I would detour to see it again. There was nothing like that about Paghman, nothing grotesque, nothing that anywhere approached such bad taste. No, there was simply no taste of any sort whatever in its well-built, well-meant, subdued, and assiduously imitative solidity.

Greek pillars and Palladian windows and chalet gabling and wooden porches and even some nice little onion domes were just tacked onto sturdy block masonry by men who had no particular feeling for Greek pillars or gables or porches, but who had been persuaded that these were the adornments of intellectual culture most improving to picturesque sites. They must have been disappointed that these dabs of decoration did not transform four-square solid brickwork into paragons of stylish grace. Or perhaps they were happily unaware of that. But the over-all effect was rather that of a plain, comfortable grandmother who had been persuaded by her children to have her hair done fashionably.

This failure, which is simply a vacuum of certain esthetic sensibilities, was not unique to Paghman. Wherever one looked, modern Afghanistan had little architectural distinction and indeed little gift for any of the visual arts except gardening. Paghman, or the palace of Amanullah in Dar-al-Aman, or the new buildings going up in Kabul, the houses, even the tomb of Amanullah's martyred successor Nadir Shah—these are solid, they are sometimes imposing by sheer solidity, heaven knows they are well intended! But they have no grace, no style, they speak with no voice whatsoever. One feels that they are the work of journeymen with no sensitivity to proportion and balance who are trying to make things look right without the esthetic instinct to assess their own work. One can imagine them asking, "Do you like it? Is it fine?" Well, yes, it almost is, but it is also dull.

This, in a country which once had glorious art and magnificent architecture! The Blue Mosque still stands at Mazar. Fragments of other monuments still exist. Why then should a people lose such feeling for the creation of beauty by the work of their hands? I could only speculate.

Of course the Pushtuns—and for two hundred years the kings and therefore the court with its patronage have been Pushtun—have always been hillmen, not townsmen, at heart: fighters—and fighters travel light; they are not devotees of masonry.

As for the rest of the people, perhaps they have seen their work destroyed too often in every trampling back and forth across this ground. It is conceivable that eventually they gave up the love for their own handiwork because it was too painful for them to keep it. There may be a limit to how often one can see created beauty utterly destroyed and still hold on to the will to create it again for yet another destruction. Afghanistan's past is buried like a vast Pompeii, but with this difference: in Pompeii the earth rose to engulf the city whole, ashes poured from Vesuvius until the land reached up and swallowed the works of man. Here, the cities were razed to the level of the earth. They were crushed and hammered, ravished and burnt and trodden down, until they were driven into the passive earth. Moreover, Pompeii fell to an inscrutable cataclysm of nature; Afghanistan saw the creations of men destroyed by men. It all comes to the same thing in the end: the earth takes everything. But there is a difference nonetheless.

One may suspect that the brand of despair was finally burned into the memory here by the Mongols. A Westerner can barely conceive of what those names mean—Genghis Khan, and a century later, Tamerlane, and their hordes. Nothing was ever the same again after they swept through. They were the Juggernaut. They were the Apocalypse. They were death.

Where they drove their war horses there was desolation, and the very hoofprints were wellsprings of blood. They cut a swathe across the land like a scythe, from Turkestan to the Indian Ocean, and every flower fell beneath the grisly blades of the harvesters of death. It is seven centuries and more since they passed this way, and still people shudder at their names. Until Nazi Germany in our own time, there was nothing like them.

No matter that their grandsons piled up new splendors, for before Kublai Khan could dazzle Marco Polo with his palaces in Cathay, his grandfather must build pyramids of skulls in the Afghan hills, and turn the southern grain fields into desert. He did it all methodically. It is said that Genghis Khan killed a million and a half people when he took the city of Herat and razed it; and after he had done that and gone, he sent back a contingent of troops to wipe out the trembling few survivors who had crept out of their hiding places in the rubble. And the city had hardly put one brick back upon another when Tamerlane came.

Listening to the old stories, one wonders where it all ended. It has never entirely ended. What was lost could never be truly restored. The land had been depopulated, its people were dead, fled, or enslaved; the very soil had been murdered, deliberately turned to desert. Cultures had been erased from the face of the earth as casually as lines from a piece of paper. Ghazni now is little more than a village, which once was a gorgeous court. Balkh, the Mother of Cities, is a heap of rubble for archaeologists to dig in. The scholars were gone, the artists were gone, the poets, the heroes, the kings were gone, the land was stripped of life, the fields were ruined and barren. My horrors die with me, yours with you, but such horrors as these are ineffaceable, and heal, when they heal, like an amputation.

It is true that Tamerlane's descendants rebuilt, and rebuilt splendidly, in Herat, making it the artistic center of their time. (It was left to the British to something about *that*. In 1885, when they concluded that the Russians were about to advance on Herat, the British advisers to the garrison there got it into their heads that to defend the city they must blow up the Timurid academy and minarets which had reglorified it. The invasion never occurred—a settlement was negotiated—but of course one never can tell about such things, can one? The shattered minarets stand in blasted isolation now, or lie piecemeal on the ground like great truncated limbs of a vanished body, stretching across the plain of Herat. Bright bits of colored tile gleam like shiny flowers among the weeds that overrun them.) But the Timurid court in a reborn Herat had the power and wealth to draw on the best resources of the whole surviving Islamic world, and to create new ones; around it the countryside slowly drew its breath and began to live again. Elsewhere, lacking such resources, the will to build beautifully seems to have withered after the Mongols had swept the world away. Slowly or quickly the earth buried the reminders of what had once been. With the creators dead and the creations gone, the chain of tradition was broken, the esthetic nerve was severed.

So when, so much later, the moment to build had come again, the new creators can hardly be blamed for their literal artlessness, for their fond ineptitude, for their uncritical borrowings, their overeager enthusiasms. After all, they no longer had the eye, the hand, the turn of mind to do much more; like musical virtuosity, these require constant practice. It must have been delight enough just to be building again.

Moreover, when they emerged at last from the long isolation which had been imposed upon them, and realized that they had been left aside in a changing world, the Afghans were too proud not to be embarrassed; so they rushed to accumulate what that world had in the meantime stamped as accepted goods, in art as elsewhere. It was touching to find my own world so enthusiastically imitated, and with such eager faith that we were really, truly worthy of wholehearted emulation. I felt the sort of private self-consciousness that a woman might feel about being complimented on her chic when she knows that her skirt is held up by a safety pin.

Now, of course, archaeologists are burrowing about and digging up bits of the Afghan past: Kushan statues, robed and booted like the men of the north today; exquisite Buddhist sculpture, fine carvings, the lineaments of the murdered palaces at Ghazni and the buried temples of Alexander's satraps; a minaret that miraculously survived to stand alone in a remote gorge where once the Ghorid kings had a splendid capital; and more undoubtedly waits to be found. Who knows? Perhaps their secret survival and the vitality they still contain will stir the Afghan imagination to life again. At least, one hopes that before the relentless functionalism which so often treads on the heels of modernization can stultify it once again, that sensibility which responds so beautifully to a flower will recover its response to other creations once more.

14

*T*he summer months were studded with holidays, some sacred to Islam, others to Afghan independence. Almost every holiday here celebrated faith or freedom, one or the other.

The month of Ramazan was a strange inversion of life, an interlude of stultified days and hectic nights. This is the holy month of fasting throughout the Islamic world; between the rising of one new moon and the next, each day from dawn to sunset the faithful are forbidden to eat, to drink, even to smoke. The natural responses of life are reversed: the rising sun closes in upon people, damping them down under the burden of their abstention; the light of day lies heavily upon them, while shuttered night releases the springs of life again—in darkness. There is no real hour of repose.

The dates of Ramazan are set by the lunar religious calendar, so that the fast falls in different seasons year by year. These are wearing weeks whenever they come, but hardest in midsummer, when days are so long and nights so short, and the heat may not be relieved with a drop of water from dawn till sunset. The burden of each day's fast is added to the accumulated weight of those already past and each torpid day drags ever more slowly, until everyone is worn and edgy, waiting wearily for the end of the month. Meanwhile, life is attenuated into a strained alternation of erratic energy and exhaustion.

Ramazan came in June, announced by the cannon on the mountainside as the new moon rose thin and fresh over the hills. Families gathered for a predawn meal and then, as the first day dawned, the city settled heavily into its devout duty. Offices opened as usual, shops opened as usual, men bargained and bought and sold and sat down to their desks as usual—at least in the beginning. During the first days they pushed themselves stoically against the strain. Through stifling afternoons, perhaps shopkeepers fanned themselves somewhat more languidly, nodding at the backs of their shops. Perhaps clerks in government offices might be a bit slower than usual. But the cool night ahead still promised to restore them.

Shops and offices began to empty early as men went home to rest before a long festive evening, but when the sun finally dropped behind the mountains and most of the bazaars were shut, food shops and teahouses burst into exuberant life. In the byways where dusk and quietude usually walked hand in hand at this hour, music blared feverishly from dozens of radios. Bare bulbs blazed beyond midnight in every busy shop, throwing garish stripes of yellow glare across the black alleys. Crowds of cheerful men surged into the patches of light and vanished again into darkness. They were not rowdy; then I never saw Afghans rowdy. They were soberly gay. They congregated at kabob shops, bakeries, teahouses; they strolled the avenues along the river, singing and laughing, celebrating their relief late into the cool night.

Day after day the city drooped like an unwatered plant in the heat, and night after night it came to life again, the sudden release surging up and overflowing, as people tried to cram a whole day's living into the short midsummer night. That was impossible, but breaking the fast resurrected them, tempting them to see the night through. Behind the high walls one could hear the gaiety of family parties. What sleep there was had to be snatched in the hours between midnight and dawn, which meant little enough rest for anyone, anyhow; for when the first light appeared the fast began, so those who did sleep had to rise again soon in darkness to take a last cup of tea before the stars had faded.

Three days, four days, a week . . . the pace of days began slowing down, the cheerful nights began to sound less spontaneous and then to fade away. Faces were shadowed with weariness, nerves were stretched tight, tempers stiff. The bank teller was suddenly, inexplicably rude. The laundryman lost twice as many socks and handkerchiefs as usual and did not even have the energy to invent an excuse. Bargaining banter with a shopkeeper ended abruptly in an unexpected ultimatum. At school the students were slow in answering. They had visibly to gather their thoughts and force themselves to consider the lesson, and I hadn't the heart to press them. Each day seemed hotter than it was. The month wore on. Some offices closed, others went onto short hours. Shops failed to open. Streets languished half empty in the dull heat of midday. The city dozed.

Mercifully, the Ministry closed the schools at last. Everyone was counting off the days that still remained. The sickle moon that had risen, had slowly waxed and slowly waned and finally vanished.

It was time for it to rise again. As dusk settled over the city on the last day of Ramazan, everyone roused himself and waited to hear the cannon announce that it had been seen. Then the slow echoing boom of the gun floated over the quiet city. Ramazan was over. It was the Eid, the day of rejoicing. The city awakened with delight, the bazaars filled again with light and music. Children ran out laughing.

The Eid is time for the new turban, the new shirt. Gul Baz will receive a new karakul hat tomorrow, to wear with the swank new jacket he has been saving for weeks. The gardener gets a new outfit; so does the batcha. On the street outside the house, a troop of horses clatter by on their way out from the nearby cavalry barracks; their hoofbeats sound gay and lively as they have not sounded for days, driving the dogs into a frenzy of resentful barking ... or perhaps they are celebrating too? The fast is over, and the life of the city bursts from behind the dam of duty, pours out over the town, sweeps away weariness.

One crosses a desert, one finds a spring.

Summer had begun with Independence Day, when the Army paraded on the fairgrounds at the far end of the Jadi Maiwand. We sat with officials and other guests in the reviewing stand—a red-and-white-striped tent, a very pretty oven—watching the troops pass by.

I suppose that a more military-minded person than I would have found much to shrug at. The soldiers marched well enough, but their units had none of the snap and verve of precision drill. Their equipment was old. Afghanistan had received little co-operation from the rest of the world in its attempts to obtain equipment and modernize its army. They had had to make do with what they could get, and so fast does the world make progress in such matters that these arms seemed almost antique. Some small items had been donated by the Germans in the 1930's when, like the Kaiser a generation before, Hitler's Reich hoped to disturb the borders of India. (No matter that the faces were not fanatically set, the march not a strut: the unexpected sight of men in the high domed helmets of the Wehrmacht gave me a sudden icy shock.) For the rest, most of what the Afghans had been able to garner was surplus matériel left over from the First World War. The gun carriages were horse-drawn; the few old British biplanes which passed slowly overhead had been hopelessly outmoded for decades.

But then, Afghanistan's strength had never really lain in a regular army but rather in the independent fighting man with his rifle and bandolier and his unswerving determination to hold his land. Militarily, this is undoubtedly a fault and out of date; but humanly, I find some virtue in it.

Indeed, as far as the lineaments of war can ever be human, there was something human in this march that pleased me as perhaps the handsome gloss of spit-and-polish drill would not have done, although I suppose that the Ministry of Defense would—quite properly—have preferred the latter. But I was moved at the thought that just such men as these conscripts, who looked so uncertainly military as they marched beside their aged equipment, had and could and would rise formidably if they were called on to fight for their own.

Meanwhile, they had wreathed the artillery barrels with flowers, and the wheels of the gun carriages, too; and the cavalry rode beautifully on proud handsome horses whose bridles were studded with roses.

At the other end of summer came Jeshin Istiqlal, the week-long national holiday, also celebrating independence and freedom. Then too there were parades, but there was much more. The vast parade ground suddenly took on the appearance of a country fair. Big display sheds went up as every governmental department put forth exhibits of its current projects, with charts and maps and scale models and demonstrations. Booths sprouted everywhere, and the improvised promenades were strung with colored lights. Merry-go-rounds appeared for the children, vendors offered food and souvenirs of all kinds, and Pir Ahmad's curio shop was eclipsed as every shutter in the silent arcade flew open on a temporary teahouse, embroidery shop, boot shop, photographer or candy stall. Sightseers poured into Kabul from every corner of the country. The broad half-paved Jadi Maiwand was for once filled as people streamed toward the Jeshin grounds, milled around the plazas in front of the movie houses, jammed the bazaars and the caravanserais, and camped about the outskirts of the city.

The Afghan people is a mingling of many peoples, its face is the face of the world, and all of it was to be seen in those crowds. Men who might have ridden by with Alexander or with the Arabs, with the Yuehchis, with Darius or Ashoka, or on the heels of Marco Polo. Blue eyes, gray eyes, brown eyes. Black hair, fair hair, red. Everyone who ever passed this way, whether or not they stayed— here was their legacy.

Villagers in tribal dress, bewildered by the bright lights and traffic, their guns half forgotten across their backs. Children in new turban caps clutching at toys or—the very little ones—clinging to a father's shoulder as he strode along and looking very small and solemn with their tight bright embroidered baby caps and kohl-smudged eyes. Old *hajjis*—men who had made the pilgrimage to Mecca—identifiable by their beards dyed orange with henna. Faces marked with the ravages of smallpox or bleared with trachoma. Weatherbeaten farmers in worn gray cotton and tattered vests, clerks in blue serge, students in ill-fitting school uniforms. Women—but the women were all anonymous bundles in their chadris, individuals only below the hem, where one sometimes saw thick ankles and rough shoes, sometimes trim silk-stockinged ankles above fashionably high heels. Old and young, rich and bitterly poor, everyone was in the crowd, and the crowd was everywhere.

One day when the streets were filled and the crowds had spilled onto every byway, I saw a black palace limousine edging its way slowly through the throng. In the back seat, beside the window, was an old man—obviously old, yet with a peculiarly *preserved*, beardless, waxy face; he was smiling slightly, looking out at the hectic street, speaking to someone unseen beside him. With a shock, I knew that he was a eunuch. He must have been one of the last, perhaps indeed the very last, surviving from the long-gone days of the royal harem for whose services his life had been channeled into this strangely nonentical identity. Although he was no longer needed, he could not be cast out upon the world thus, and so he was living out his days on the household staff in some capacity or other. There was a cosseted look about him, as one might perhaps see on the face of a very old Chinese woman whose feet had been bound beyond repair in childhood and whose modern family, pitying her, cared for her gently so that she might not know that she was pitiable. In a moment the crowd shifted, the limousine passed, and he was gone, moving through the present but a survival of time past and blotted out, a great auk living, a coelacanth suddenly brought to light from the human sea.

And the crowds moved on. With all their human variety, there was—is—yet a characteristic which the people of this country seemed to share. One sensed it in their differing faces and in their bearing, marking them all as Afghan. It is, I think, the same quality which makes one always remember Afghans as tall, although of course they are not always tall: a compound of pride and dignity which one may see in almost any face. Even in a coolie bent double under his load. Even—or already—in the children.

This dignity draws the sting of humiliation from the direst poverty: there are many who are poor, but Afghanistan is a country without beggars.

Perhaps this strength comes in part from their ancient code of honor and from the traditional Islamic brotherhood of Afghans. Perhaps it comes in part from that sense of the individual which makes this old tribal monarchy at its root so essentially democratic. But I think that it must be born, too, from the relentless struggle with stony mountain and arid plain by which they have survived in a land where survival itself may be triumph.

15

During the Jeshin celebration, and once or twice at other times
during the summer, the schools would close for holidays. Most of
the students stayed on, of course, but there were no classes, and for
a few days, only the dormitory staff was needed. Some boys who
lived near enough to Kabul might go home, and the rest spent their
time at the fairgrounds.

One afternoon, when we had spent the day looking through
handicraft exhibits with Joan and Abdul Kayeum and they had come
home with us for dinner, Abdul suggested that we all go traveling.
It took only a few minutes to decide that we would get on a bus
and ride up into the Panjsher valley as far as the road would take
us, and only a few hours to get ready. Kayeum went off to make

arrangements for the bus, messages flew back and forth through the evening, Gul Baz packed up a blanket roll for us, and early the next morning we set off for the Kayeums' house, where the bus was to stop and pick us up.

Shortly after we got there, there was another knock at the gate. "Ah, that must be the Professor," Abdul said. "I thought he might like to come along, too. He lives alone, you know, and I think that he must often be rather lonely."

I had met the Professor once or twice at parties. He was a tall, very gentle-mannered instructor at the university. From a number of years spent studying in Paris, he had brought back the wistful aura of a most infinitely modest *boulevardier*. He was probably, as Abdul suggested, often lonely: he was a bachelor, and very shy and diffident. In company he usually retreated into smiling silence, although there was something so pleasant about him that his withdrawal never made others feel ill at ease.

However, when I saw him, as I often did, bicycling home at noon, he always looked nonchalantly debonair in neat tweeds held precisely with bicycle clips, his starched collar unwilted by the midday heat, a narrow-brimmed Panama or a sola topee set smartly on his head, and wearing spotless fawn-colored gloves appropriate *pour le sport.* Then he would smile and bow as he pedaled by bumpily on the dusty road, waving an elegant gloved hand and calling out a cheerful, *"Bonjour, madame, bonjour!"*

This morning he came in as impeccably complete as ever, only ungloved. He put a strapped bedroll on top of the heap of blankets in the hallway, shook hands, and said *"bonjour"* all around, after which he lapsed into shyness again.

The bus arrived late. The driver was honking impatiently, and no wonder, for it was already full of passengers who were eager to be on their way and had been detoured to pick us up. Their baggage had already been piled onto the rooftop baggage rack, their bundles of chickens, tied together at the spurs and carried indiscriminately upside-down or right-side up, were squawking and restless, their babies were thinking of getting hungry and were tentatively bawling, and the boys who had taken cheap passage on the roof, on top of the goods there, wanted to know whether to climb down and stretch their legs or to stay up for immediate departure—which would be better, because they had a goat up there.

Joan and I looked at each other and shrugged.

The Kayeums had decided to take their cook along, and he was already clambering in, heavily encumbered with kettles and ladles and a sack of rice, which he wedged around himself with some difficulty. The driver picked up the rest of our goods and hoisted them up to the fellows on the roof. Then we all climbed into the bus, squeezed onto the crowded wooden seats, assured one another that we were splendidly situated, and the bus set off, the driver pumping joyously at the rubber bulb of his horn.

Although Afghan buses were uncomfortable, they had a compensatory charm all their own. Only the cabs and chassis were imported; the bodies were erected locally on the frames. The side and front panels of the bright blue bodies were painted as elaborately, if not quite so skillfully, as the ceilings at Versailles, with exuberant landscapes, genre views, and scrolled calligraphy in bright primary colors, scalding pink being a favorite. The front window and driver's mirror were often decked with paper flowers and, sometimes, tasteful pin-ups of Indian movie actresses, who incline to palpitating languor. This riotous artistry distracted one in some part from the fact that the seats were hard and fractionally too narrow for an ordinary human bottom, and without much leg room.

But the most impressive thing about the buses—as about all motor vehicles in Afghanistan—was the drivers and their relationship with engines, wheels, transmissions, axles, and the other essentials of the machines they drove. They could keep anything moving no matter what happened, and they did it when necessary with bits of wire, with string, with linseed oil, with spit or, at the last extremity, by sheer willpower and nerve.

As we bumped and swayed onto the road that led north to Panjsher, the driver had a few delicate adjustments to make. Once or twice, without stopping, he leaned out the window to shout up to the passengers on the roof, who responded to his instructions by redistributing themselves, their goat, and the baggage to eliminate a noticeable list to starboard.

It was a beautiful day for a trip. The summer sky was, as always, clear blue and cloudless. The sun was brilliant. Along one side of the road the mountains lay rose-brown and gray, crisscrossed with a faint tracery of shepherds' trails beaten hard by the sharp little hoofs of numberless sheep and goats. Furrows on the distant slopes stretched into cracked gullies crossing the road—the channels of springtime torrents which had burst across the roadbed to water the valley a few months before, now lifeless dry beds, bone-dry, baked hard, their pebbles shimmering with stony light in the full glare of the summer sun. On the other side of the road, fields were laid out across the valley as neatly as truck-gardens, each field precisely rimmed with low mud walls and laced with little irrigation ditches to carry the hoarded water, and colored by late summer ripeness.

Against the treeless stone-colored landscape brilliant little blue-green kingfishers flashed like bits of irridescent enamel as they swung on the telephone wires along the road, while the ever-present big black-and-white magpies stalked about the fields.

We passed Istalif, its green woods tucked into a ravine; and Charikar, where fine knives are made; and stopped at Gul Bahar, at the mouth of the Panjsher River, in the park where the rivers meet. With kabobs from the bazaar—lamb and young kid, crisp and still smoking—and slabs of fresh bread, and melons, we feasted under the trees. When we set out again, the bus had lost some passengers, including the goat, and picked up a few others. We crossed the rushing waters and started up a tortuous road hewn heroically into the mountainside, up through the valley of Panjsher, while below us the river tumbled past.

The landscape changed. Everything cooled and paled—air, light, and color. On either side, high above, the rocky escarpments were hard yellow-gray in the sunlight; but their lower flanks were covered with trees, and wherever the valley reached out from the river and poked fingers of earth among the roots of the hills, there was green: rich glowing leafy living green, as exciting to find as gold shining in the silt of a miner's pan. The further we went, the richer it grew. As the afternoon waned, the high peaks overhead, rising in majestic order toward the ranges of Badakhshan and the high Pamirs, cut off the sun from the lower gorge. There were shadow and water and verdure and beauty into which the spirit could sink luxuriously, soaking in rich green peace. It was miracle; and the miracle was simply a river which never ran dry.

You must live in a dry land to know what a garden is. The very word *paradise* comes from the Persian word for "garden," and Eden must have been much like the valley of Panjsher: an island of sunlit greenness and coolness and flowing water; that is what Genesis says: that Eden had trees and a river. It is a definition. The men who set down that story knew such landscapes as these, and for them the wilderness beyond Eden must have been like the waterless plains which I had seen stretching to the horizon, a land where there is no sustenance but what can be wrenched from the earth by endless labor and unrelenting struggle. That was the wilderness they knew, and they must have had a precise understanding of what I could here begin to comprehend: the terror of Adam and of Eve, driven from such a world as this green valley out onto the sun-blanched rocky earth which they had hardly glimpsed, and never heeded, beyond the leafy edges of their paradise; and forbidden to return.

The road wound upward as the valley rose slowly toward the great peaks in the distance. We stopped for a few minutes in a tiny village. Everyone got out and stretched. Two or three shops tucked under the trees made up the whole bazaar, but Joan and I found there some white quilted, embroidered turban caps which we had never seen before, for they were made only in the valley and not sold in Kabul. We each bought one and put it on, refreshed in vanity if not in the legs.

When the bus started again, the road was bucking and winding along the side of the rock, dipping down toward the river only to twist up higher than ever. The gorge was in sunset shadow and we could not see out to the last sunlight tipping the ranges overhead. Finally the driver stopped at the top of a steep narrow cut and shouted to the remaining rooftop passengers. They clambered down to the road behind the bus, the driver shifted into first, and with the gears screeching we careened down the hill and around a curve where the road was cut under overhanging rock which would have knocked off roof-riders like chessmen swept from a board. The driver stopped again until the men on foot caught up with us and climbed back up. Then in the gathering dusk we rattled off around the last curves and up into the village which stood at the end of the road.

We looked around for a place to sleep. It was a very small village. However, overlooking the road there was a two-story teahouse whose portly owner was willing to rent us some space on the second floor. He led us to the foot of the outside stairway. Or, it had once been a stairway; that may have been before the rains. Whatever it had been, now it was a long uneven chute of dried mud-clay, lumpy here and there where steps had once been, with heel marks dug in where climbers had made a foothold. We made our way up, using knees and elbows, and found ourselves on a flimsy covered balcony supported by frail-looking wooden columns. The floor trembled under every footstep. The Professor looked unhappy. "What about earthquakes?" he murmured to Abdul. "This whole thing would fall down."

The owner heard him and reassured us at once. "Oh, no. Perfectly sound. We've had lots of quakes here and it never even cracks." He demonstrated with a stamp of his foot, the entire structure quivered, and the Professor looked more unhappy than ever. The owner gestured to several doors along the balcony wall. "Fine rooms in there." We looked in. They were musty, stale little cubicles. We chose the balcony.

Then there was the matter of food. It was too late to get much tonight, the man said. Far too late for any chicken or lamb. But with luck he might be able to scare up a few eggs and some tea. In a while. We decided that we might as well go exploring in the meantime, so we assigned the cook to take care of the eggs, dropped our blankets on the balcony floor, and, taking a flashlight—for it was completely dark by now—we slithered blindly down the stairwell and set off down the road, tired and aching and hungry and happy.

The night was beautiful. The starry black sky, luminous from a full moon, was clasped between the ranges on either side of the gorge; the river gurgled and splashed over the rocks below, and a sweet mountain wind swept down the valley, carrying the scent of water and leaves and the ice fields on the high peaks far away. We walked past a corn field. We turned down to the river, where the dark rushing water was invisible except when it foamed and eddied around rocks and caught the starlight. We pulled leaves from the bushes and trees to crush in our fingers and smell, and we remembered being small children.

When we finally returned to the teahouse, the eggs had just been put on to boil. By the time we had eaten them with bread and tea, we were almost asleep. We scrabbled our way upstairs again. As each of us pulled a blanket off the heap, no one noticed that the Professor had picked up his bedroll and disappeared. The rest of us took off our shoes, loosened our belts, and rolled up in our blankets, moving as cautiously as possible to keep the floor from shaking. It quivered at every step in the house below; it shook even when a donkey trotted by on the road. We had exchanged a few thoughtful remarks on this circumstance and were just about to say good night, when the door of one of the little rooms opened and the Professor emerged. He was wearing freshly laundered pajamas, a robe, and slippers, which had apparently come out of the bedroll he had under one arm. He had a lantern and an alarm clock in his other hand. He set down the clock and the lantern, unrolled a sleeping bag, unzipped it, folded back the hem of a fresh white inner sheet, pulled out a nice white pillow, plumped it, and put it into place. As the rest of us watched in awe, he picked up the alarm clock, wound it carefully, checked it by his watch, and politely asked us if six o'clock would be an agreeable hour to rise. We nodded, he set his clock and arranged it with his lantern at the head of his bed, turned back to us, and said to each one in turn, "*Bon soir . . . bon soir . . . bon soir*," He folded his robe neatly ard hung it over the balcony railing, which he tested gingerly for strength, sighing audibly at the result. He slipped into his sleeping bag, and distributed one more round of "*bon soir's.*" Then he blew out his lantern and went to sleep.

We all slept, waking once or twice perhaps at some fancied tremor, but too tired to stay awake and worry. A brilliant sun woke us—except for the Professor, who awoke precisely when his alarm went off. We put our shoes on, tightened our belts again, and, ready for the day, slid downstairs to get breakfast.

While we were drinking our tea the proprietor appeared and took Kayeum off to one side to present his bill. We heard an exclamation of outrage and saw Abdul gesticulating angrily. There was a sputtering exchange of rapid Persian: the charges for food were apparently the equivalent of a dollar per egg, while the rental might have been more appropriate for Palm Beach. In the midst of the dispute, someone had come up the road and stopped quietly to watch. A voice said, "Sir . . ." and I looked around to see one of the older students from Darul Mo'Allamein standing there, holding an enormous basket of grapes. We called to Abdul, who turned, broke off the argument, and came over to greet the boy.

"Why, Din Mohammed," he exclaimed, "I didn't know you lived here."

"Oh, raïs-sahib," said the boy, "I don't live here. I live on the other side of the mountain—over there." He nodded toward the range behind us. "But last night in my village I heard that you were here with some of our teachers, so I came to bring you some grapes and say welcome to Panjsher."

He put his basket down in front of us. There must have been twelve or fifteen pounds of grapes. Din Mohammed looked at them thoughtfully. "I'm very sorry that I couldn't bring more than this," he said, "but I couldn't get a ride and this was all I could carry walking. If I know that you are coming again, I'll arrange to bring you more."

"How far is your village?" Abdul asked him.

"Oh, about twelve miles, no, maybe ten."

Abdul looked at the mound of grapes. "Thank you," he said, and we all said "Thank you."

"Raïs-sahib," the boy said, looking toward the proprietor, who had been watching the whole scene in surprise, "is this man giving you trouble? Excuse me—let me speak to him." He walked over to the man and spoke to him for a moment in a very low voice, scowling.

The owner's face changed. He rushed over to us and seized Abdul's hand. "Oh, sir!" he cried. "Please accept my apologies! I didn't know that you were the raïs of a school! I didn't know that your friends were teachers! I'm honored to have you in my house, to offer you food—I can't think of charging you! You are my guests!"

Abdul looked at him with distaste. "No thank you," he said. "We'll pay. We'll pay fairly." The man looked horrified and, chattering more hasty apologies, rushed away to bring fresh tea. Din Mohammed rejoined us, looking satisfied.

Kayeum grinned at him. "All right," he said, "what did you say to him?"

The boy grinned back. "Oh, I just told him you were my teachers, and if he took a single afghani from any of you, all the students would come here and kill him."

Din Mohammed did not stay with us very long. He had to walk back over the mountains to the village he had left long before dawn. So after a cup of tea he said good-by and set off.

The grapes he had brought were delicious, pale green and solid and sweet. After you have been asked if Afghanistan does not have the finest melons in the world, you are certain to be asked if it does not have the finest grapes. It well may. There are hundreds of varieties. The fruit shops have them piled in a rainbow of colors and there are many kinds I have never tasted anywhere else. Those which Din Mohammed brought were particularly fine. We carried big bunches of them down to the river and dangled them in the water a moment to make them icy cold. Then we sat on the rocks and paddled our feet in the foamy snow-fed river while the sun filtered green through the trees and bushes and the world around us was beautiful.

The valley of Panjsher was as lovely as a legend. It could have been named for five real lions as easily as for metaphorical ones, for they might well have come here to lie down with the lambs. It would seem too a proper home for unicorns, which are at once wild and gentle like the valley itself. We wandered about eating grapes, and rode on patient little donkeys up into the hills, and spent beautiful quiet days there, until the bus returned and it was time to go.

On the return trip, the bus was not so crowded. It left late and traveled slowly, stopping for the night at a small town near the lower end of the valley.

When, late in the afternoon, we pulled up in the village bazaar, two students stood there, smiling and waving. Assadullah, from my eighth-year class, explained that all arrangements for our stay had been taken care of: we were to spend the night in his father's garden and to have breakfast with his family the next day. Dinner was ready for us now.

"But how did you know we were coming?"

"We heard that you were in the valley. We knew that you would pass this way."

So we went with them to a walled garden orchard by the riverside. Rope-strung beds had been set up for us under the trees and a feast of pilau and chicken and fruit was waiting.

I lay awake for a long time that night, looking up through the leaves to the stars, listening to the water rushing by, not wanting to fall asleep and lose any of it; thinking how far I was from home, and how near.

In the morning the bus, guided by the two students, came to pick us up. We drove out into the countryside to one of the high-walled farm villages I had often seen from the road. They look like fortresses; they once served as fortresses. Like medieval manors, they stand self-sufficient and invulnerable-looking, turning their backs to the world and conducting their life around the inner courtyard. The clay walls are fifteen or twenty feet high or more, and thick, and windowless. At the corners there are stubby towers, narrowly windowed, and the courtyard is lined with household and farm buildings, sheds, granaries, and stables.

Assadullah's father was obviously a khan and the leader of a large family clan. We went through a high gate and across the yard where one or two donkeys were tethered waiting for their daily duties to begin, then into one of the towers which was part of the house. Upstairs, in a big square room lined with carpets and cushions, a number of men were waiting for us. We were greeted and seated, and then the servants began to bring in food: tea, eggs, fresh bread, big bowls of clotted cream, meats, and a multitude of fruits and melons. For almost two hours we ate and talked, while with politely covert glances our hosts curiously observed the foreigners, two of them unveiled women, one of whom was teaching a son of the family.

Finally they escorted us back to the bus, where the driver and the other passengers had been waiting with amazingly cheerful patience. Assadullah's father thanked us for honoring him with our company and at last inquired about his son's studies.

"I hope he is working hard," he said sternly. "I want him to become an educated man."

Kayeum gravely assured him that his son was doing well. I found a chance to half-wink at Assadullah, and, behind his father's back, he smiled. Then we left them behind us and drove away to Kabul.

16

One morning the teachers' bus was stopped by a road block half a mile or so from the school, and, grumbling, we all set out to walk. Then we looked ahead and began to run. Fire engines were pouring a last trickle of water into what had been the chemistry laboratory. Before dawn, flames had engulfed it, sweeping up the staircase and almost trapping the chiprossies who slept in the storerooms on the second floor. Kayeum, arriving within minutes of the alarm, found it blazing so wildly that he feared dynamite might be needed to stop it once it struck the laboratory itself; but students raced in and brought out the chemicals before the flames got to them. That probably saved the rest of the classroom building and perhaps the whole school from ruin, although the two-story section was completely gutted.

Now everyone was standing around, watching the firemen play their hoses through the shattered windows of the smoldering blackened shell. On the edge of the crowd the school storekeeper was wringing his hands and bemoaning the loss of the old school records, which had been stored in the upper rooms. No one had looked at those documents for twenty years; there was little likelihood that anyone would ever have wanted to look at them till the end of time; like the heap of worn-out tennis sneakers which he kept preserved in a cupboard of the supply room, they were dust-covered and long-forgotten. But, like the sneakers, they were his responsibility; now they were a sodden mass of ashes, and it was certainly true that if anyone, whether on earth or perhaps before the Throne of Judgment, should ever demand to see them, the poor man would be utterly unable to produce them; so he was miserable. It may well be that even to this day he wakes up sweating in the night, having dreamed of a Voice thundering, "Where are the records of Darul Mo'Allamein for the 1930's!" and himself unable to answer.

There were no classes that morning, and the stench of waterlogged charred wood hung over the school grounds for days.

It took time for the Ministry to find the money for emergency repairs, so the shell was still desolate, the school walls still smoke-streaked, a few weeks later when the King drove by on his way to Paghman and noticed how bedraggled the place looked. He gave personal instructions that the laboratory should be rebuilt at once and the whole school repainted and spruced up.

When Kayeum stepped into the English office with the good news, we indulged in a brief orgy of delight at the prospect of a fresh coat of whitewash, inside and out. In the midst of rejoicing we had an idea—oh, a tremendous idea! Cheap powdered pigments of the sort used in poster paints could be gotten in the bazaars; couldn't we add some to the whitewash and have colored classrooms? Magnificent thought! Grand innovation! We were so dazzled by our own audacity that Kayeum, carried away, made a decision: we would not stop at one color, we would use many. Pink, yellow, green, blue: each classroom would be different. In our minds' eyes we could see them looking like the models of advanced design shown in the architectural magazines. Underneath, of course, there would be the same old mud-brick walls; but what a surface!

When word got around among the students it set off a tremolo of excitement that matched ours. Looking back now, I wonder at it: could it have been such a few years ago? And was it really possible for grown people with serious responsibilities, and students mature in austere realism, to have been so delighted, so exuberant, even triumphant, merely because a few pennies' worth of colored powder was to be added to some whitewash?

But then I remember the drab, ugly, cheerless rooms in which the school lived and worked day after day; that their chipped and dingy walls had never been anything but soiled flaking whitewash, and even that an improvement on un-painted adobe; and that nothing better had ever seemed possible; so that those garish rainbow walls were more than paint. They were a herald of untold possibilities; they said silently, "Not always only this." And yes, it is true: we felt daring, as though we were doing something grand and unheard of. And we were. We were moving the dream a quarter of an inch, and who knew what miles might not follow?

The students were fascinated but puzzled; what was the reason for the colored rooms? They asked Kayeum. Perhaps it would have confused them more to tell them what had really been in our minds: "Because it will be bright and pleasing and there is little enough around you that is simply bright and pleasing." At any rate he said, "It is sound educational theory." That was impressive; they asked no more; fortified with a new pedagogical dictum, they began to look forward to something bright and pleasing.

The masons went to work repairing the burned-out building, slowly, brick by brick, week by week. When they were finally done, one day the painters appeared. They had a limited but tenacious grasp of their work, a profound resistance to change, and no interest whatsoever in educational theory. Schools were whitewashed. They could with difficulty acknowledge the possibility that the whitewash might be colored. But that every room should be different, and the colors rotated—that was unheard of. It was ridiculous. They balked. They declined to understand what was wanted, arguing that it could not possibly be wanted. Explanations did not move them. At last Kayeum, exasperated, simply ordered them to it; at which they put the whole project down to an eccentric whim and unwillingly went to work, expressing with every look and movement the exaggerated indulgence people use for humoring intractable madness.

The boys inspected the sample color splashes on a corner of the building and waited eagerly to see what color their rooms would be. Class 9A even sent a delegation to me to ask respectfully if they might have pink walls. I dared not reawaken confusion by interfering with the painters' precarious obedience to a rigidly fixed color rotation, but I surreptitiously worked it out on my fingers and was happy to tell the envoys that their classroom would indeed be pink.

The next morning one of the same boys burst in on me during a class, begging me frantically to come at once, something terrible had happened! I rushed after him into the hall. At the door of their room, his classmates filled the hall. Their faces shared a peculiar sickly expression.

"Look, sir," they said, and pointed.

I looked. Inside the room the painters were at work, and their resistance had apparently snapped. The whole idea was so crazy— pink, blue, yellow, green, pink, yellow, no two in a row—well, if madness was the order of the day, why stop halfway? So they had dumped all their leftover colors into one bucket and were busily painting the room an appalling shade which might have been called mauve and then again might have been called puce, and was unquestionably to be called disgusting.

The boys spent seven hours a day in that room, six days a week. They looked at me reproachfully. "You promised us, sir," someone said softly, "that it would be pink."

I spoke officiously to the head painter. The man gave me a blank look and went on with his work. I told a student to get the raïs-sahib and he raced off, returning breathlessly with Kayeum, who had been summoned somewhat incoherently and rather expected to find blood. By this time another several square yards of wall had been made hideous. Abdul rescued the situation at once. At his sharp orders the painters stopped. They listened to him and looked at one another, shook their heads significantly, and reluctantly departed to dump the offending bucket of color into the nearest gutter. The room was repainted pink, the class was saved from disaster, and my word was vindicated.

The paint plan was only one of many which sprang to life in the little English office. It was a veritable Jupiter's head for ideas springing to life, full-blown and armored. The room had originally been the raïs's office, but Kayeum preferred to operate informally on the move or from an easy chair in the main office next door, where the staff and students had easy access to him; so he turned it over to us. When he wanted to escape the telephone for a while, however, or to discuss an idea, he would drop in.

A cadre of the younger teachers also took to stopping in there, to relax and talk and turn up new ideas. Some were transmuted into reality, more were not, but they were the sparks thrown off by the wheels of enthusiasm which turned constantly and spontaneously in the school. It might be a design for a better school uniform, or a plan to write some badly needed textbooks, or another to plant fruit trees around the grounds. We schemed endlessly and futilely to get hold of window screening for the kitchens, the dining room, and the latrines: dysentery and its fellows were a constant scourge among the boys. A day, an idea, an attempt.

Sometimes students came to see Kayeum when he was there, and if he had to discipline a boy he often preferred to do it in this room, away from the gaze of the staff. Sitting in a low armchair, he would look up at some great husky young man standing in front of him, shake his head sadly, and say, "I'm disappointed in you!" and the student—as likely as not, big enough and strong enough to have broken the raïs-sahib in two without much effort—would hang his head, reddening with shame. He was their friend. It was terrible to fail him. That was his discipline, and nothing more was needed.

When he was in the English office and a student came to see him, they would often, in deference to me, talk in English. One day it occurred to me that this was the only place in the school, or anywhere else, where a boy had a chance to use the language he was so laboriously learning; and then it occurred to me that there ought to be such a place, one where the students could go regularly. So we decided to start a reading room. We would get books and magazines in English, and make a rule that within those four walls the boys would have to speak English only, and maybe even try to enforce that rule.

There was no sense calling the project a library: we had absolutely no hope of finding enough books to make a real library. Besides, the school already had a library. True, it was never open; the librarian was personally responsible for every book, so naturally he kept them all locked up tight and safe. But the library was there; it had to keep its prestige as well as its sanctity; we must not trespass; so this was going to be just a reading room. I managed to scrape together a few dozen books and good David, at the embassy library, donated a huge stack of old magazines and two or three subscriptions to keep us supplied. Within twenty-four hours Kayeum had assigned me a big empty room near the dormitory and located some extra tables and benches and a lopsided bookcase which, propped up with a brick under one corner, was quite usable. The equipment being complete, we could start.

No project was ever left to stand alone. There were too many things that could be done and perhaps should be done or at least might be tried, to leave anything to itself and simple. Between the time any idea was first conceived and the time it was actually attempted—which might not be very long—other ideas would crystallize around it until the original thought was encrusted with them and had itself been reduced to a mere core for them, like a rock left in a salt mine. If the reading room began with the purpose of providing a place for the students to practice English and have access to reading matter, almost at once we saw other possibilities it offered. It could be a first exploratory experiment in self-government: let a student committee run it. Which opened up another innovation: class elections. The boys were accustomed to waiting for instructions from their elders and betters, and stepping carefully within the bounds set by them. For the first time we would put a project into their hands and ask them to carry it. Even with a degree of judicious assistance from the wings, this amounted to dumping innovation on them with a startling thud; but the job was small enough and unessential enough that the worst that could result from its failure would be just that—its own failure.

If we could make the plan work, the committee members might begin to develop some initiative, some independent responsibility, perhaps even a sense of organization— "teamwork," that sacred panacea—which would filter through to their classmates. I thought I might sneak in a small blow at the tradition so old here and so imbedded that it was almost taken for a law of nature: an educated man does not use his hands, it being far below his dignity to put a shoulder to the wheel, let alone a nose to the grindstone. Of course, there is a virtue to such respect for learning, while such privilege has a seductive appeal for all who can take advantage of it (including, there and then, myself); but it is a crippling encumbrance for young men who want to work miracles of change in a cosmic moment, particularly if some of those miracles are rather badly needed. It puts theory on an exalted plane with no relationship to action, so that the man who knows the theory of the pulley would never think of building one for a bricklayer or a miner to actually use. Literally, he would not think of it.

My lever to move them was, if worse came to worst, the invariably courteous acquiescence I could demand as a foreigner with my own strange foreign ways.

The students, of course, had no idea of this mélange of purposes. They knew that (1) we were going to create a place for them to read English; (2) they were going to do something connected with it; and (3) they were prepared to do it if they could only find out what it was they were supposed to do, which, they trustingly expected, would doubtless be told them in good time.

The first task was to get each class to elect its committee members. It was not easy to explain to the boys what was wanted, let alone why. Anyone takes his own customs so much for granted that the logic behind them is presumed to be self-evident, when of course it is not, not at all. For an American, who starts his voting career by selecting the kindergarten milk-monitor and steadily ballots his way through clubs and classrooms until at last he can greet the voting booth like an old friend, a secret ballot seems like a simple, standard, obvious technique, the natural way to decide things. It is neither so simple nor so obvious and certainly not particularly natural. As a revelation of the democratic process, trying to explain the reasons for it was at least as instructive to the teacher as to the students.

Our one previous grappling with American electoral processes had proved confusing to all of us. That was the summer of 1952, and the Kabul newspapers had reported the nomination of General

Eisenhower for the presidency. The boys thought he had been elected. When, a few weeks later, Adlai Stevenson was also nominated, they wanted to know why the United States had suddenly begun to use two presidents at once. With laborious effort, I thought I made everything clear. When I discovered, however, that they were now in a state of profound awe at Mr. Stevenson's temerity in daring to oppose a candidate who must surely be supported by the might of the American Army, I did not feel that the electoral process as I knew it had been fully illuminated for them.

Voting itself was not new to them. Afghans are familiar enough with that in the *jirga*, or council, at which local, tribal, even national affairs are decided—but by an open vote, a show of hands. It was difficult to explain to the boys why they must, instead, write on little bits of paper, fold them up carefully so that no one could see, refrain from looking at their neighbors' votes, and drop the papers into a hat; only to have them promptly unfolded again for counting and then, oddly enough, when it was all over, secretively destroyed. Despite my best efforts, I did not feel that I was getting the philosophical concepts across. So I finally suggested rather lamely that there was more than one way to do most things, and it was worth while to try various methods and compare them.

They were listening earnestly, still surprised that they were being asked to make these choices at all. A jirga was for grown men; they were students. Why didn't I just appoint the committee members? That was the way it was always done when duties or honors were being passed out. The teacher decided, and it was not a very hard decision to make, because, as everyone understood, one of the two or three scholars who stood at the head of their class would always be chosen. In fact, as I struggled with my explanations and they with the muddle that emerged, some of the boys suggested sympathetically that we might as well do it the usual way; since everybody knew anyhow who would be elected, that would save me a great deal of trouble.

I started to argue, then I just said no, uncomfortably aware of falling back on that same sheer authority to push them into some self-reliance. Irritated, I exclaimed, "You say you want to do great things for your country. How can you if you can't do a little thing like this in school?" They concluded at once that they had angered me; they accepted the rebuke and the decision and tried to make amends. Now they wanted me to know that they were sure that it would be good to do things my way simply because it was my way and I recommended it. That was further exasperation, precisely the sort of polite acceptance of my authority which I hoped to shake, but if I told them so, they would only get unhappier.

We muddled on. The boys listened intently to learn just what it was that they had to do: nominate, write, fold, keep silent—and in every class it was the same. They went through the procedure several times, at first with absolute confusion, then with less confusion until at last, getting the knack of it, they voted. Then came the revelation, far clearer than anything I could ever have said: in almost every class the students were surprised to learn whom they had chosen. The top students, who had looked so assured when the votes were being cast, were crestfallen when they had been counted. The effect was remarkable. Suddenly the boys realized what they had done and wondered at it; no further explanations were needed. That much I could see. But what I could not see, and only faintly sensed, was the discussions they held among themselves—in the dormitories, in the dining hall—about this instrument for speaking one's mind with the openness of privacy. Was this perhaps related to the word "democracy?" They found no sure answers, but they thought about it and they did not forget.

One afternoon I came back to the school for the first meeting of the Reading Room Committee. I found the members waiting for me in our big empty room, one corner of which was filled with the magazines and books, another with benches and tables piled high. We pulled a few benches into a circle and sat down. I began to explain their job to them. I would advise them, but they themselves were to run the room: they would make the rules and enforce them, take care of the reading materials, decide on the program, set the hours for every class. I was as simple and plain and specific as possible. They listened docilely, ready to be helpful, waiting for instructions. But I was explaining, not instructing. I asked them for questions; they had none. I asked them for opinions; they had none.

One must start somewhere. Take something concrete.

"How shall we arrange the tables and benches?"

No answer. My fault—I should know that was the wrong way to put the question. Reframe it. "Shall we put them next to the pillars?"

Enthusiasm. "Yes, sir. That would be very good, sir."

"Or should we put them by the windows?"

Enthusiasm. "Yes, sir. That would be very good, sir."

"Which way do you think is better?"

No answer. Respectful attention. Whatever they were learning, I needed some lessons in patience. I sighed, then I stood up and started toward the heap of furniture. "Let's put them by the pillars and see how they look," I said.

"Oh, sir, that is chiprossies' work! I will go and find a chiprossie tomorrow to put the tables in place."

"We won't be here tomorrow," I said. "Besides, that's wasting our time today. Let's do it now."

"But there is no chiprossie here now, sir."

"Then let's do it ourselves."

Surprised, they sat still until they saw me actually pick up a table and start across the room with it. Then they all jumped up to take it from me and went to work lugging the tables and benches and the tottering bookcase into place. They looked sheepish; they were clearly too surprised at themselves to conceal their surprise; this was unheard of. But it would have been worse, far worse, to allow me to do such work, a teacher, a woman, a guest in their country. As it was, they were constantly dropping their own burdens to snatch something from my hands. Yet somehow I did not appear to think it was embarrassing for any of us.

First day, first lesson.

I begged some colored posters from a Swiss travel agent in the city. They were scenic, mostly of Alpine valleys filled with prosperous milch cows but no people, so I hoped that they could be put on the walls without being condemned as graven images. I held them up against the walls.

"Do you like this?"

"They are nice pictures, sir, but that one is crooked."

"Yes, I know. Put it up that way, at an angle."

"Crooked, sir? But don't you want them straight?"

"Well, let's try it at an angle for a week and see how you like it. There are different ways to do things, you know."

While the boy twisted his head, trying to straighten out the picture—and the whole idea—in his mind, I pushed a roll of tape into his hand and he found himself putting up posters every which-way on the walls.

"I never thought of that before," he said later. "I didn't know it was allowed. But it is interesting."

The committee boys might still wait for instruction in every duty, they might leave every choice and decision up to me, but at least they were acting. A schedule of hours was written out elegantly by a boy whose hobby was calligraphy, and posted prominently on the front door. The magazines were laid out on the tables, and on every wall peremptory signs said, SPEAK ENGLISH ONLY! in English—and in Persian. The room was opened and the students came in.

Kayeum was in the English office one morning when a chiprossie knocked on the door and stuck his head in to say that two students wished to see the raïs-sahib. Kayeum waved them in. It was the two cousins from Laghman, the inseparables of my tenth-year class. I had gotten to know them better by now—or at least one of them. Introspective, habitually silent, Mohammad-jan with his Donatello face was still hard to reach; Ismatullah's good-natured charm and his ready smile seemed to provide enough gaiety for both of them. But Ismatullah was not smiling now. He was walking carefully, leaning on his friend's shoulder, one hand pressed against his abdomen, his face tense with suppressed pain, Mohammad-jan's with concentrated sympathy. We helped the boy into a chair. Since dinnertime the night before he had had that pain. It could be a gastric attack, or it could be something more, perhaps dysentery or appendicitis. Kayeum quickly scrawled an order for admission to Ali Abad Hospital nearby, where the students were sent in case of illness.

"You be sure to go with him," he told Mohammad-jan superfluously, "and let me know right away what the doctor says." Mohammad-jan nodded and carefully pocketed the note. Ismatullah rose to his feet again, wincing with pain, and smiled at us thinly but as brightly as he could manage; and then they left, the tall, strong boy leaning heavily on his slight, fragile-looking friend as they walked slowly down the corridor. Mohammad-jan turned once at the door and gave us a reassuring look; he returned later to say that it was only something intestinal. Ismatullah had been put to bed.

Late at night there was a pounding at the gate of our house and the batcha opened it to Kayeum. When he came in, his face was drawn and anguished and shocking.

"Ismatullah is dead," he said abruptly. "I thought I'd better come and tell you—I didn't want you to get the news in class tomorrow." Then he sat down and put his head in his hands and did not say anything more for a long time.

I had heard what he said, I knew what he said, and yet I did not know it. I just sat stunned.

Gul Baz brought in a tray of tea but Abdul waved it away. When at last we all looked at each other, he slowly, grimly, told us what had happened. A re-examination had shown appendicitis after all. The doctors operated, but the appendix had already ruptured and peritonitis had set in. The boy did not come out of anesthesia. Kayeum arrived to find him in a coma. He never awoke.

"And there was nothing I could do!" Abdul said. "Nothing— except watch him go. I grabbed every doctor I could get hold of, but there was nothing . . ."

After a while he went on, quietly. "I remember last winter," he said, "when I was down in Laghman and those boys came to beg me to let them come to the school, to go to their fathers and persuade them to let them come up to Kabul. I told their fathers I would take care of them. And now I'm sending him home . . . like this."

"Where is Mohammad-jan?" I asked.

"He's with Ismatullah. He's taking him home. They've left already. I made the arrangements, then I came here to tell you.

I thought of the long road to the east, and a lorry driving into the evening; and of the two boys who had grown up doing everything together, together now for the last time: the sure, laughing boy and the quiet one, so deeply reserved. I could not yet comprehend that Ismatullah was dead, and I wondered if Mohammad-jan could. His face, the voice of his silence, had already been touched with melancholy; now that he was alone, who now would make him laugh?

In the morning I walked into the tenth class. The students rose to their feet quietly. We looked at each other. They needed to say nothing, I dared not try for fear of breaking into helpless incoherent rage. I gestured to them to sit down. I took my seat. First desk, first row by the door: empty. I opened the textbook. "Turn to page seventy-three," I said. "Alam, please read the first section."

One day Mohammad-jan was at his desk again. He looked gravely at me for a silent moment; I looked back into his eyes; other than that, we never spoke of Ismatullah again. For a long time he sat alone at the double desk; then one day a boy moved from the back of the room into the empty seat beside him. Mohammad-jan's face seemed more finely drawn than ever, the only sign of what had happened; and perhaps even that was only my imagination. But he appeared wrapped around an inner core of stillness which no one outside could reach.

And as always, things moved on. That's the worst of it, in a way: there are so many times in a lifetime when it seems that now, this once, just for a moment, the earth must have stopped turning or the sky must have changed or the landscape been marked; when we look up it is somehow quite terrible to see that it has not paused or changed after all, not at all, and that the days have passed as usual and they still do. A cold pulse now beat in the morning air, and the fields turned yellow and faded to brown with early frost. Classes moved outside to catch the pale warmth of the autumn sun. The students threw chipons over their shoulders, and rubbed their cold hands. Suddenly one saw that they had outgrown the uniforms they had been given last spring, wrists and bare ankles stuck out. It was getting on toward final examination time. The boys worried and worked harder than ever as the weeks went by. If they failed one or two courses they would have to repeat an entire year; if they failed a second time, they would be dismissed from the school; and there was so much for them to prepare.

I would have liked to spare my students that examination ordeal, first a written one and then an oral examination with an inspector from the Ministry sitting beside me to observe them, to interject a question, perhaps use words they had not yet learned. I had worked with them for months. Whatever they still lacked, they had at least been released from the chains of dumbness in the English language; and of one thing I was certain: no boy had given me less than his best. They deserved something for that.

My family had sent a quantity of pencils with the name of the school embossed on them in the school colors, gold on purple; I had intended to use them as an incentive, an award for every student who made ten points above the passing mark. But when I brought one to school and showed it to them, and saw their faces, I knew that I must give one to every boy—to every boy in the school.

So on the last evening of the school year, when all the examinations were over, my husband and I returned to the school with the box of pencils and a big stack of bright picture magazines David Nalle had given us. Kayeum and the mudirs were waiting in the main office. For five hours or more I sat like a Renaissance prince distributing largesse while the whole school streamed past, five hundred boys or more: young men of eighteen or twenty, some growing their beards and mustaches for their winter at home; little boys barely visible over the desk-top; boys I knew and boys I hardly had seen before; boys in school uniforms, in old American Army jackets, in quilted chipons and felt wraps, caps and turbans. Even the chiprossies were there: one or two, I knew, secretly nursed a wish to be students, and tried to study and learn with the boys.

Each of them, his eyes bright, came solemnly up to the desk, bowing politely, thanking us, then breaking into a smile, looking down at what I could put into his hands: a purple pencil stamped in gold, and a magazine. Some of those pencils would return with them in the spring, unsharpened and unused—and still be pristine in their pockets a year later.

The next morning the staff came to see the students climb into lorries for their long journeys home, shouting and waving at us cheerfully. The teachers stood in the roadway and waved back, watching them drive off in a cloud of dust, under a wintry sky—back to every nook and cranny of the land. Then we all shook hands and exchanged good wishes and went home. The school stood empty and, astonishingly, a year had passed.

17

The Khyber Pass had to be driven by daylight. In spite of the system of treaties and blockhouses and air patrols inherited from the British, Pakistan would not be responsible for the traveler in the Pass when darkness fell. No one was allowed to enter the Khyber before dawn, or less than an hour before sunset.

That is why travelers from Kabul to Peshawar began their journey at night. With luck, barring blowouts or washed-out roadbeds or any of the myriad of delays that could befall a car on the road, the two-hundred-mile drive could ordinarily be made in about eight hours: one would arrive at the Khyber with the morning light and be in Peshawar for breakfast. So, in the silent midnight, one mounted that great lump of mountain, the Lataband Pass, twisting slowly away from the string of lights along the ancient city walls which for hours marked the first and last glimpse of Kabul.

Now a new road has been cut through the upper gorge of the Kabul River, along the line of march where the British Army was wiped out in 1842, in the debacle known as the First Afghan War. I am told that the tortuous climb up the Lataband is not much used any more, but in those years the new road was still being hacked from stony mountainsides and the long slow scaling of the Lataband is forever fixed in my mind as the great watershed of any journey, the dividing line between Home and Away.

It was ironic that the Lataband and, south of it, the road from Jagdalak, were driven in darkness while the Khyber could not be; for the road on the Afghan side of the border was rough, narrow, and dangerous, had one or two truly splendid natural locations for ambush, and others at least adequate for highway robbery. Yet aside from problems with drivers, brakes, and the tire-puncturing nails left along the road by the shoes of those who journey on foot, we drove it without qualms. One rarely heard of anyone being stopped along the way or of violence, and when it did happen the Afghan government would take blunt quick action to prevent further incidents. For the most part, travelers went their way with impunity.

When I speak of "travelers," I mean, of course, those of us who climb into a car or bus for the trip, to whom the point is to get from here to there, crossing the intervening miles as expeditiously as we can, our eyes fixed on our place of arrival. There are other, different travelers who fill the passes in their season, traveling the caravan paths on the slopes beneath the roadways—the Kuchi, the Pushtun nomads, winding their way down the passes and across the plains into the northern Punjab on their great ceaseless migrations. There are hundreds of thousands of them, and for perhaps two thousand years, perhaps more, they have plodded north with the springtime and south with the autumn, from Tartary to Hindustan, driving their flocks before them on their trek to pasturage, surging with the seasons like the ocean tide. To us, this was a thoroughfare; to the Kuchi, it was the background to their lives.

I often saw them passing through Kabul, and occasionally they might pitch their black felt peaked tents just outside the city, near the school. One viewed them only at a distance, for the camps are guarded by huge ferocious dogs which could easily bring down and kill a man and which are trained to attack anyone who crosses the invisible line demarcating the territory of the camp. Left alone, the dogs only growl menacingly; and they—and the camps they guard—are left alone.

Usually, however, the caravans passed through Kabul and went on. Long lines of great shaggy Bactrian camels swung along, laden with household goods, folded tents, and babies. The women walked proudly beside them—unveiled, vivid, dressed in black and scarlet and decked with silver bangles. In the city, where purdah sent local women fluttering shyly from attention, the proud indifference of these handsome Kuchi women seemed imperious. It could be disconcerting, almost mocking: one day a Kuchi woman, her shirt open, her baby at her breast, walked into the American Embassy compound and wandered about—why, nobody ever found out. The flustered diplomats were nonplused as to how to get her out again; no one dared touch her even to lead her to the gate; she spoke to no one and seemed disinclined to leave. Then, apparently amused at the sensation she had created, she just as unexpectedly departed.

But ordinarily the nomads appeared indifferent to the life of the town; they did not pause or veer from their steady course. The city was just one more phenomenon on their continuing way; the trip to Khyber was a function of their days, which slipped along, endlessly circling through the seasons, the years, the centuries, like the beads slipping round on a tasbeh in the hand of a Muslim telling his prayers.

In that December, however, I was one of the travelers from Here to There.

As soon as the school year ended we began casting about for a ride down to Peshawar. In Kabul the skies were still bright blue and the ground untouched by snow, but on the Paghman range we had for weeks watched the snowcrest creep lower each day from its permanent hold on the peaks. The morning breeze from the west brought the scent of winter, of cold earth and ice, cutting through the early sunlight that shone thinly on the last marigolds and sunflowers withering along the streets. Before the snows of winter closed us in, we wanted to be off to the roses of India.

Two or three times a week there was usually some diplomatic car making the trip to Peshawar, and with luck and a bit of inquiring about, one could sooner or later hitch a ride. We found that friends were taking two station wagons down to be overhauled, and there was room for us and for Gul Baz Khan, going home on holiday. We arranged to meet one midnight.

At night, the silence in Kabul is almost a sound in itself, and the darkness seems palpable. The December air was cold and still, the sky hard and polished like black obsidian, with glittering stars fixed in its rigid surface. Our little cluster of travelers spoke hardly at all and then only in hushed whispers. A dog barked on the other side of the valley. As the bearers packed the cars according to some private organized scheme of disorder, the two station wagons with their interior lights shining looked like two isolated little worlds in the silent chilly night. With hardly a word the bearers shepherded us all into the proper places and climbed in themselves. I sat by the window, behind our driver.

The drivers, who liked to play daredevil, gunned the motors, there was a sputtering roar, and we shot off into the darkness, heading east past the hills of Bimaru. The headlights caught only the endless clayey brown of the walls lining every street; nothing stirred; even the street dogs had disappeared. Then suddenly we were in open country, bumping along toward the blackness of the Lataband. The whole night was to be a study in blacks: black, blacker, blackest— how does one go on from there? Everyone sank into some position for sleep; once one has learned to travel the rutted tracks across the desert, it becomes a rather easy matter to sleep through them. Only I sat awake, staring out into the darkness—I, and the driver; but he said nothing, his only distraction the occasional scratch of a match on the dashboard as he lit a cigarette.

It was past midnight and the moon, far from full, was already sliding downward toward the ranges behind us. There was nothing to see beyond the windows, but still I stared out until my eyes, like a cat's, had focused in the darkness and the shadows began to have shapes.

Slowly we wound up the first approaches to the Lataband; then we were climbing steeply. The narrow road sloped out toward the left: just beyond my window the precipices dropped away into the folds and crevices of the mountainside. To the right, the mountain stretched upward, blocking the last glow of thin starlight. Looking out and down, I could see, far beyond, palely discernible, the flatter shadows of the plains; but between our mountainside and their broad darkness, the humps and gullies of the cliffsides seemed like a night-born landscape in some chilling tale of strange imagination. Darkness seemed eternal; morning, sunlight, life seemed incredible.

Then, as the road twisted higher up the mountainside I began to sense—not really to see—darker patches in the gullies: geometrics, squares, curves, sharp angles. I opened my eyes wide against the darkness. There they were again: the tents of the nomads, black by day but what in this unutterably black night? The immobile silhouettes of camels emerged, the tent peaks, and then, occasionally, the small red glow of a half-covered watchfire and the silent shapes of men asleep beside it. Not a camel bell broke the stillness, nor the slightest sound from the guardian dogs. Like a tableau the peaked tents lay clustered on the sharp-angled slopes.

And why should they rouse for us, even for a moment, as we hurtled by? We were wayfarers bound to the rock-hewn road, tied to the little tunnel of light we threw out before us. Since time unknown and untold they have passed this way, southward to the plains of the Indus and northward to the Oxus again with the turning year, planting as they journey downward and reaping as they return. Trains to catch? Two-week holidays? What are these to a people whose lives run together into eons, whose measuring rods are the seasons, and whose clocks are the snows on the mountain tops?

With their black tents and red carpets, their Turkic saddlebags, their dress, and now, the dull red embers of their fires in the night, their lives seemed drawn in red and black. In Kabul they did not stop: the city—any city—was an intrusion on the unending rhythm of their life. Now I saw them as they chose to be, scorning a caravanserai, planting themselves on the precarious slopes, impervious to all worlds but their own.

We did not touch upon them; we could not if we wished; we hurried past. Yet never in Asia did I ever feel myself an intruder, and in a foreign land, as I did in those hours when our very existence, our motor, our planned arrival at the Khyber at a given hour, seemed an intrusion and an affront to an entire way of life.

The thick yellow light of teahouse lamps was like a blow as we pulled up to break our journey. The air was cold, the tea steaming and aromatic. When we climbed back into the cars I was still wide awake, while the others returned to their dozing. At the top of the Pass the driver stopped again, at the little hut where white rags drooped feebly on their poles. It would be unthinkable, and tempting fate, to cross the Pass without a gift to the holy man, but here there was no light and no one awoke. Our obeisances quickly made, we started off again, downward.

It was still dark as we rumbled dustily through the gorge of the Kabul River and crossed at Jagdalak onto the southern plains. This was the spot where the tiny remnant of the British army which had escaped ambush struggled to make a stand in that bitter winter of 1842. Thousands set out on the retreat from Kabul, but only one man escaped from Jagdalak—Dr. Brydon, who rode fainting into Jalalabad to tell his story to the British garrison there. Around the bazaars of Peshawar and Kabul one often sees copies of an old steel engraving of Dr. Brydon, slumping half-dead on his exhausted horse as he rode into Jalalabad. It is rather bad art, drawn to the sentimental Victorian taste for patriotic pathos and doubtless intended to inspire an admiring tear. In Kabul it serves rather as a triumphant warning to those who would conquer the Afghans. But here on the Pass with the awful plains stretching ahead to Jalalabad, the sentimentality of the picture is sloughed away and Brydon's ordeal and his heroism become real.

To the east, across the Kabul River, the green fields of the Laghman Valley lay hidden in the night, and beyond them, the mysterious mountain valleys of Nuristan. The people who live there are still an enigma to the rest of the world and, it seems, even to themselves. Less than seventy-five years ago they were kafirs— infidels—worshiping, it is said, carved wooden idols, making wine, and thoroughly isolated from the rest of the country; their land was the almost legendary Kafiristan. Afghans claim that their language is completely unlike Persian or Pushto. Some say that they are the Lost Tribes of Israel, but in this part of the world as elsewhere that is the immediate explanation for every group whose roots are not apparent; for that matter, the Afghans sometimes make the same claim for themselves. Again, one hears that the Nuristani are descendants of the soldiers of Alexander the Great, who did pass through their land on his way to India; and that archaic Greek words are to be found in their language; but this also seems to be more legend than fact. When Abdur Rahman invaded their land to conquer and convert them by the sword, the Kafirs sent emissaries to the Viceroy of India, claiming British aid on the grounds that they were fellow Christians. But after losing two Afghan wars, the British were not inclined to get involved again, and no one really knows if the Kafirs were perhaps remote Nestorians or if their claim was just an expedient. Anthropologists are still searching out the truth of them. Much of their original culture was destroyed in the invasion, although they still live in elaborately carved wooden houses, and a few of their stiff strange wooden funerary figures survived and stand awkwardly now in the Kabul Museum to intrigue and puzzle the curious.

Today they are called Nuristani—the People of Light—being, presumably, enlightened at last by Islam, and are more or less integrated into the country, but they remain shadowed, isolated, and aloof—one of those jigsaw puzzle pieces that always intrigue scholars and travelers alike, that turn up here and there in Central Asia and cannot be fitted into place. Their territory is almost inaccessible to ordinary travel, and since they seem to prefer their isolation, they may remain a mystery for a little while longer. Occasionally a Nuristani comes to Kabul to earn some extra money—one boy worked for us as a batcha for a short time—but they keep to themselves and say little, and soon go back to their mountains.

It was barely a dim winter dawn as we passed through the sleeping city of Jalalabad, but the air had lost its cold edge and we were unmistakably in the south. Grass grew along the streets, and orange trees and acacias were green. Beyond the city we set off across the desert plains of Batikot, along the rutted track marked out by stones. In the pale gray half-light every rock and pebble stood out with unnatural clearness. Now and then a jackal skittered away from the road as we approached, and once a small gazelle leaped from behind a rock.

Suddenly, huge and looming in the pallid dawn and still miles ahead of us, the ranges of Khyber rose, stretching across our path, walling the world. The peaks rose and fell across the horizon like a great wave: here was the end of one world and the beginning of another—it could be nothing less. They rose stark out of the plain, warning, holding, barricading.

To come upon the Khyber from the south has no meaning and tells you nothing; I had come up from Peshawar and been in the Pass before I knew it. No wonder that travelers set forth from India so readily through the ages, going outward, upward, to the north, carrying Buddhism and philosophy and trade with them. It seems so easy from the south. But to come upon the Khyber from the north is to face India in full force, and find that massive hand reaching out to block the path. If the world were indeed flat and had a barrier rim to save us all from falling off, it would look like this.

It is awesome. It stuns. I stared at the mountains hypnotically. They seemed to come no nearer, although we were driving straight for them. This, I thought, is what the Vedic Aryans saw four thousand years ago when they rode down from the steppes to create India. What thoughts were behind their eyes? For before their eyes was the same vision I was seeing; it likely has not changed much. No pass was visible; how had they dared to push on against this utter wall? And what of Alexander's men, and all the other conquerors? Alexander himself, and Tamerlane, chose the green valleys to the east for their crossing. But Mahmud of Ghazni marched here to bring terror and ruin and a new faith to India, and the Ghilzai, who conquered in Delhi; and then Babur swept down to found the Moghul Empire, and his grandson Akbar, to reclaim it. The empress Nur Jahan passed this way in silken luxury; she, who ruled the world she knew with glittering splendor—was she, too, awed by the sight? Or was it for her the footstool of her majesty? Chinese pilgrims braved this desert and those mountains, looked at them as I now looked, approached them at a camel's pace, to seek the new-minted wisdom of the Buddha and carry it back to the Yellow River. That wonderful English gentleman Mountstuart Elphinstone—in the jumble of the ages he almost seemed to have passed just a moment before me—rode back this way to report to the British East India Company on the conditions in the Kingdom of Caubool.

Probably they too had approached at sunrise, most or all of them: the tribes in the Pass were known raiders when the Macedonians passed by. Four thousand years! How many must have seen the ranges of Khyber at dawn, as I saw them now! Turks and Tartars, Mongols and Persians, Romans and Franks and emissaries of the Holy Father in Rome; young English soldiers retreating wearily in defeat, emperors and would-be emperors, sages, pilgrims, merchant adventurers—and now, from the heart of a land barely born when this path was already ageless, how did I come here to catch my breath at the same moment in space?

Suddenly, where the walls of rock thrust their sharp ridges against the southwestern sky like a chipped Neolithic flint, the sun, rising, struck the peaks, and all at once that cutting edge of the earth blazed gold—a stream of gold, dazzling against the somber rock and the colorless sky behind it. A river of gold seemed to run across the peaks as, one after another, the snow-topped ranges caught the bright rays.

It lasted only a few minutes; I think it was too splendid to endure for long. Then the earth turned, and the sun rose, and light filled the mountains and the desert. We were almost at the border, and then we were there, and the night was over.

The Afghan customs post was surrounded by nomad tents, awake and mundane in the morning sunshine; across the border, the Pakistani officers offered us tea and nan while they leisurely checked our papers. Everyone wakened and stretched and began the day. Every perspective was changed: the road was smooth, the mountains rose around us, the driver was cheerful at the sight of macadam. We sped through the Pass, its walls carved with the records of the regiments of Her Imperial Majesty Victoria Regina, who was and somehow always will be, there, The Queen; and of battles bravely fought and nearly forgotten. A Buddhist *stupa* along the road seemed no more than a crumbling ruin out of a long-ago past.

But once there was an echo of the night and the dawn, to tell me they had been real: as our car headed for a hairpin turn that bent against the mountainside, a great eagle settled on a rock straight ahead of us. Then he spread his wings and they glowed bronze and gold in the sunlight as he slowly rose and majestically soared away and across the river gorge, and into a brilliant blue morning sky.

18

*W*henever we returned from journeying and thumped a clamorous happy tattoo on the front gate, Gul Baz came rushing out to hug us home. The dogs attacked us joyfully with tongues and paws and wildly wagging tails. Ahmed-jan smiled from the obscurity of a doorway. Shaban, mysteriously informed, arrived for tea within the hour. We would sit far into the night, till the lights grew bright and the sky grew dim, while Gul Baz, who was our eyes and ears, told us everything that had happened while we were gone—in the house, in the town—until we were firmly set in our firmament again and, glutted with news, were willing at last to sleep. Breakfast the next morning would be lavish, and the sun always shone brightly when we had come home. Gul Baz would sit down at the long table with us to elaborate on the news he had already sketched in, and then he would bring forth any less appealing items that he had temporarily withheld: one pedal, the seat, and both handle-bar grips had fallen off the bicycle, which he had warned us not to buy; he had had it repaired, but further collapse must be expected and not complained of; or, more distressing, the Afghan hound had slipped out the gate and vanished; and always, "that damn boy" was back, having appeared, with his usual unerring instinct, at the precise moment of our need and of his: Maullahdad repeatedly fell upon evil days, thanks to his unreasonable faith in his own cleverness. He would be dead broke again, and we would be the beneficiaries of his misfortune.

If we had been away for more than a few days, we would find the social scene shifted, for the foreign colony had suddenly begun to grow enormously. Old friends wound up their duties and went home or were posted elsewhere, while the burgeoning of various international programs brought numbers of new people. All sorts of people. A free-wheeling, free-spending American pilot who wanted to start an airline. Two sisters, French, very lively at parties: one always carried her ouija board about and levitated tables while her sister was proving that she could bend over backwards till her head touched her heels. A Chinese sericulturist and his two beautiful daughters, who wore their high-collared silken cheong-sangs slit up the sides to the hipbone, thereby bringing all activity to a lurching halt when they strolled through the bazaars. A stateless Pole who had served with the Free French, cordial, cheerful, utterly cynical. A loquacious and amiable Greek handicrafts expert with a difficult name and an impossible accent. There was a new influx of American teachers as implacably virtuous as their predecessors, who rapidly were not invited to parties. A Danish anthropological expedition led by Prince Peter of Greece arrived and disappeared into Nuristan. Occasionally an American Congressman drifted by, and correspondents of the various world press services and major newspapers came for brief visits during which they went from party to party, asking for news, then left to write yet another story about multitudes of beautiful women hidden and forbidden behind enticing veils. Previous ambassadors left, which produced fine farewell parties. New ambassadors came, which produced fine welcoming parties. An efficiency expert who had been sent to reorganize an important international program was to be found at all of them, uncomprehending and despairing as he ticked off his problems methodically. And at the French Club the French could be heard complaining that they were being overrun.

There were always guests in our house: teatime visitors of course, and often people who stayed for a while. Beds and mattresses were cheap; we kept two or three extras in a storeroom, and there was always room. People we had met on our travels came to visit. Omar Pound, the poet's son, arrived unannounced from Tehran, and promptly collapsed with a recurrence of an old malaria. He stayed with us while Gul Baz nursed him back to health, wandered the city for a week or two, and then left, vaguely in the direction of the Americas. He was very quiet, and deceptively, fragilely young in appearance, with unexpected deep pockets of learning and naïveté; and when, rarely, he did join a conversation, his remarks were extraordinary.

A charming and sardonically witty linguist, Oscar Luis Ramon Chavarria-Aguilar, generally known as Chevy, came to Kabul to study Pushto, and lived with us for several months. Gul Baz objected when Chevy moved in, and took me aside in the kitchen to mutter suspiciously about how house guests were likely to hit dogs on the head and make them bite people; but in a matter of hours he forgot his objections. After my husband and I left for school every morning, the two of them would have long, leisurely conversations in Pushto, and while Gul Baz was our friend, he and Chevy became buddies. It was as though there were some cheerful conspiracy between them. Perhaps it was because of the Pushto, or perhaps it was because they both agreed that the world was slightly mad and they were not; but it may simply have been that each of them amused the other and both of them knew it.

Among our teatime guests there were often teachers from the school, at ease with us by now. Boys who had graduated the year before began to stop by too, shyly and tentatively at first, not knowing how to drop their student deference and adjust to being simply friends; but they learned. I remember Anwar Shinwari, intense, needing more laughter, who said little and listened much, his handsome face set with concentration, determined to learn anything which would make him useful to his people. He had two rare qualities: by sheer nature, he was intellectually honest; and he had no malice. I had never realized how rare that was until I found how strange it was to talk with someone who had no malice at all.

And there was Hassan Kakar—angular, sallow, his thin pockmarked face lit with eager intelligence and high good humor. Hassan had fought his way out of tuberculosis; and though the disease had cost him a scholarship abroad, he was not going to let it cost him an education. He gorged himself into near-indigestion on books and ideas, and came to argue them energetically.

Shaban, of course, came often. We still played cards, but many evenings he sat quietly, his face thoughtful. We went to his home for the Passover meal and ate unleavened bread as thin and brittle as an autumn leaf. Shaban said, "When is it that you are leaving? I really must go by then, too. No, this time I mean it. I must apply for a visa . . . I will write to my wife . . ."

So there were changes, but we saw them only as shifting colors in a kaleidoscope, which keeps its pattern as it turns. Which was not unusual: most of us pretend that our lives are fixed and somehow permanent, even if only for a moment. For if we let ourselves think of life as it is, shifting always, not for two moments the same, there is no place to take hold; one might not even dare to try. This is even more true when we move into a world where everything is new and strange. Then we convince ourselves that everything around us is solid and sure, that we are the one volatile element, that once we fit ourselves to the environment, we will have a secure niche. So we create the illusion of permanence just as we spend our lives assuming *terra firma*; and then we begin to believe in it. We settle down, plump up the cushions of habit and arrange them for comfort, and are always unprepared for what comes next.

The pattern of our daily life seemed set, and nothing of importance was likely to change much.

The landlord had begun coming around at all hours to badger us. As badly as he had wanted to get us into the house, he now wanted to get us out. The new members of the foreign colony, arriving all at once and looking for houses, were casually paying rents that were astronomical by the standards of even a few months before. He preferred to get rid of us, or at least to double the rent, which we could not afford. But the lease he himself had written made it impossible for him to do either. To his intense irritation, he had tied his own hands, and no compromise satisfied him. So he tried to bedevil us out. He came in whether we were at home or not, and complained of us to any guests he found there. He bemoaned his losses, and declared that we were ruining his property, and called upon them to be witness. It was indecent, was it not, to paint a room that color; the dogs would destroy his garden; we were always having guests, and who knew who they were or what they did here; look, there was a scratch on the newel post—no, look there! Smiling forever from sheer habit his Cheshire-cat smile, he feinted his verbal claws at us and lashed his tail in frustration. We tried to ignore him; and he suddenly gave in and stopped troubling us.

A few days later the dogs were poisoned.

One evening, as we sat with Shaban over leisurely after-dinner coffee, Gul Baz screamed in the yard. "Khanum, come quick, Tossy is crazy!"

We rushed outside. Gul Baz was staring in horror at the big dog stretched out writhing in convulsions, foaming at the mouth. We flung the houseboy out for the veterinarian. In the few minutes it took Dr. Somer to arrive, poor Tossy collapsed into exhaustion and was seized with agony again, rolling his eyes at us in bewildered terror. Dr. Somer needed only one look. It was strychnine, a massive dose: there was no hope. He called at once for the other dogs. As they came running, they stumbled and dragged their legs with paralysis and I heard my own voice scream. Somer quickly decided they might live. He took them inside and shut them each in a dark room alone and told us not to look at them till morning.

It was a long night. Between Tossy's convulsions Gul Baz, blank with shock, sat stroking the leonine head of the gentle clumsy dog he had loved best. Finally the men sent me off on some fabricated errand, and when I came back Tossy was dead. The other dogs, locked away, were living or dying, we knew not which, until at dawn my husband crept in to see them and they looked up, still paralyzed but alive, and we knew they would recover. Then we tried to sleep.

When we came downstairs in the morning, Gul Baz was standing in the hall where Tossy had been. The tears rolled slowly down his face and we all sat down on the steps together, our arms around each other, and wept.

"He's never hurt anybodys, khanum," Gul Baz said over and over. "He's never hurt anybodys."

Maullahdad passed through the hall and looked at us curiously. "What are you all crying about?" he said. "It was only a dog."

Gul Baz started up in fury. I grabbed at his hand. He stopped and stood rigid and trembling, glaring at the boy. Then, "Maybe he was only a dog," he cried in a choked, cold voice, "but by God he was a better man than you!"

Kayeum was unexpectedly transferred from the school. He was appointed to administer the Helmand Valley Authority, a great hydroelectric and land reclamation project beyond Kandahar. The news stunned the school. The teachers—even those who disagreed with him—had come to count on his support with their problems. As for the students, they were dismayed: they loved him. They talked of getting up a petition—they were not quite sure to whom, but to somebody, the King or the Prime Minister, perhaps—to keep him at the school. Then they learned that the appointment was official and final; he was needed in the south; there was nothing they could do. He had been transferred. He was leaving. And the students feared they might be losing more than a man they thought of as their friend: Kayeum had put before them his dream of the future, and they needed that dream, they needed the future. Without it they might readily be ground by the opposing blades of pride and shame into bitterness and cynicism.

Afghans have a great sense of their own history, and from childhood it nurtures their pride. The traditional sources—legend, epic, reminiscences told and retold from each generation to the next—make even the unlettered rich in the lore which conveys a nation's passion; and if it may at times be flawed in scholarly detail, it is spiritually true and therefore as significant as any other form of history; for to a great extent we make ourselves into what we believe we are.

So they grow up proud, proud in their nature and proud of the triumphs and glories of their past, as though it were just a moment ago that they held sway over India or brought the Persian Empire to its knees. Then—for some—education or chance reveals to them that the rest of the world regards this land to which they are so devoted as an exotic backwash, its drama of little concern. And they discover that the clock slowed there, and all but stopped, some time ago. Such a young man might not learn much of the happenstances of geography and economic change, and of the complicated needs of other nations busy writing their own histories, which had made his once-central country a strategic pawn remote from the centers of the modern world, and had kept it isolated. But he might easily discover that the world condescended to his pride, pointed to unpaved streets and outside privies and called him backward, and seemed at times to imply that because his land was poor he should be not proud but apologetic and, desirably, grateful for any attention whatever. This would be hard enough to have to learn but it is harder still to discover that, having told him this, the rest of the world, busy with its own concerns, does not care.

Pride and self-contempt mingled are a cruel burden to bear. Chauvinism may be taken for granted as the sometime price of national pride anywhere, but xenophobia grows from such twisted roots as these. It has a darker, uglier hue and sows tragic seed. There were a few Afghans—I imagine they may well have once been among the most sensitive, the most hopeful youths of an earlier generation—who, brooding blindly on their bitter realizations, had come to imagine some Machiavellian conspiracy of the world to shut their people off in a mountain prison forever. The Germans, always eager for strategic friends in Asia, had played hopefully on this at times, especially during the Nazi era: putting a comforting arm around the Afghans when they could, murmuring soothingly of undying friendship between two brother nations of true Aryans whom the envious mongrel world conspired to thwart. Few were willing to clutch at such a sodden twig of debased consolation.

Still, when a man has become so embittered, his pride is reduced to a gauzy scrim behind which one sees the sullen glow of envy, and envy of that unconquerable protean foe, the world. And if such profound bitterness was rare, there were more who had been touched at least and scarred, and left irascible and suspicious. Resentfully aware of their disadvantaged present, they saw a sneer behind every word. Admire anything that was their own, and you were likely to be accused of mockery or hypocrisy, or a desire to lock them in the past like quaint relics in an international curio cabinet. Praise change, and you might be understood as denigrating once again their own and original selves, as implying (and they had reason; some foreigners openly said it; my own fellow countrymen were prone to do so), "You improve as you get more like us," which also means, of course, "Your own uniqueness was nothing very much worth having."

So far, there were not many who had been so incurably wounded, and those few were, it seemed to me, most often men who had already exchanged hope for cynicism a decade or two before; but, few or many, they were to be met, and they seemed to warn that bitterness and despair were the trap which might await a larger number, younger men. When I met such a man I wondered sadly if this lay ahead one day for any of my students.

For when, in the early days, the boys asked me, "Do you like our country? Are you happy here?" I could see them watching, my eyes as I answered, to read my real answer. And when they no longer needed to ask me that question, they still apologized sometimes:

"We are very backward in this country, sir. Please excuse the trouble it is for you," or, "I hope you will forgive that rude man— we are uncivilized, I know."

Even when that was said with irony it was a two-edged knife, cutting the speaker and cutting me, making me party to the humiliation of his self-respect. It was the only thing that could drive me to anger with the boys; I knew there was not much I could do about it, yet I could not allow this to pass and by my silence appear to agree. I would try to remind them that time stops everywhere sometimes, in various ways; and that it starts again, moving now slowly, now swiftly; and that either may happen as a matter of chance. In the long stretch of human history, even of their own history, it had not slowed down for them so long ago; if they had to run to catch up again now, that was no shame, and they were not alone. All of us were running, all of us were behind someone, in some way, even if it was only ourselves. They looked curious and half-believing: perhaps they were wondering if I were not just being polite. Would I be angry if I were mouthing courtesies? They could see that I was angry. Perhaps I meant what I said. Though they were touched by the inner conflict, they had not yet given way to it; they would turn from it if they could.

But words and reassurances—certainly my words and reassurances—could never keep them from bitterness and despair. Only one thing could do that: hope, faith in the future—that it could bring change and growth, and that they could help to shape it. That was what Kayeum had been giving them; that was the dream.

He was not unique, of course. He was part of a whole new generation, knowledgeable and realistic, who were beginning to wind up the clock again and set time to marching on the double in the country, men in a variety of fields, in every ministry. But of these men, Kayeum was the one the students knew; for them, he was the one who had put the dream before them and he had made it theirs. He had put it into action at the school wherever he could, and he had been there every day—not only in the office and the classroom, but at the dinner table or out on the soccer field kicking a ball with them—finding every chance to tell them and show them and to make them believe it: that the future would be better, and that they would have a part in building it.

Now that he was leaving, it seemed for a moment that all of this might go with him. What they did not realize, then—nor, I suspect, did he; none of us really did—was that the dream would remain when he had gone: that his students had become the dreamers.

Like everyone else, I wondered how things would go now at the school. The Hazrat-sahib, who had been principal of the upper section, was appointed as the new director. He was, after all, a conservative man, traditional in his background and his training, and now he had the opportunity to return to the accepted ways of the past. But it soon appeared that the new raïs was doing his best to continue along the road Kayeum had charted. He moved uncertainly: nothing in his background had prepared him for this. But he had observed that the new road led to the future, and he would try to find his way.

It is neither usual nor easy for a man in his middle years to struggle with his own mind and try to transform lifelong habits of thought, a whole outlook. When he has an established position as a pillar of conservatism and has spent long years in his profession, it is doubly rare for such a man to set himself to learn from someone younger and less experienced. I thought it was even more remarkable because there was no necessity forcing him to re-examine his thinking: a raïs has great autonomy; the Hazrat-sahib would have been free to reimpose tradition. So if I was sometimes less than happy with some of his policies, I could not help being impressed and moved by what he was trying to do—and, slowly, doing.

The school was not the same, of course; for the moment at least, development had changed to a holding action as the new director felt his way, and, of course, old patterns did re-emerge here and there. The mudirs and others assumed more of their old authority. There was no one now who could discipline the school with a word of reproach or use sheer personal influence to replace the rods which had been taken from the teachers' hands.

A new man from another school took the Hazrat-sahib's place as mudir of my section of the school. I had not met him before, but the boys knew him by reputation and were unhappy about his coming. I met him in the office one morning—a rather tall, self-important man with black hair and bright blue eyes who might have been good-looking if his face had shown any light, any thought. But it revealed only a certain crude cleverness, as shapeless as an unlicked bear cub, and he was slovenly, as no other teacher was. The school—teachers and students—mocked him nervously behind his back. He was excessively polite to me and he never interfered with my work, but I always had a sense that he would have done so if he had felt free to do it. But of course eventually I would leave and he would stay; eventually all those who had been touched with ideas might go, and he might be able to outstay them all.

Meanwhile, in my own bailiwick everything went along much as before: the classroom, the reading room, each day with the boys. Only the adventure of experiment was missing, and of course my contract had not guaranteed me that.

While Kayeum was raïs he had often urged the Ministry to give scholarships to the students from the provinces. For many years, only the graduates of the Kabul lycées had been considered for advanced studies abroad. If education was the key to the future, then those boys had a monopoly on its greatest hopes. Our students knew it, and if they had not known it, they were told it often enough. The lycée boys mocked them to their faces as country cousins, small-town hicks; they condescended from the superior authority of their blue serge suits, flaunting their urbanity before the provincial boys in their clumsy uniforms. How many soccer games ended in fist fights! Our students won the fights as they won the games, but they knew it was a hollow victory.

Now, in the Helmand Valley, Kayeum was given grants to train specialists needed for the enormous reclamation project, and the Ministry agreed at last to experiment by sending three of the outstanding graduates of Darul Mo'Allamein. The effect on the students was electric. Boys who had been their classmates last year were to be sent to American universities. Now the future might hold every opportunity for any one of them if he only worked hard enough to earn it.

Abdul asked us to help the chosen students get ready. For weeks they came to our house every afternoon, and half the evenings, too, while we wrote to their colleges, arranged their travel, supervised the tailoring of flannels and corduroys, and stuffed their whirling minds full of every random bit of information we could think of that might conceivably be of use to them. Awed and thrilled by the opportunity and the burden which were theirs—to study at a great university and to do so well that others could follow them—they sat dutifully, week after week, memorizing an indigestible hodgepodge of advice.

By the time they climbed into a bus, clutching tickets and suitcases and written instructions, and cheered on by a crowd of schoolmates, they were dazed with excitement and exhaustion. As we waved them on their way, we silently prayed that nothing vital had been overlooked and that they would arrive safely.

From their schools they wrote us at last: "At the Orly Airport in Paris, France, the officials said that our papers were not correct and we would have to go back. But we did not agree. So now we arrived at the university."

Since then I have often heard those words from other students. It delights me: they do not agree, and they get there.

Every morning at recess the students were given copies of the daily papers. They read them eagerly, carrying them back to class and putting them aside reluctantly when the bell rang.

One day Ghulam Dastagir, sitting alone near the back of the room, was so absorbed in his reading that he did not hear old Baba Ghulam pounding away at the gong. The other boys tucked their papers into their desks and took out their books, but Dastagir read on.

"Please put your newspapers away," I announced, staring pointedly at him. The class turned and stared at him too. I cleared my throat noisily. We waited. He was oblivious. This was the first time anything remotely like a discipline problem had come up, so I was completely unprepared. I supposed I should do something. I improvised. On an impulse, I gestured to the class for silence, then started down the aisle to where Dastagir sat buried in his paper.

In retrospect, it was a long journey. As I stepped off the dais, an absolute silence fell over the class, like the paralyzed unnatural stillness of the last moments before a tornado. No one moved: only their eyes followed me. With some corner of my mind I was aware of the hush—it was a muffling blanket of stillness over the room— but I did not really notice it. I was too occupied with wondering what I was going to do when I got to Dastagir's desk. I hoped that he would hear me coming, but he did not. I got there, and looked down at him sternly. He read on. I had not the slightest idea what to do. I was struggling not to giggle. There was no sound in the room behind me. I had to do something, now that I was here.

So I leaned over and shouted "BOO!" right in his ear.

Dastagir jumped. He blushed. There was a momentary vacuum of silence. Then it was filled with a roar of student laughter. I was laughing too, a little, as Dastagir grinned sheepishly and put his paper away. But the laughter around us was rising hysterically, breaking in battering waves across the room, and I turned to stare amazed at the limp, helpless hilarity on the faces of the class.

Then in one clear moment I understood. The silence I had heard had been a tension gripping them like a vise as I walked down the aisle and stood at the boy's desk. They had been rigid: they had been holding their breath. And I understood that they had thought I was going to strike him.

They had braced themselves against the shock of that expectation: braced themselves to see the whole fabric we had built up together torn to shreds, and our friendship revealed as a mask. I knew now that they trusted that friendship. But I knew, too, that if they could not imagine me—as myself—beating a boy, they had not expected authority to do anything else: that was how things were for them now.

I felt as though I had crossed a chasm sleepwalking. Suddenly waking and looking into the gulf, I was heartsick. I had no power, and actually I had no fact—only knowledge. There was nothing I could do.

A few weeks later I came out of the English office to find the corridor blocked by one of my classes. The blue-eyed mudir stood before them, a willow switch in his hand; behind him a chiprossie held a bundle of switches. The mudir raised the whip and it whistled down and cracked on the outstretched palms of one of the boys.

I stopped, appalled, rooted to the spot, as the boy stood rigid and braced, his face impassive, barely wincing, his hands scarlet and swollen already with welts; and as the rod rose and fell, the mudir's eyes shone with satisfaction.

In the first frantic moment my mind tumbled pell-mell: fury, horror, revulsion, outrage, knotted in the pit of my stomach. I must stop this. I have no authority. I must stop it at once. How can I? Then, another knowledge: if I stop him—if I even could—this man will revenge himself later, somehow, somewhere, in the dormitory, in the classroom, with no one to intervene. His face told me that if he were denied his satisfaction now, he would take it eventually, and with interest. I had never before seen sadism unconcealed. I felt ill. My own hands flinched with every lash. I had physically to stop myself, one set of muscles holding back another, to keep from grabbing one of those whips and turning it on the mudir. So I stood there: I could not get by, and it would have been a cowardly betrayal to retreat to my office and shut the door on this.

The mudir did not see me—or rather, I think, he pretended not to see me—until he had finished with the boy. Then, before he called out the next student, he greeted me casually, and offered to make way for me to pass by. I was afraid my voice would shake and betray me. I spoke very carefully.

"I know these boys—I teach this class. What have they done to be punished so severely?"

He smiled. "They have tried to get out of class, and then they lied about it. They are extremely unruly and untrustworthy boys, and they need to learn a lesson."

"May I question them?"

"Of course. Only, you can't trust them."

I turned to the students. In front of me was Ghulam Jilani, a nice boy with a pleasant, open, ingenuous face. I asked him what had happened.

"It was our time for athletics," he said. "We went out to the playing field but the sports teacher did not come. We did not know where to go, so we waited there and the mudir came along and asked us why we were not in class. We told him, but he does not believe us. He says we were trying to escape from our duties."

I turned back to the mudir, weighing my words cautiously. "Perhaps there has been a mistake. Have you spoken to the sports teacher?"

He smiled condescendingly. "You are a very kind lady with a soft heart. There is no need to speak to the sports teacher. These boys will not tell you the truth—they are lying. I know them."

I could not answer, "No. They might lie to you but they won't lie to me." It was true, though it could hardly be proved, but in any case he would do what he wanted to do. And if I had said it, and he had asked me why they would not lie to me, he would have laughed at the answer: "They will not lie to me because they know I will believe them." Although that too was the exact truth.

"It is an unpleasant duty," he went on smoothly, "but I must teach this class a lesson." He gestured to the chiprossie for a fresh switch. I knew that if I stood there one moment more, I would strike him; so I pushed by. He laughed. I heard him tell Jilani to put out his hands, and as I walked numbly down the corridor toward the staircase, I heard the willow whip whistle through the air again and strike.

Like an automaton I blindly walked down the steps and out into the dazzling sunlight. Choking with fury at my own helplessness, I got across the school yard, across the road, to a little cigarette stall there. I handed the man a coin, got a packet of cigarettes. Then I stumbled around behind the shop, where I was hidden from sight of the school, where no one would see me. I tore roughly at the cigarettes, got one out, lit it. Then I broke, and stood puffing furiously, shaking with anger and impotence and shame, while tears poured silently down my face, and silently, over and over again, I cursed. I ground out one cigarette, lit another, and still the flood did not stop.

I don't know how long I was there. I felt a hand on my arm and turned. It was one of the boys I had seen upstairs.

"Don't cry, sir," he said softly, "it didn't really hurt much."

Then he was gone. I got control of myself somehow and mopped my eyes, my face. I put on fresh lipstick, and walked back to the school and in to my next class.

19

At the stroke of noon the midday gun boomed out over the city and men everywhere made their way to the mosques or knelt in quiet corners to pray, oblivious of passers-by. On the streets the mullahs appeared in their severely handsome garb of black and white, the color of script or of print, of The Word itself made plain. In the crowded bazaars when one saw a Sikh or Hindu merchant, he was isolated by his bright turban in a land where man, beast and earth share the same somber hues—ochre, gray, umber—the colors of clothing, of walls, of turbans and camels and mountainsides. Wherever one looked, whenever one looked, there was a constant awareness, constantly renewed, that this was a land of faith and that the faith was Islam. It seemed an inevitable conjunction: the austere land and the austere faith. The hand of God was severe, but He was close: He was raised upon no altar, for His hand lay on every man's shoulder.

Islam has ruled here for almost nine hundred years. It was hard to realize that the Buddha had held this land in his uplifted palm for nearly as long, or longer.

Much of Afghanistan's history before the coming of Islam is like a landscape wrapped in mist, in which one can discern scattered rocks of knowledge solid enough to stand on, linked by unsteady bridges of theory and speculation. No one knows just how much history lies buried in Afghan soil: the archaeologists dig, and with each spadeful of earth the story as it has been known is transformed. In 1952, for example, rumors got around in Kabul that a French expedition had made an important find. The archaeologists themselves, cornered over a drink at the French Club, smiled deprecatingly and noted that every time you dug up an old pot there was always someone who was sure that it was filled with gold. As it turned out, they had indeed struck a veritable Klondike at Surkh Kotal: the ruins of the Kushan court of the first or second century. They were merely hugging their secret to themselves until they could get it safely into print in the academic journals, where scholars fire deadly footnotes at one another over the bodies of wounded and dying theories. There the implications of that discovery are still being argued today, and they will shape the histories written from now on.

So discovery follows discovery. This land has been more than the funnel through which the world poured into India and the valve through which India released its own creations, although it has certainly been these things. But Afghanistan has in itself repeatedly been a creative center from earliest times until relatively recently—Zoroaster taught here, and Avicenna—and it has besides transformed the cultures it has received, sending its own influence out along the historic routes of trade and civilization in every direction. Lapis lazuli from the Afghan hills was counted among the treasures of the Pharaohs before the time of Moses, and ideas travel in the same pack with precious stones.

There is much more to know than the fragments available so far, but a great many of the secrets of history in this land have yet to be wrenched from the silent grasp of time. Yet not everything is thus buried. Bamian is not buried.

One of the visible rocks in the historic landscape of Afghanistan is Alexander's passage. In 330 B.C. he swept across the land like a wind and soon, like the wind, was gone, leaving little of visible permanence behind him. But in his wake, what is today one country was left in two, with the great central mountain ranges dividing them. In northern Afghanistan, Macedonian officers had remained to establish a satrapy in Bactria; but with Alexander dead, the Bactrian kingdom centered around the Oxus plains gradually slipped its Greek moorings and established ties with a new power which had risen to the south of it, the great empire of Gandhara.

Gandhara stretched from the southern slopes of the Hindu Kush across the plains of the Ganges to the Bay of Bengal, binding together all of northern India; and in India the rising tide of Buddhism was already threatening to overwhelm the ancient Hindu faith. Ashoka, the greatest emperor of Gandhara, was converted, and by 250 B.C. he had proclaimed Buddhism as the faith of the empire. For the next eight hundred years it held sway over the lands of the Hindu Kush both north and south. Indeed, as Hinduism in India recovered its strength and drove Buddhism out of the land of its birth, Afghanistan, at the core of Gandhara, became the great Buddhist heartland.

Under Ashoka and his successors and then under the converted Kushan kings who ruled the empire in the early centuries of our own era, missionaries went forth from Gandhara to spread the teachings of the Buddha across Central Asia into China, Korea, Japan. Pilgrims poured in to visit the great shrines and schools and monasteries here. The landscape—Afghanistan was green then, lavishly blanketed with forests—was dotted with stupas, brilliantly painted and rich with sculpture. There are parts of the country where even today a farmer can hardly plow his fields without turning up some bit of statuary from that vanished past.

If Alexander's actual mark on the land was debatable, he had certainly left a memory and an influence. He had reminded the worlds of east and west of the channels between them, and those channels were kept open and enlarged: the Kushans are said to have had intimate ties with imperial Rome. Thus in Gandhara the two worlds met at the very moment when Buddhism was searching for artistic forms into which it could pour its symbolic content; and the techniques of Greco-Roman art stood ready to hand. Together, mingling the serenity of the Buddha with the grace of Apollo, they created a new art of exquisite beauty.

In the heart of this heartland of a vigorous faith full of creative vitality, the valley of Bamian lay high among the mountains, a graceful pause between the exhausting heights of the Hindu Kush and the Koh-i-Baba ranges; and Bamian became perhaps the greatest monastic and artistic center of all. Some even think that it was here that Buddhism emerged in its dominant sophisticated form.

It stood on the ancient Silk Route which led to Balkh, where the northern and southern branches of that great artery met. As the caravans wound their way through the mountains, they paused at Bamian to gather strength between the rigors of the passes on either side. Men of every land mingled there before they moved on across Sinkiang to the Celestial Kingdom, which guarded the eastern edge of the world, or to Malabar in the south, or across the deserts of Persia and Syria to Tyre and later Byzantium, gateways to the Roman world of the West. Those were the fringes then, and this was the center. The valley had its citizens devoted to the traveler's mundane needs, and to commerce. The rubies of Badakhshan and the silver of Panjsher must often have changed hands here, with a portion of the profit going, perhaps, to the glorification of the faith—and of the Valley. For while the royal cities of Gandhara were elsewhere, Bamian was great in the faith.

The valley was scarcely twenty miles long and perhaps a mile wide, guarded by royal fortress-cities at either end, and filled with thousands of the devout from every nation. Along the pink sandstone cliffs edging the valley a vast honeycomb of monastic chambers was carved into the mountainside itself. From here saffron-robed monks and pilgrims, merchants and artists came and went in every direction, outward to China, north to the Gobi, down into India, departing, returning, teaching, learning, mixing and mingling all that they carried with them and gathered along the way, as bees make their busy way across wide fields and return to pour their gathered nectar into the common honey of the hive; and then go forth again to cross-pollinate as they pass, to fertilize, to create a new flowering.

Here without a doubt the faith of the Enlightened One stood triumphant. Who could question its permanence when, among the hundreds of cells cut into the valley wall, the monks had carved two colossal standing figures of the Buddha as Lord of the World— one nearly one hundred and seventy-five feet tall, the other a little smaller; covered with gold leaf and brilliantly painted—which must surely proclaim the glory of the faith forever.

In the fifth century one Fa-Hsien came the long road from China, and found ten thousand monks in Bamian. The valley was at the height of its splendor: the monasteries were flourishing, the great Buddhas towered magnificent in their vaulted niches, surrounded with splendid frescos, and the face of the cliff into which they were carved was studded as well with smaller niches holding lesser figures of the Buddhist pantheon, behind which lay the honeycomb of rooms, elaborately plastered and painted and busy with life and thought.

A century later the White Huns smashed their way across the land. They left the monasteries in ruins, the survivors of their butchery broken. When in 632 another pilgrim made the long trip across the Gobi and down through Turkestan, he found Bamian in decay—its people devout, but its monks few and its life feeble. The two great Buddhas still stood: he noted in his journal that the golden surface and precious ornaments dazzled him from afar. But the monasteries and stupas were ruined, overgrown with weeds. The great age of Bamian was over, and with it the great age of Gandhara art.

Buddhism lingered in the land for another five or six hundred years, shattered, struggling for survival among other faiths— renascent Hinduism, Mithraic cults, Zoroastrianism, the first Muslim footholds in Afghanistan, and other sects obscured and long forgotten—until in the tenth and eleventh centuries Islam became dominant and bit by bit the others dwindled away. At last Genghis Khan came to the valley and murdered it, and the story was ended.

One day during a midsummer holiday we set out with Shaban and the Kayeums to visit Bamian and, beyond it, the lakes of Band-i-Amir in the Hazarajat. Shaban had as usual arranged for a car, and had indicated his own readiness for roughing it by adding a pith helmet to his customary brown business suit: thus outfitted, he looked extremely uncomfortable with himself. We drove along the now familiar road through the Koh-i-daman valley, past Istalif to Charikar; but this time we turned west into the gorge of the Ghorband River, which leads to the Shibar Pass and Bamian. The road lay along the bottom of a deep slot carved by the river between sheer cliffs. The stream tumbled away from us and narrowed as we climbed toward its headwaters.

Early in the afternoon we reached the town of Chardeh, whose houses clung to the slopes at the widest point of the valley. Karim, a young teacher, lived in Chardeh; he was at home visiting his family, and he had asked us to stop as we passed through. Parking the car in the midst of the bazaar, we found a loitering boy and sent him off to locate Karim, who came to guide us on foot up through a maze of narrow alleys, just wide enough for a panniered donkey to squeeze between the high mud walls on either side. The door he opened to us was one of many similar battered, unprepossessing wooden gates in the otherwise blank walls. We stepped through a dim passageway and found ourselves on a vine-covered veranda overlooking a garden which fell away in terraces down the mountainside. The upper terraces were bedded with strawberries and flowers; roses scented the air. Below there were orchards, where a few sheep and skittish goats browsed under the trees. Along one side of the garden a brook tumbled in its channel from terrace to terrace, turning tiny water wheels as it went.

Two young boys were already busy spreading cushions and pillows in a corner of the veranda. Karim's brother and uncle were waiting, and by the time we were all introduced and settled among the cushions, children began bringing trays of food: fruit, almonds, and pistachios, roasted sweet corn, and pots of rich sweetened milk, flavored with cardamom and rosewater. Other children appeared with brass ewers and basins; we washed; ewers, basins, and children vanished again. We sat back comfortably, talking and laughing and sipping our hot milk, while the dust and ache of hours on the road slipped away from us like an unwanted skin shed by a happy snake. Meanwhile, a constant stream of children sidled in and out, apparently drawn from every corner of the neighborhood, looking for excuses to take a peek at the company. They refilled our cups or suggested that we needed more fruit; they added cushions, removed cushions, and rearranged cushions; they looked hopefully for flies to be shooed away; and when they ran out of ideas they just gathered shyly inside the hallway peering out, content as long as no one seemed to notice them but bursting into giggles and running away if any of the guests was so inconsiderate as to smile at them directly.

We stayed too long and were urged to stay longer, but by late afternoon we knew we must go or give up hope of reaching Bamian that night. So out into the dusty world we went again, and drove on through the narrow throat of the gorge.

Along its red sandstone walls, fantastical stripings of dull crimson, orange, purple, ochre, and russet dipped and writhed across the cliffs, telling in the florid palette of their stratification a geological story far older than the ancient country and its ancient peoples. The red light of sunset struck the rocks aglow with a strange wild burst of bloody color. Then the canyon ended as abruptly as a tunnel, and in the evening dusk we wound our way over the Shibar Pass and on toward Bamian.

A few miles before we reached the mouth of the valley we emerged from another defile and stopped to rest at the foot of a mountain. An overgrown footpath wound upward: in the fading light we could just make out on the cliffs above us the crumbling turrets and desolate walls of Shahr-i-Golgola, the City of Clamor and Lamentation.

When Genghis Khan led his army into Bamian in 1221, the fortress cities refused to yield and fought for their lives. In the midst of battle a luckless arrow struck down and killed the Great Khan's favorite grandson, and in his fury Genghis proclaimed that this valley would be known forever as the Valley of Sorrow, that the city would be known forever as the City of Sorrow. His orders went out: no looting in Bamian, and no taking of prisoners. When the valley fell, everything was to be destroyed and no living thing left to live. And so it was. Every man, woman, and child was put to the sword; every dog, every cat, every sheep, goat, bird; the trees were cut down, the barley slashed to the root. No living thing was left to live where the grandson of Genghis Khan had died. Such was his revenge, more complete even than his destruction of Herat—for at Herat, if a million and more were killed, forty are said to have survived. In Bamian: no one and nothing.

For more than a hundred years his curse lay upon the abandoned valley, and the city was known, as he had proclaimed, as Maobaligh: the Accursed City, the City of Sorrow. When men took up life in the valley again, they built little farming villages among the neat fields. The ramparts of the destroyed cities remain forever empty under the spell of their terrible fate; and it has come to be said that in the night their broken towers echo again with ghostly sounds of murder and the lamentation of the doomed.

Darkness fell before we entered Bamian itself and drew up at the hotel, which was set on top a low hill directly across the valley from the Buddhist ruins. The lobby was filled with an ebullient crowd of German engineers and their families on their way back to Sarobi from a camping expedition at Band-i-Amir. They assured us that we would find Band-i-Amir delightful: it was beautiful, and there was wonderful fishing. You just exploded a few fish bombs and scooped up all the trout you could eat. In fact, they would have stayed longer but the lakes were so full of fish that their bombs had killed thousands, and the stench had driven them away. By the time we got there, they assured us, the smell would undoubtedly be gone. They offered us their left-over fish bombs, which we declined, and then went off to their sleeping bags in the main dining room, where they were thriftily camping in *en masse.*

The manager screened off a corner and set dinner for us. We ate hastily by the light of a kerosene lamp, speeded by our own weariness and the gentle snores and murmurs that emerged from the darkness around us. Then we went directly to our rooms to sleep, planning an early start for the next day.

When I had blown out the lamp and was about to go to bed, I stopped, and went to the window. I found that it looked straight across the valley to the sculptured cliff. The moon was high, and by its pale light I saw for the first time those two great figures, tiny from afar, standing like rods of silver in the dark shadow of their niches. For a long time I stood looking; and, touched with moonlight, they calmly and steadily seemed to return my gaze.

In the morning we stood halfway up the cliff, at the foot of the greater colossus, looking up, up—beyond the gigantic legs, the togalike robe, the shattered arms, to a blind face far overhead: ephemeral Lilliputians in awe before an eternal Gulliver. The gold leaf which once covered the figure had long since disappeared, the colors had weathered away. Of the brilliant frescoes which had decorated the stucco surface of the niche, there were now only faded remnants high up in the arched dome. The statues themselves had been literally defaced: much of the faces, the uplifted hands, and great pieces of the trunk and legs were blasted away over the centuries by zealous Muslim sharpshooters bent on the holy work of idol-breaking: it is singular that so much of what man has created in the name of the glory of God has so often and everywhere been despoiled in the name of the glory of God. On the great face so far above us only the mouth and chin remained, the full lips curved in a serene enigmatic smile.

We had come from the lesser Buddha a mile or more away, past the cliff pocked with empty niches and entrances to the hundreds of chambers within. A few yards from where we stood, a door in the wall led into a half-ruined staircase which wound upward through the cliff to the top of the statue, where a doorway opened out onto the huge head. A schoolboy from a nearby village offered to guide us, and we started up the long, ill-lit climb.

Part way up, a window looked out into the niche: before us were the shoulders of the statue, and on the walls above we could glimpse bits of fresco. Further on, a crevasse gaped across the passage where the weakened face of the cliff had started to split away. The walls had been propped and the passageway strengthened with timbers, but the only way to go on was to leap the crevasse. I must have made some sort of sound, because Joan turned to look at me and said, "You're green. Sit down." I took this advice abruptly; apparently my knees were trembling. Shaban, who had been climbing without any visible enthusiasm, promptly said, "You should stay here. I'll stay to keep you company. Let them go on." But I managed to get across the chasm at last, and we all continued upward. The corridor leveled out, and we found ourselves at the doorway overlooking the head of the statue, more than big enough for half a dozen people to sit on.

On the walls and vaulted ceiling overhead, the faded colors of the old frescoes swirled in fragments of sinuous gesture. The arch itself framed the view before us like a Byzantine panel: below a crescent of blue sky the valley was unrolled like a green silk carpet at the feet of the Buddha. Birds caroled in the poplar groves far below and miles away. It seemed as though we looked out with the eyes of the great stone Buddha itself, and saw a vision of peace.

The road to Band-i-Amir led westward for another fifty miles or so into the central massif of the Hazarajat, across an empty landscape of tawny, barren mountains—rock-strewn, utterly lifeless, weathered and worn into an ocean of stone waves. Only the faint track of the road marked the vast tangle of mountain desert. There was not a spring, not a trickle of water, not a drop of it; not a withered shrub or a clump of tough mountain grass to say that life had ever been sustained here. Only mile after mile of mountain lying defenseless under a merciless sun. The heaving landscape was like the bony structure of the earth itself made visible under a thin, taut shell of rock.

Then suddenly in the heart of a barren valley there was a chain of brilliant blue lakes, sparkling and glittering and dancing in the sunlight like a bracelet of sapphires thrown into a clay bowl: Band-i-Amir.

They were incredible. They could not be real, but they were: intensely blue, lapis blue, cerulean, sapphire, aquamarine, rising one above the other, each spilling into the next with a crystal fan of waterfalls which glistened over the rocks in a multitude of streams. Where the lowest lakes spilled over into the valley, there were faint streaks of dull moss-green for a little distance until the desert blotted up the water. Other than that, nothing: absolute desert wrapped around brilliant jewels of blue: no stream flowing into them, none flowing out. A handful of lakes in the middle of a desert ten or eleven thousand feet high—just simply, fantastically there.

At some places barren brown cliffs fell away straight down to the blue waters, and on down into their bottomless depths; at others, there were low craterlike mineral formations which held the lakes above the valley floor as a setting holds a gem. Around these shallower sides, the edges of the lakes were rimmed with the green of water plants, while farther in and under the surface there was a shimmer of frosty white where minerals had crystallized like white lace coral.

There were a few poor huts along the shore, one of them a crude little mosque, and a few men stood casting for fish: Hazaras, the Mongol people who give the area its name. They are said to be descended from soldiers of Genghis Khan who settled here and they have a well-earned reputation as fighting men, but on their high plateau now they are impoverished farmers, and in the cities they do menial work.

We drew up near the fishermen. Seen close, the lakes seemed even more unbelievable than when they were seen from a distance. The water was transparent as glass. Except for the white mineral formations, there was no shelf at the shoreline: the walls of the lake dropped vertically down, and through the crystal-clear water one could see pale silvery fish gliding past far below. Then the waters darkened into deep and deeper blue, and hid whatever lay in their depths. The water was icy: we had hoped to swim, but when Abdul plunged in among the rushes at the shallows, he had not gone three yards when he turned back and climbed out blue-lipped, numb, and shivering.

There was absolutely no visible source for the waters, or for the fish that swam in them. I suppose they must be fed by springs, very deep, but if the source is known, all I was ever able to learn of it was what the fishermen told me:

Although most Afghans are members of the Sunni sect, which dominates Islam, most Hazaras are Shi'ites, who particularly revere Ali, the Fourth Caliph, over whose presumed tomb the Blue Mosque rises in Mazar-i-Sharif. When Ali visited Afghanistan, oh, hundreds and hundreds of years ago (the fishermen said), he came this way, across the Hazarajat, and through this very valley; and in his great footsteps the lakes miraculously sprang forth as testimony to his holiness.

The fishermen were casting for trout with a long weighted line which they wrapped around one hand, whirling the weighted end above their heads and flinging it out with a quick twisting movement of the wrist. The fishing was not as good as it had been, they said, for the foreigners' bombs had killed so many fish and frightened off the rest. Still, they caught enough to give us some, and shared their barley bread, too. We offered the fruit and eggs we had brought from the hotel, they made a fire, and with the fish and the dry barley cakes, we all had lunch together.

We left Band-i-Amir before nightfall and returned to the green valley, its pink walls, its lonely colossi. In Bamian I thought again of Pompeii, where it is possible to imagine that life might at any moment take up again just as it left off: where one would not be at all surprised to turn a corner and bump into a Roman matron on her way to market. In Pompeii, life seems suspended.

Bamian is dead. Nothing waits in its empty halls. In Bamian, death blew out all the lamps, and they were never lit again; silence descended, and it was never broken. One thinks: from the hand of God, many survived; here, at the hand of man, none.

Yet this valley is serene. It is, I think, the most peaceful place I have ever known. Its tranquillity floods the soul.

At the foot of the sculptured cliffs the houses turn windowless backs to the great statues. The people of the valley know them not, and look elsewhere now. But still the blind Buddhas look out across their valley, towering, faintly golden in the sunlight and pale beneath the moon, silent before the unassuming grace of fields and running brooks as once they were silent before the unspeakable: forever blind, forever seeing; forever silent, forever an echoing voice.

20

*T*he great games are on horseback. Like the Parthians and the Scythians who rode out of Central Asia before them, and whose heritage they may well bear, Afghan horsemen ride with a reckless ease which suggests that the saddle is their birthright and the horse an extension of their will. There are few places in the world where you can see such brilliant riding and nerveless daring, and all carried off with a casual élan that puts bravado in its puny place.

In the south, it is tent-pegging, a wildly murderous testing of absolute skill, of eye and nerve and reflex all concentrated toward the single moment when a rider races full speed down the course, lance in hand, to spear the stake and wrench it from the ground as he goes—or to break his neck.

In the north, the game is *buzkashi.*

"Have you seen buzkashi?"

"You must see buzkashi—it is our national game."

"You have perhaps heard of our national game, buzkashi?"

Yes, I had heard of it: everywhere, ever since I arrived. But as to seeing it: it was played, vaguely, in the north; at times and in places unspecified and unspecific—"in the valleys or the plains"; "when the weather is right"; "when the men have time."

Shaban came to the house. "Tomorrow afternoon we are going to the buzkashi match," he said. "I have borrowed a car. I will call for you at two o'clock."

"What buzkashi match?"

"Why, the one in honor of the King's birthday. Haven't you heard? It is the first time they will play in Kabul, out on the field beyond the golf course. The teams are coming down from Badakhshan and Katoghan."

"Just what is buzkashi, Shaban? What's so special about it?"

"Well"—vaguely—"*buz* means goat, and *kashi* means—you know, you pull? pulling? dragging? Yes. Well, they kill a goat, and . . . I'm not good at explaining it," he finished lamely. "I have never seen it myself."

"Look," I said, "I haven't the slightest interest in watching anybody kill a goat. As a matter of fact, I'm sure I wouldn't like it. I think I'll stay home."

"But you must go! It is in honor of the King, it is an extraordinary thing, and, besides, everyone will be there. I will come and have lunch with you and we will go direct."

In class the next morning the boys looked at me expectantly.

"Are you going to see buzkashi?"

"Yes. Tell me, what is buzkashi?"

"It is our national game."

"It is a hard game, sir."

"It is very dangerous."

"Yes, but what is it? How do you play it?"

There was a moment of silence; then the boys nudged one another and looked toward the back of the room.

"Mardan-gul can tell you. He is a buzkash—he plays."

Mardan-gul? Shy, retiring Mardan-gul? He flushed at all the attention.

"Do you play, Mardan-gul?"

He turned a shade redder and nodded. "Sometimes. I am learning. I have a horse."

Gradually I drew a patchwork explanation from him. The game sounded simple. It did not involve killing a goat; that was done in advance, and the carcass was simply the object used in play. Most often a goat wasn't used at all, but a calf, which had a better weight—a hundred and fifty pounds or so. The game was played at the gallop by mounted teams on a big field. The carcass was placed in a shallow pit at one end of the field; each team tried to seize it, from the saddle, and carry it around a goal post at the other end of the field and back to the pit again. That was all.

"Are all of you going?" I asked.

"Oh, yes, sir. You will see us there."

"All right. I'll see you at the grounds this afternoon."

After lunch we drove the few miles to the great *maidan* on the outskirts of the city, where the game was to be played. It was a beautiful autumn day, sunny and clear, the sunshine a hot varnish on the cool fresh air. The road was jammed with buses and cars, gawdis and bicycles, and hundreds of people in a holiday mood trudging along on foot, cheerful in spite of the dust and pebbles thrown up by every passing vehicle.

At the near end of the field a pavilion had been put up for the royal party: the King, the Cabinet, ambassadors, and other guests. Next to it there was another tent, filled with folding chairs for the rest of the foreign colony if they wanted it. In front of the royal pavilion a trench had been dug, seven or eight feet across at the top and perhaps six feet deep at the bottom of its sloping sides, as protection in case the players broke through the ropes when the game was at full speed. The other tent was only roped off, but then few people were in it or expected to be: you would watch this game on foot, shifting about to get a view. Beyond the trench the playing field itself was roped off waist-high, and the rope was hung with red cotton cloth as a warning to the fast-riding players.

The hills surrounding the maidan were already filled with people, and thousands more were swarming up the slopes to find vantage points. Our school bus was parked near the tents. Its roof was crammed with teachers and students who shouted to us and waved, while others were scattered through the hurly-burly of the crowds.

The field itself—the level valley floor—was perhaps a mile or a mile and a half long, and almost as wide. The low hills on either side and the mountains rimming the valley seemed its only visible boundaries; but at the far end I could just make out a tall pole like a solitary upraised finger, the goal post. Just beyond the red cloth barricade the riders were getting ready: tightening saddle girths, lifting a hoof to inspect it for a stone in the frog, checking the placement of a bit. There seemed to be about a hundred men, tanned and grizzled, not youths. One team, made up of men from Mazar and Kunduz, wore maroon trousers tucked into their boots and wrapped at the waist with crimson cummerbunds, and, over their white shirts, heavy quilted jackets of green-black silk. Their round helmet caps of polished golden leather, gleaming in the sunlight and rimmed thickly with black fur, would identify them in play. The other team, from Badakhshan and Katoghan, was less elegant but more brilliant. They wore scarlet shirts and black trousers, and red scarves swathed around helmets of some tawny fur, like lynx.

To one side, watching, supervising, and quietly waiting, the two captains sat their horses. They were magnificent. The leader of the Mazar team, wearing a long, brilliantly striped silk coat of many colors, his turban twisted high, sat, a whip in one hand, the other reining in his fine black stallion. His polished high boots were set in heavy engraved steel stirrups. The horse had been groomed till it shone like watered silk; around its neck the bridle harness was held by a collar made of squares of heavy brass, damascened and studded with semiprecious stones, alternating with squares of fine brass chain-mesh. A matching piece looped down from the pommel of the saddle to a spiraled ornamental breastplate, and the elaborate saddle itself was set on a saddle-pad of bright flowered stuff.

His companion, the captain for Badakhshan, was equally splendid on a beautiful glossy bay. His left arm was in a sling, and when I came over with my camera, I pointed to it and remarked that it was too bad that he would not be able to play that day. He lifted his injured arm slightly and laughed, and said he would not have played anyhow; neither captain would play; but it had been foolish of him to break his arm half an hour before game time on such an occasion. I admired his horse and took his picture and then, on an impulse, asked him if he would like to come to tea. He said he would be very glad to, so we set a time and I invited him to bring some of his men if he liked, and he said he would.

Then I had to get back behind the barrier. Several referees were walking toward a sort of crow's-nest observation platform at one side of the field; others, cavalry officers—natty, but, by comparison with the players, drab in their khaki—were riding out to clear away spectators and get the teams in order. The field was staked out with slender poles from which colored pennons drooped in the afternoon heat, some sort of boundary markers or directions for maneuvers, I supposed. As I walked back toward the ropes, I saw the carcass of a calf which was to be the object of play. The animal had been beheaded a day or two before; the carcass had been soaking in water since then to make it slippery. It lay now in a shallow pit directly in front of the royal tent. To my surprise, I was not in the least disgusted: there was no gore; the animal had ceased to be a living creature and had become simply a bulky object, black, its legs four long slippery handles, just what was required for play.

I had gotten off by myself on the field. As I ducked back under the barrier, into the spectator area, I looked for the rest of our party but they were lost in the crowd, so I stayed where I was, with full view.

On the field the riders were taking their places in a long single line which stretched away at an oblique angle to the royal pavilion. The captains rode out before their men; the cavalry officers called out last instructions and withdrew; a sword was raised, and lowered, and at the signal the entire line broke into a slow steady trot and began to move forward. Steadily, steadily, men in golden helmets and men in scarlet rode forward, their bridles jingling like chain mail. Slowly, steadily, they rode forward; their unbroken line swung around till they faced the royal pavilion, where the red, black, and green of the Afghan flag hung overhead; and they came onward with their captains in the van to pay formal homage to the King, for whose honor and pleasure they rode today. As the King rose and stepped forward, slender and straight, to take their salute; as the horsemen rode steadily on in ceremonial order; as the banners fluttered and the harness clinked against the steady thudding rhythm of hoofbeats; there was a strange hush, as though beyond them, marshaled in phantom ranks on phantom chargers, there rode the armored chivalric knights and the paladins who had long since vanished into the past like a ghost at cock-crow: the merest echo of an echo, the ghost of a ghost, hovering in the haze of dust struck up by the horses as they wheeled into position.

The ceremonies were quickly over. The game began.

Around the pit where the carcass lies, a hundred horsemen are milling, jammed together, jockeying for position, struggling to seize it. Horses rear. Men shout and curse. Whips are flailing in the air. The mass swirls. It heaves. Suddenly a shout. A horse plunges through the pack at a gallop, its rider hanging onto the carcass. Whipping up his horse, he races down the field and after him charge a hundred others—his opponents galloping hell-for-leather to grab his prize or make him drop it, his teammates running interference.

That carcass has to go around the goal post a mile away, and back again. If a team loses it and regains it, they will have to carry it again from the spot where they dropped it—if they can get it back that far.

They are all over the field now at breakneck speed. With one hand the carrier is wielding his whip. He lashes alike at the flanks of his horse and at any horse near him, trying to drive them off. With his other hand he grips the slippery carcass. It drags him half out of the saddle. The reins? Clenched between his teeth. Riders are closing on him. Suddenly there is another melee. Galloping horses, pulled in, rear back wildly, almost falling. They turn. The carcass is down again. Again the scramble. Again the seething pack. Again the breakaway—one man racing for the goal. Rules? There are no rules. The whips swing out in every direction. Hands reach to grab. God alone knows how they stay in the saddle. One rider wrenches the carcass from another. It pulls him down till one heel in a stirrup is all that keeps him tied to his galloping mount. They gain on him. They reach out to tear the carcass from him. Horses charge from every direction. The carrier dodges like a broken-field runner as they hurl themselves at him.

When they pound past us or struggle at our end of the field, the tumult of shouts and curses and whinnies and hoofbeats and the thwack of leather whips rises over the roar of the crowds on the encircling hills. Then they race down the field again, a hundred men, all focused on one. They charge across the rock-littered plain. Who has the carcass now? They are so far away that they seem a mass of toy figures, entangled, wrestling back and forth in the midst of a cloud of dust. Back and forth they swing. Turbans stream in the wind. Horses are lathered with sweat. Horses and riders go down, and are up in a moment and riding again full speed. Hour after hour it goes on, an exultant trial of will and skill and daring for rider and horse welded into one; until one team races in, flings the battered carcass back into the pit, and gallops away in triumph.

When the ancient Greeks first saw the mounted men of Asia, they created the legend of the centaur. Watching the buzkashi riders, one can understand why.

That afternoon the men of Badakhshan won. The final dash came so suddenly, from halfway down the field, that many of the spectators were caught off guard, wandering around while they waited for the action to come our way again. The triumphant team, racing in at full speed to win, veered off, too swift and too exuberant to be able to rein in, and circled the field at a racing gallop again as the losing team drew up to one side.

"What happens now?" I asked someone in the crowd.

"Now the King will present a special banner to the winners. You'll see—they'll come riding up to get it."

I checked the film in my camera and slipped around the end of the barrier trench, under the first set of ropes, and up to the line of red hangings at the edge of the field, to get pictures of the winning team as they rode in. Fifteen or twenty other people had the same idea, and we gathered in a corner of the ropes to watch the Badakhshani come in. They were still riding at a gallop, shouting and cheering, some of them waving the red scarves they had torn from their helments. Suddenly they were there, and they couldn't stop, and the horses broke through and were on us. We tripped, we ran, as the riders tried to rein in and their horses reared above us, pawing the air. I leaped into the trench with the others, and heard a yell; one of the horses came crashing down into the trench behind us, almost on us. I dropped my camera, and in one of those hyper-lucid moments of catastrophe which have the clarity of dreams and the time-sense of a slow-motion film, I stopped, and stooped, and recovered it.

Then there were hands thrusting over the edge of the trench high above me, shouts and hoofbeats and horses leaping somewhere overhead. In the chaos I seized a hand, I was yanked forward, I saw the face of our friend Marshall, I thought my arm would burst at the shoulder socket, I was up the side and safe out of the trench, and momentum hurled me forward until someone caught me just as I was about to fall upon the startled figure of His Majesty the King. It had all happened in less than a minute.

By the time I had my wits about me, I was sitting on a chair outside the pavilion. No one, I learned, had been injured; but it had been a narrow thing. Marshall stood there, looking at me oddly.

"Here is your camera," he said. "You dropped it again." I thanked him for that; I wonder if I ever thanked him for saving my life.

When the final ceremonies were over, and the Badakhshani had received their prize, and the Mazar team had been praised for their game, the sun was setting. Shaban and Gul Baz and my husband and I found one another and started back to the car. While we waited for the chauffeur, students passing by stopped to say hello.

"Did you like buzkashi, sir?"

"Oh, yes!"

"I think, sir, it is a very game."

"Yes, indeed, it *certainly* is a very game!"

The next morning I looked at Mardan-gul with something like
awe.

"Do you really play, Mardan-gul?"

He flushed and smiled and looked away and said softly, "I am
learning. I have a horse."

That afternoon the teams presented an exhibition of horsemanship
at the stadium. From the grandstand we had a close view: it was
pure riding, riding raised to the ultimate power. The teams could not
attempt a match in such close quarters, but they rode as recklessly
as ever. One fine black horse broke its leg in a fall and was led
outside. The crowd was subdued as the crack of a pistol sounded
beyond the gates; but a moment later, a beautiful chestnut stallion
was led into the stadium and presented to the unhorsed rider with
the compliments of the King, who had been watching from the
royal box.

The next day half a dozen of the riders came to tea. They arrived
on horseback, which I had somehow not expected: one rarely saw
riders in Kabul. As the batcha swung open the heavy gates and they
rode into the yard, the landlord appeared outside, astonished and
angry, until stolid Maullahdad swung the gates shut again in his
face. Then he rapped sharply, and Gul Baz opened the small door
a crack.

"What are those horses doing here?" came the shrill demand.
"They will ruin my driveway with those beasts!"

Gul Baz coldly informed him that the men he was speaking of
were undoubtedly the greatest buzkashi players in all of Afghanistan,
in Kabul to ride for the express pleasure of the King, and that he
should be honored that they even deigned to visit on this street. The
landlord's voice promptly dropped into cajolery, and Gul Baz came
over to where we were greeting the riders, who had dismounted and
were tethering their horses in the garage.

"The Brigadier-sahib is very anxious to meet these gentlemans, khanum. He's say can he come in."

"I'm very sorry," I said, raising my voice to carrying pitch, "but I'm afraid I have no room for any more guests."

With grim satisfaction Gul Baz repeated my message and bolted the gate, leaving the landlord to spend the afternoon hanging around in the street, calling to the gardener from time to time to ask him what was happening inside, to which the gardener replied, "They are drinking tea."

We were. Gul Baz had set a fine table. None of the players had met foreigners before, and they looked about with polite interest but with reserve; and unlike some guests, they seemed very much at ease and self-assured—as I suppose anyone must be who can ride in that game. Besides, they were accustomed to attention: the buzkash is a hero. Since everyone likes to rub shoulders with a hero or two, I had invited some of the students to join us, and they were eagerly helpful in translating and explaining when the conversation got complicated.

The riders looked pleased when we told them how much we had enjoyed the match and the exhibition; they asked if we did not have such games in our own country. We told them about cowboys and rodeos, and about other American sports, but we had to admit we had nothing to match their game—which pleased them again, of course.

But they laughed when I asked, "Do you always play with such big teams?"

The match we had seen had not been big, not at all. In the big games—at Mazar or Kunduz or Faizabad—three or four teams would take the field, nearly a thousand men sometimes. The Kabul match had been modest: picked men from the best teams, chosen for the occasion. They felt the game had gone well, considering that they did not know the field and it was a bad time of year. "Playing in hot weather is not good for the horses."

"When do you usually play, then? Not in winter, surely."

"Of course in winter."

"But what about the snow?"

"Snow makes it better. Besides, there is not much work you can do on the land in winter, you know," the captain explained. "So then we have time to play, all through the winter and in spring, too, until Nauroz comes, and planting time."

They were not professional players, then? The men looked puzzled, and so did the students. We explained about professional athletes, and the boys labored to transmit our explanations, which seemed to surprise them. They were farmers and villagers, who played for the game itself, or sometimes for a prize; but they certainly could not live on prizes.

"You see," one of the boys said, explaining back to us, "if there is a wedding, or a new son, perhaps the family will make a game to celebrate. They will pay for the calf and give a prize, but not a big prize—maybe a new turban, or twenty afghanis, like that. Then the game will be in their honor."

"With thousands of men?"

"Oh, no. Those are the big matches. In the villages the games are not so big. Sometimes like the one you saw, sometimes smaller. Sometimes there are not even enough to make teams—only twenty or thirty men. Then each man plays for himself to win."

How, I asked, did one become a buzkash? It didn't look like the sort of game someone could casually drop into.

They started as boys, riding on the fringe of village games: on Fridays, through the winter, there was always a game in one town or another. After a while they might play in and, if they were good, go on to the big matches. But of course that took years of practice. As I had noticed on the field, it was not a young man's game; most of these men were in their late thirties or forties, and some were even older.

"But practice is not the most important thing," one of the men said emphatically, and the others nodded in agreement. "The most important thing is to have a good horse. The horse is more important than the rider. Rather a bad rider on a good horse than a good rider on a bad horse. Even the best rider would not be allowed to play if he did not have a trained horse. He could hurt himself, he could hurt others. Men could get killed."

Their eyes lit up as they talked about their horses, which were specially bred for the game, for a combination of strength and speed; only stallions were used. When the horses were two or three years old their training began, but it took several years before a horse was ready to play.

"The horse must know everything," they insisted. "He must know how to leap into the middle so we can get the calf. He must know to start galloping as soon as his rider has the calf. He must know without the man telling him what to do. He must know to do everything by himself."

"And most important of all," the captain added solemnly (and the student grew solemn as he translated), "the horse must know never to step on a man on the ground. Otherwise we could be dead. If the rider falls, the horse must stop. If there is any man on the ground, always the horse must know not to put his foot on him. That is the most important thing, because when we are riding, we are wild, we are excited, we are not always thinking about these things. With the right horses, not many men get hurt.

"Sometimes it happens, of course," he added as an afterthought, "and of course, if the men get angry and start to fight, then look out!" He made an expressive grimace, then laughed. "But most of the time—some bumps maybe, but not really hurt." Then he realized that his own arm was in a sling, and pointed to it. "This was an accident. It can happen anywhere."

"What if a player doesn't have a good horse? For instance, if his horse is sick, or dies. Can't he play?"

"Not without the right horse. But you see, rich men sometimes like to raise the horses for the honor of it. Then they look for a buzkash who wants a horse, and he rides it for them. Then if the player is a good player, they all get honor: the rider, the horse, and the man who owns the horse."

"The horses you have here—do they belong to men like that?"

He glanced around, and each man shook his head. "No, these are our own horses."

They told us that they played wherever there was open space for a game. The big matches were played on the enormous Oxus plains: at Khanabad the field was two or three miles long and nearly as wide. But in the village games . . . One of the men smiled. "We play wherever it is flat, and if we get excited we play where it is not so flat—up and down the mountainsides, and in and out of the rivers, if they get in our way."

"Isn't that against the rules? Or are there any rules?"

"Oh, we should stay in the boundaries, I suppose, but when you are riding hard you don't always think about that. It's not very important, anyhow. There are just two important rules, but they are very important. Never you must hit a player with the whip— it happens sometimes, an accident, but never you must do it on purpose. The other rule is, never you must try to knock a player off his horse. That happens sometimes too, an accident, but it is very dangerous and never you must do it on purpose." He thought a minute. "It would start a fight, and that is very dangerous too."

"And are those all the rules? Just those two?"

"Yes," he said.

But another man spoke up. "Sometimes there is a rule just for one game. Like, if it is a very big game—seven hundred, eight hundred men—they will let the buzkash use a rope to catch the calf, like . . . you know, like . . ." He tried to demonstrate.

"Oh, like a lariat. That's what we call it."

Translation.

"Lah-ree-yat?"

"Yes. Our cowboys use them in America."

"Ah, you use them in America, we use them in Afghanistan." He looked pleased at establishing the bond. "Well, if there are so many players it is very dangerous to try to get the *buz* with your hands, so they make a rule for that game that you can use a lahreeyat to catch it and pull it to the goal."

"You keep talking about the *buz*—the goat—but it seems that you always use a calf. Why do you call it a *buz*?"

"Probably it used to be played more with a goat. Sometimes we use a goat, but a calf is better. It is stronger when you are pulling it around, and, besides, it is heavier, too."

"Then why don't you change the name of the game?" We all smiled because we all knew the answer to that: because buzkashi is buzkashi.

"You should see the games in the north," said the captain. "When winter comes, why don't you come up to my village? You could be my guests, and see some good matches." And the others added their own invitations.

"That would be wonderful, if only we could. But this winter we will be far away in America."

"But you will come back to Afghanistan?"

"Oh, certainly we will come back."

"Then when you come back you must come to visit us in the north, and we will take you to see buzkashi."

When they left, we went out with them to look at their horses. As a rangy stallion nuzzled my hand, I saw that its right eye was milky-white. "Your horse is half blind!" I exclaimed to the owner.

"Alas, yes," he said. "It happened long ago, an accident in a game."

"But how can you play with a half-blind horse? How can he see what to do?"

"He knows what to do. He knows the game. Better a good horse with one eye than a bad horse with both eyes. He knows the game, he likes the game. We have played together for fifteen years. If I did not let him play, he would be unhappy and so would I."

When they had mounted, we took some photographs.

"It will take three days to get the pictures," we said. "Will you be in Kabul that long?"

"No, we leave for home tomorrow. Bring them to us in the north when you come back; we will look for you there one day."

21

On Fridays we often used to walk out beyond the city to the rice fields stretched across the valley; or we would ride in the Babur Gardens with a friend, an announcer for Kabul Radio, who kept his own stable of horses. In spring and summer the rice fields were shimmering tender green, the mulberry trees around Babur's tomb on the hillside a thick shade. Now the days were cooler, the trees had turned yellow and brown, the rice had long since ripened to gold.

At harvest time the Kayeums and their children came up to Kabul and we went together to Abdul's family home in Laghman: he wanted us to see it before we left. It was as beautiful as he had promised, a valley sheltered beneath the fierce peaks which guarded Nuristan beyond. We lived in a summer house just outside the compound walls of the estate, a grape arbor cooled by a running brook, walled and roofed by gnarled old vines and shaded by enormous trees. I was taken to meet Abdul's stepmother, who lived in complete traditional purdah behind those compound walls despite her educated modern sons. She was nearly eighty, yet from her seclusion she had managed the family estates with a firm hand through years of widowhood. Withered, frail-looking, the old lady sat in the sunlight of an inner courtyard where she could keep a watchful eye on the busy servants. She took her visiting grandchildren on her lap and listened seriously while they seriously told her of their affairs, as though they were all old ladies together, before she sent them off to the kitchen for sweetmeats. Then she took my hand and smiled, her eyes bright and curious: we needed no translations; and she teased us all gently—Joan and I, and Abdul too—as though we were children. When we left, she drew me down and patted my cheek, and thanked me for coming to see her.

Our contracted time in Afghanistan was drawing to an end. The Ministry of Education asked us to stay on, and for a time I hoped that we could visit the United States during the winter vacation and return in the spring. But it appeared that our affairs would keep us in America for a year or two; we must go, and be gone awhile before we could return. We booked passage. It seemed odd to say that we were going "home."

"You are going to America, sir? You will come back again?"
"Yes. Of course. Not right away, but in a year—maybe two years at the most. Before you even finish the twelfth grade."
"Truly, sir, you will come back?"
"Yes, truly. I promise you."

"You were not unhappy in Afghanistan?"

"Unhappy? Of course not. We want to come back—we will come back!"

"Truly, sir, you will come back to Afghanistan?"

"Yes, truly."

But until we did? I felt guilty, knowing that we were leaving work begun and unfinished, not knowing what would happen to it while we were gone.

The reading room had become a school center. Student musicians performed there. It was open in the evenings. David had alloted money for books: we had ordered them and waited months for them to arrive. Now they were on the shelves and students flocked to get them. The committee had learned their job—they followed my instructions easily now. But still they waited for instructions. Who would be in my place next year? What would become of it all, the books, the center, the little push toward independence? Would the room be locked into uselessness like the library upstairs? Or dismantled and the books dispersed and lost? Would it be there when I returned?

One morning I went to the reading room at an hour when it was not scheduled for use, but I found the door unlocked. Some of the committee boys were inside. They had just finished rearranging the room. Bookcases, benches, tables, wall displays—everything was different. I stopped, surprised, then thrilled with the realization of what had happened.

"Is it all right, sir? We thought this would be more convenient, and you were not here for us to ask permission."

They were uncertain, looking to me anxiously for approval. How could I explain to them what they had done? What old bonds they had shaken from themselves? Organization, initiative, responsibility— flabby officious words which could hardly suffice for a triumph. My clever young friend from Herat was looking at me sidelong from his narrow, knowing eyes, and I rather thought that he knew what I knew: it was theirs now. They had finally made it their own and one way or another, they would keep it.

The flowers withered. There was frost on the morning grass. No more postponing: we must get ready to go. We would have to decide what to take with us, and pack it and arrange to ship it down to Peshawar. The rest would have to be sold. When we came back, we would start over.

But it was hard to begin. It seemed impossible to believe in the necessity of doing it, when our life was going on as usual. Maullahdad had disappeared again, but we were all accustomed to that. Anyhow, Ahmed-jan brought his younger brother to fill the vacancy, and Abdullah-jan turned out to be the alert and teachable boy Gul Baz had always been hoping for. The household was actually running more smoothly than ever. It was a time to settle down, not pack up.

I went through the house, making a list of all the things to be disposed of. Nothing was for the taking yet, but people began coming a good deal ahead of time to reserve items they particularly wanted or needed, as they always did whenever they heard that someone was planning to leave. But it was all words, an odd sort of joke, to put down buyers' names next to the items on my list. Strangers wandered in and out, some of them neighbors who came only to look around and ask questions. Meanwhile, every chair and table stood in its own place, where it belonged, where it had always been, and it was preposterous to imagine that it might ever be somewhere else.

The school year lasted well into December, but the autumn was long and the skies remained clear. The classes moved out of the chilly rooms into the sunshine. And every day, from one boy or another: "Really, you will come back?"

"Yes. It won't be long. You'll be surprised how soon."

"I hope we were not bad students, sir. I hope you were not unhappy in Kabul."

"Of course not! What makes you think—? Do you think that's why we're going? You know that isn't so!"

"Then why do you not stay?"

"Because . . ." How could I put it in their terms? "Because our families want to see us."

"Oh, of course, sir. Now I understand. It must be very hard to be so far from your family. But you will come back?"

"Yes, I will come back."

On the last day of classes before the examination period began, the last day when the school was all together, a group of teachers approached us during recess. The white-bearded old poet laureate led them, and the calligraphy teacher, a distinguished gentleman with a discreet goatee who was known respectfully as the Agha-sahib. On behalf of the faculty, they had come to give us a scroll on which the calligrapher had inscribed in his most beautiful script the passage from the great *Gulistan* of Saadi, which begins, "All of humanity are as limbs of the same body, created by one hand, of one clay . . ."

The sunlight was thin, no longer enough to warm us, by the time the examination period began. The English tests were scheduled for the first week, with an entire day given to each class. In the morning the boys wrote their papers with fingers stiff from the cold; in the afternoon they came one by one to sit across the table from

me for an oral examination. It was my last chance to talk with each
of them, so perhaps it was fortunate that I could not linger. I could
not: before the afternoon was far gone the sun would slip down
behind the mountains, and the early evening breezes from the snow
fields of Paghman would chill the boys who still stood waiting their
turn, shivering in their cotton uniforms. I had to be brief; I already
knew their work; so it was really less an examination than a last
greeting, and an *au revoir.* A few minutes, a few good wishes, a
joke or two, and a personal word, a handshake, no good-bys. Only,
"Good fortune on your journey, sir. Come back soon," and "Keep
well, good luck, till I see you again."

The last day, the last class to be examined: they were eleventh-
year students now. They had been my first class on the first day. It
was these boys who had made the joke about Bluebeard, who had
broken down the walls and taken me in; and Ismatullah had sat
in this class. Somehow the oral examinations went very slowly.
The afternoon waned, and still there were boys waiting, chafing
their cold ankles with numb fingers. The sun was gone. Purple
shadows stretched across the fields and grew longer. The early dusk
of December was gathering and in the dormitories the lights were
already on. I must quicken the pace. The sky was fading, but there
were only one or two boys left now, and they had been waiting all
afternoon. I had been unfair to take so long, not to let go.

As a boy rose and shook my hand and left, someone came walking
swiftly through the dusk from the direction of the dormitories:
Mohammad-jan. He had finished his examination long ago; he knew
his grade, knew he was near the top of his class; what could have
brought him out again into the evening cold? Since Ismatullah's
death I had never known him to speak unless a question called him
forth from his reserve. "Yes, Mohammad-jan? Is there something
you forgot?"

"I came to say good-by."

Taken aback, I extended my hand. "Why, that's very nice of you, but didn't we before?"

"Before, I said, 'Good luck till you return,'" he said quietly, "but I think you will not come back to Kabul again, so I came now to say good-by. May God go with you."

He took my hand, and then was gone.

Ah, the truth-tellers of this world! They will not be silent, and they break our hearts.

The house was empty, and Gul Baz was not there. A family emergency had called him to Peshawar for a few days, and then he had an attack of sciatica and could not travel. He sent messages to us every few days, saying that he expected to be well tomorrow and to return; but he was not, and could not, and we did not see him again until we reached Peshawar.

It is so strange to think that he was not there at the end, for wherever I look in my memory of those years, I see Gul Baz Khan in his old sleeveless pullover and blue jeans, his karakul hat at a jaunty angle: hurrying to deal with some emergency or sitting on his heels, cigarette in hand, for profound discussion; leaning against the doorjamb and tipping me a sympathetic wink over the head of an interminable visitor, or signaling melodramatically that the dogs had eaten up all the tea sandwiches; doubled up with laughter at some nonsense and still chuckling to himself in the kitchen; chiding, guiding, philosophizing, remonstrating—wherever I look he is there, the Greek chorus to our days. Perhaps that is why I understood at last that we were leaving: Gul Baz was not there.

The skies turned gray and dark with waiting snow. People who, weeks before, had bought our furniture came and took from the house, one by one, things which now belonged to them; so that at first there seemed to be odd gaping holes in every room and at last there was nothing left but the bed and a few old crippled chairs and tables and odd cups and pans. A strange thing, this dismantling of everything which has formed itself into a home. If it had been possible, if we could have afforded to do it, I would much have preferred to leave it all intact and just close the door one day on the life that had been there. It must be a peculiarly human self-torment to break up the framework of our lives from time to time and cast it away in pieces. Even the birds, when they fly forever from their nests of a season, do not pull them apart into sticks and grass again.

Everything that would go with us had to be packed and sent ahead. My husband was out of the house all day long, going to one office after another, getting visas, arranging to send our things to Peshawar on a British Embassy lorry. Mohammad Anwar came almost every day to help me with the packing. One evening in the cold dimness of the lower hall we were packing books into an old steamer trunk. I picked up a one-volume Shakespeare and asked him if he would like it. He thanked me gravely. The next day he arrived pallid with lack of sleep but alight with exhilaration. He had read through the whole night, discovering one play after another.

We had to do something about the dogs. Ahmed-jan asked to take Blackie to his home in Bimaru, but we could find no home for Jenny. The only place for her was on the streets, where I had often seized astonished little boys and shaken them angrily for pegging rocks at stray dogs. We looked at her and said, "Jenny, would you put us out on the street?" and she looked back coyly with her odd golden eyes. We booked a kennel for her on the ship.

When the heating stoves had been taken away by their new owners, a damp chill settled on the house. In the empty living room I spent hours burning old papers of every sort. There was nothing of importance in them, but I knew that the landlord would come looking through anything left behind, and I wanted to leave nothing for him. Besides, although the fireplace smoked dreadfully, the blaze warmed us a little. At last we began to break up the old chairs and burn them piece by piece. There was nothing left now but the dust in the corners, and the pale squares on the walls where pictures had hung. I sat on the stairs with my typewriter on my lap and wrote enthusiastic letters of reference for Ahmed-jan and Abdullah-jan, who could not read them, of course, but smiled hopefully, wanting them to be favorable. I asked Anwar to translate them for the two men, who were pleased and put the envelopes carefully away in their pockets.

Friends still came often: Shaban, Anwar, Hassan, Marshall and other teachers, students who had not yet left for home. We stood around in our overcoats, shivering, drinking tea, which Abdullah-jan kept constantly steaming on the little charcoal brazier which was our cook-stove now. It was not much hospitality to offer, but people came.

There were still errands to be done in the city. I often went to the bazaars to try to do all the things for which it had always seemed that there was plenty of time in the future, now that there was no time at all. I had ordered coats of black Persian lamb for myself and my mother--gifts from my father. Shaban had selected the skins, gathering the finest he could find over many months, and now they were being made up, stitch by hand-sewn stitch. I would go for a fitting and Shaban would arrive to inspect the coat scritically, pointing to a tiny spot here or there, saying, "I don't like that. It doesn't match." So the furrier would snip it out—half an inch this way, an inch the other—and cut into another skin of silky fine-curled karakul. I was sorry only that no one would be able to see the interlining when the coat was finished—flamboyant Russian flannelette smeared with garish colors like an Easter egg dyed by a madman: orange, electric blue, acid green, purple.

We made a special trip to Paghman to buy a sitar and then, on a cold, damp afternoon, went with Hassan Kakar to a cubbyhole in a crevice of the Shor Bazaar where a musical-instrument maker was repairing a *rabob* for us—a handsome bouted instrument, an ancestor of the violin family. The rabob-maker was a fine craftsman, and very good-natured and cheerful, although he was half dying of tuberculosis. He sent his apprentice to bring tea for us, and as he polished the ivory inlay with which he had filled a crack in the instrument, he said, "You are not the only foreigners who are interested in musical instruments. My friend who makes sitars in Paghman said that some crazy Americans came and bought one from him the other day."

So we came and went on familiar streets and saw people we knew well, and still lived in Kabul; yet the life of the city somehow appeared to enclose itself from us, not unkindly but inexorably, as though it knew that we had no business with it now but to prepare to go away from it. We had forfeited our share in that life; and land, city, the very streets and walls, the movement of crowds, everything around us, had withdrawn—taking back into the common store whatever portion of their life we had briefly held. We came and went but we belonged already to another world, and a far one. Before we left this land, it left us; and I could feel myself trying to cling somehow, trying to keep my hold till the very last moment.

The new year came and one morning it began to snow. The skies sank low, sodden, lead-colored. By noon they were hidden in a blizzard. It snowed all that day and that night, and the next, and on for six days. The winds blew out of the north and froze the world. The passes were blocked. The city was buried in snow, and nothing moved.

In the cold house we burned the last sticks of furniture and went at night to a friend's home to sleep. Every morning we fought our way through the storm and the snowdrifts to the embassy—a five-minute walk ordinarily, almost an hour now—but the news there was always the same: in every direction the passes were blocked. The city was cut off. In the mountains the drifts were higher than a man's head. Nothing could get through. The snow stopped falling and there was a rumor that the snowplows would have the Lataband clear in two days. Then it began to snow again.

Not a wheel turned in the streets of Kabul. The winds, channeled between the high walls, drifted the snow hip-deep or deeper. Unless he must, no one went out to plod through the drifts; only a few figures were to be seen occasionally, wrapped in quilted chipons with scarves tied across their faces against the stinging wind. Life was reduced to essentials: to keep warm, to get food. The bazaars were silent. From beneath the muffling blanket of snow only the bake shops sent up here and there a wisp of smoke from the bread ovens to signal life within. The city was a white limbo, frozen to sudden stillness—softly, thickly, absolutely white and still.

The snow stopped again. The sky cleared. Snowplows pushed through the main avenues, and when the wind drifted them back over, narrow pathways were trampled between walls of snow. The city stirred faintly in its white sleep. Rumor said that the snowplows had gone to the Lataband. At the embassy we learned that the American diplomatic courier, who had been caught in Kabul by the storm, was determined to try to go over the Pass on the second day, using a station wagon with a four-wheel drive. No one but the courier himself could authorize any passengers to travel with him, let alone—what? a dog! We had to catch a boat; we would not leave the dog. We went to the courier. He said he would take us.

On our last night in Kabul we made our way to the little shop by the river where Shaban was waiting to oversee a final fitting of my coat. In the city the wind had already undone the work of the snowplows. It seemed impossible that the Pass would be clear.

Long after midnight we left the furriers still sitting cross-legged under the yellow light bulbs, stitching, stitching the last bits of fur into place. It was too late to awaken the friend with whom we had been staying. We turned instead toward our empty home, stumbling one step after another against the wind, slipping, laboring endlessly through the icy silence. Not another soul was out on the streets. I remembered stories of wolves, driven by winter to leave their mountain haunts and come down to roam the streets of the villages and towns; but we saw nothing and no one, heard only the sound of our own feet, slick on the snow, and our own heavy breathing. The cold air burned in our lungs. The snow itself lighted the black night with its unearthly cold radiance. On the mountain top the pointless string of lights burned on undaunted. We struggled through the drifts for nearly two hours until, exhausted, we beat at last on the familiar gate to arouse the sleeping batcha.

Inside the house there was nothing but the suitcases, which stood ready in the middle of the hall, and the rope bed upstairs. Our breath hung in the frigid air, our voices echoed from the empty walls. Wearily we pulled off our boots and shook the snow from our overcoats. Then, still wearing our coats, we flung ourselves on the bare mattress and called to the dogs. They came running up the staircase and jumped up beside us. We snuggled them close, one on either side, and in their warmth we slept.

The next day I went from room to room of the abandoned house to see that nothing was left behind. Nothing was left. Shaban came, Hassan, a few others. The servants took the luggage to the embassy. There was no more to do. When night fell, we put the dogs on their leashes and Ahmed-jan and Abdullah-jan took them to Shaban's house. Then my husband and I went to a farewell party at the United Nations mission. It was a large party, and a jolly one. That is, everyone else seemed to enjoy it. Most of the guests were in one way or another living an international life, so there was a great exchanging of addresses, with promises to meet and have a drink soon in New York. At midnight we went out into the silent streets again.

All the lights were on at Shaban's house. They glowed above the compound walls; we saw them from far down the street. Shaban was waiting, and Anwar was there too. A heavy tea was ready: when he felt an occasion called for it, Shaban's cook was fond of making things with a great deal of whipped cream and crushed pistachios, and there was much whipped cream and pistachio before us.

Shaban had big cloth bags of Afghan pistachios and jalroza for us to take along, for he knew that we liked them and would not be able to get them elsewhere. There was a pile of golden Herati carpets and scarlet-and-black mowris rolled up in the middle of the floor, the rugs which I had always expected to get tomorrow. I chose three from those he had selected. That gave us something to talk about: how he would arrange to ship them to us.

In one corner of the room Ahmed-jan and his brother sat drowsing, holding the leashes of the uneasy dogs. We pushed a sleeping pill down Jenny's unwilling throat. Then the two men roused themselves and rose to leave on their long walk to Bimaru. I searched my purse for whatever afghanis I still had left and stuffed them into Ahmed-jan's hand. My husband and I pulled off our rubber boots and gave them to the two servants. They left, pulling Blackie, bewildered, behind them.

We waited for Jenny to grow groggy and stupid. We tried to make conversation. We had another cup of tea. But it was no use: the time had come to leave for the embassy. Shaban and Anwar walked the two blocks with us.

"Maybe you'll get a scholarship next year," I said to Anwar as we walked. "Why, we may see you in New York before we can even get back here."

"Yes," he said politely. "Yes, maybe that is so."

One wing of the embassy was alight and busy. The car was ready. The most skillful chauffeur on the staff, one of Gul Baz's friends, was driving, and he had brought along another bearer to help him in case of trouble. He raised his eyebrows and grinned wryly when we asked if he thought we would get through. "*Insh'allah*," he said. "If God is willing." The courier was more hopeful: he was eager to get started.

It was almost dawn. It was time to go.

I had never had any physical contact of any sort with any of the students, except for a formal handshake; not even a friendly hand on the shoulder—so careful were we all, always, to maintain propriety even beyond propriety: so aware that I had done enough to come into their world unveiled. Now Anwar and I threw our arms about each other to say good-by.

Shaban was visibly shrinking into his solitude again. "Look for me in the summer," he said. "I will cable you. I have my visa. I will come."

We who were leaving climbed into the car and pulled the sodden dog in onto our laps, and shut the doors; and drove away, and did not look back.

Slowly the car made its way across the valley floor. The road was a shallow groove, only less deeply drifted than the mounds piled by the snowplows on either side. Where the plows had passed, the wind had followed, smoothing away the signs of their work. The car struggled and skidded across the plain. In the pale light of dawn the hills of Bimaru rose like white elephants watching our progress from afar. The wind swirled and spun the surface snow, set it dancing like the dust-devils of summer. Before we had reached the foot of the Lataband the sun was rising on a brilliant day, streaking the sky with gold and casting deep pools of purple shadow in the clefts among the hills. Everything else was white, white: sheer glacial glittering white. We began to climb the narrow track over the pass, the driver wrestling with the wheel as the tires skidded across the powdery drifts. Snow whipped across our path. Where the plows had gone through, the road should be passable; but the track they had cleared was already hidden, the signs of it erased by the ceaseless winds. A carpet of surface snow had wiped out the borderlines between the safety of the roadbed and the drifts on either side—smothering traps piled six or seven feet deep against the mountainside above, and treacherous shelves of ice, deceptively solid-looking, precariously overhanging the cliffs below. The road was only a guess: somewhere beneath the white carpet it lay, a feeble tightrope of safety twisting tortuously against the mountain flank.

Below, and away to the peaks like carved white jade on the far horizon, the landscape was blanketed in white, covering everything: white, shadowed blue and purple in the deep ravines, gold at the mountain crests, sparkling in the sunlight. The mountains were covered and the plains, the villages were covered and the fields, the streams were buried, and no wisp of smoke rose against the blue sky. White, white: as though for one moment the land had been wrapped in cotton so that I could lay away in my memory, unbroken, everything I had known of it.

Staring out the window as we wound along the treacherous slopes, inch by inch, hour by hour, in the muffled stillness, I could only think, How beautiful this is! How beautiful! I must have said it aloud, for my husband, who was concentrating on the car as it skidded and churned through the icy drifts, turned on me with, "My God, stop it! We may be killed—must you talk nonsense?"

After that I kept my thoughts to myself, but I refused to be interested in the danger. For hours it had been obvious that we had gotten ourselves into a foolhardy escapade which could at any moment end in death: the narrow unguarded thread of road was utterly buried, no one could see in the blinding whiteness where it dropped away into the cliffs, and even if the roadway had been visible, the skidding wheels could send us crashing down the mountainside into canyons far below. At best we were likely to get stuck somewhere in this frigid wilderness and have hours or days to fight cold and hunger before the plows could get through again, if the storm returned. The trip should never have been begun. The driver had already been told to turn back; he had answered grimly that it was probably impossible to get through but it was certainly impossible to turn. He knew better than any of us just what he was struggling with, and his face was sallow with tension.

But there was nothing whatever that I could do. So I refused to concern myself with the danger when all across the valley as far as the eye could see, to the dazzling mountains in the east, lay a beauty such as I had never seen before and might never see again— sun-struck to diamond splendor, endless, frozen and glittering, the enchanted realm of the Snow Queen.

Literally foot by foot we crept up the slippery winding track on the edge of the mountain. The bearer who had come along got out and walked in front of the car, feeling for the cliff edge with his foot. The cold was too intense. In five minutes he was back inside the car, his nose and fingertips white, nearly frostbitten. So the men took turns plodding ahead for just two or three minutes at a time, floundering sometimes among the drifts, searching out the roadbed while the car inched along behind them: a few feet, and then a few feet, and then another few feet. The drugged dog snored heavily on our knees. Sometimes we passed a bus or lorry stuck in the drifts. As we edged our way cautiously around it, the bearer would get out to talk with the other driver and come back shaking his head: "They say it's worse up ahead. I hope the plows come through soon—they have children with them."

Hour after hour through the beautiful treachery of a crystal world. We reached the top of the pass and began the slow descent. In midafternoon we saw below us the snow line. Beyond it rivulets of melted ice ran shining over sunlit rocks and bare earth. A jeep was parked there while its passengers surveyed the pass ahead of them and waited for us to reach them. Safe and unbelieving, we crossed from snow to earth and stopped at last.

The waiting men were diplomatic friends from Kabul.

"How is it up ahead?"

"Don't try it. It's suicidal."

"But you got through."

"Sheer luck. There were a hundred times we nearly didn't. The road's littered with stalled traffic. If you get stuck, you'll be there a week."

"Oh, well, maybe we'll give it a try. Where are you off to?"

"The States."

"Oh, good. That's my next post, they say. See you in New York."

So we started down through the rocks and streams, and they turned toward the snows. I looked back: the crystal landscape was hidden like a dream of fairyland. Only the white hump of the mountain was to be seen, guarding the snow world as its secret.

The driver raced across the desert now, trying to get to the Khyber before sundown. We swept through Jalalabad and on without stopping, but night fell before we pulled across the border. The Pakistani officials politely refused to let us go on. We would have to wait for dawn. The courier insisted on his diplomatic privilege:

he had already been delayed too long, he must make the next train to Karachi.

The commander of the border post went into his office to call headquarters in Peshawar. We heard him arguing for a long time.

"All right," he said when he came back. "You can go through. But I'm putting an armed guard on the car."

He waved forward a rifleman, who perched himself on the front fender. This seemed to me more dangerous than letting us drive the Pass alone. If we were by any chance held up, the last thing I wanted was someone in our party who might start shooting. But the officer had his orders and he was adamant: we would take the guard or we would not go through. So with the soldier riding postilion, we set off into the pitchy darkness of the pass.

On the highway we made good time and were already deep into the gorges when a tire blew. The driver and the bearer pulled a box of tools from under the seat and jumped out to change the tire. The squeak of the jack and the thump of the wheel coming off were the only sounds in the night—except, of course, for the footsteps of the rifleman as he paced up and down alongside the car, peering into the darkness of the mountains rising overhead. Occasionally he paused and looked into the car, patting his rifle in what was presumably meant to be a reassuring gesture.

"That guard . . . It's all nonsense, isn't it?" the courier asked uneasily.

"Probably," we said. "Possibly not."

Carrying clear on the still night air, a whistle sounded down the mountainside. Everyone heard it, and heard it answered from across the gorge. The rifleman stopped pacing and shifted his gun. The men outside stopped work for a moment, then started shoving the wheel hastily back onto the axle. High up on the slope on the opposite side of the gorge a light appeared and began to move erratically downward, like a lantern in the hand of someone picking his way among the rocks. Then another light appeared on the slope above us, moving downward.

The car door burst open. The driver flung his tools inside and leaped into his seat. Doors slammed. We roared off full speed for the end of the Pass. When old Fort Jamrud had been left behind us, brooding forever on its rock, the driver slowed to normal speed and drove straight across the plain into Peshawar City.

Each of us makes his own Eden, and of strange clay.

Behind us in the night the mountains rose unseen, hidden in darkness. Beyond them, on roads to the north and the east and west, in caravanserais where travelers rolled themselves in quilts for the night or plucked their sitars and sang impassioned melodies by lamplight, the students lay sleeping on their journeys homeward. In the high cold valleys of Afghanistan and on the passes, where the wind sweeps down over the Hindu Kush, snow lay thick and silver, gleaming by starlight in the black of night, or falling silently again to erase every footprint and wipe out every path that had been made.

The wheels of our car grated on gravel as we swung into the curving driveway of Dean's Hotel and drew up before the brightly-lit portico. Bearers hurried forward to take our bags. The warm still air of the plains curled softly around us, with not even a breath of mountain breeze to stir it. A thousand miles of gleaming steel rails stretched away before us, to Karachi and its wharves and piers; and beyond them lay the rolling southern seas.

Afterword

Did I return to Kabul? Yes—but not until more than a decade had passed and much had changed, both in Afghanistan and in my life. By the time I returned, I was no longer Mrs. Archer and a teacher: my husband and I had gone our separate ways, I had resumed my own name and written this book, and I came back as a reporter with writing assignments.

And my friends? What became of them? A few months after we left, Shaban finally sold his business interests to his Muslim partners. He gathered up his wife Sipporah and their children in Israel and they came to New York. We were at the airport to meet them. Shaban established himself as a gem merchant, and a few years later I served as a witness when he and Sipporah became American citizens.

Chevy—the witty scholar who was part of our little family for a while—became a distinguished professor of linguistics at several major universities.

Faculty and students from Darul Mo'Allamein and other Afghan friends began coming to the U.S. on scholarships and short cultural visits. My home in New York was regularly one of their first stops. "Marshall"—Ghulam Ali Ayeen, the bookish teacher—was among those who came to study for an advanced degree, as was Anwar. Hassan Kakar, determined to regain the opportunity he had lost to illness, finally won a scholarship to London, took his doctorate in history there, and followed it up at Harvard and Princeton, returning to Kabul to head the history department at Kabul University. I heard that Mohammed-jan and others had won scholarships to the American University in Beirut.

After heading the Helmand Valley Authority, Kayeum served as governor of Helmand province. He came to Washington several times on diplomatic missions; Joan came along to visit her family, and we all got together. Abdul played a major role in ending mandatory purdah in 1959. Reportedly, word reached the dictatorial prime minister, Prince Daoud, that in the HVA headquarters town of Lashkargah, where Afghan administrators and American engineers lived as in a California-style suburb, Afghan women were enjoying the swimming pool with everyone else; Daoud ordered Kayeum to get the women back under the *chadri* but Abdul told him it was too late for that and advised him to unveil the rest of Afghan women —which he did soon after.

In 1963, Daoud furiously resigned after a dispute with his cousin the king, and for the first time the king appointed a prime minister who was not a member of the royal family—indeed, not even a Pushtun—who installed a modernizing reform government, including Kayeum. This new, Western-educated generation moved to lay the foundations for a constitutional monarchy. They wrote a new constitution modeled in many respects on that of the United States; it was accepted by the king and parliament. Kayeum became minister of the interior. He, Joan and their growing family moved back to Kabul.

And then, of course, there was Gul Baz Khan. I had last seen him in a hospital bed, gripped by the pain of sciatica. We had arranged for his treatment, and gave him some airmail folders addressed to us. He couldn't write, of course, but he could hire a letter-writer in the bazaar to let us know how he was. And I had promised him, too, that we would return.

So when at last I went back, my first task—as soon as I reached Peshawar—was to find Gul Baz Khan. It had been years since any message had come from him.

Dean's Hotel was a little more worn, a little dowdier, but still a Victorian oasis. I checked in and immediately sent a message to Nevekali village.

An hour or two later, a young man wheeled his bicycle up outside my bungalow. Gul Baz had not come; it was his oldest son, Sher, whose wedding I had attended so long before. I went out on the porch. His eyes widened and he stared at me as though he was seeing a ghost.

"Hello, Sher," I said, "It's me." I took a deep breath, then asked, "Is your father alive?"

"Yes," he said.

"Where is he?"

"He is working for English people in Lahore."

So before I went on to Kabul, I backtracked to Lahore the next morning. At the airport there, I saw a familiar figure in starched, spotless white hurrying toward me through the crowd. A moment later—decorum and propriety briefly cast aside—I was giving Gul Baz Khan a hug.

Sher had sent his father a telegram the night before. His employers told me that when they read it to him, he had immediately asked for the day off, explaining that otherwise he would have to quit his job —because, he said, "Khanum-sahib is coming and I must be there to meet her." He had been at the airport since dawn, meeting every plane until he found me.

I had brought him a copy of this book, and his employers promised to read it to him. Meanwhile I sat down with him and we went through the pages. He could read his own name, which I had underlined in red wherever it appeared. And of course he recognized his picture, which pleased him, and Maullahdad's, which made him laugh. He beamed with pleasure as I told him that he was now very famous and that all over the world people knew that he was the best bearer on either side of the Frontier.

His current employers saw him merely as an employee. The lady of the house said he missed some of the dust. What? Gul Baz *missed the dust*? I took him to an optician in the bazaar and bought him a pair of eyeglasses.

We exchanged news. He had a bit of arthritis, was pleased with one son, disappointed in another. He wanted to know about everyone who had been part of our household, even the dog we had taken home. (She was living in canine luxury in my parents' home in Iowa.) He remembered everything: those years had been a good time. We reminisced and laughed. I stayed only a day or two, but I told him I would see him again when I returned from Kabul, and so I did, a few months later.

This time I didn't have to scrounge for a ride to Kabul; Kayeum had a car now and he had sent it to Peshawar to pick me up. The trip through the Khyber Pass was familiar, but the once-forbidding border post now sported a sign announcing "Welcome to Afghanistan," and a colorful billboard advised "Drink Orange Squash."

Instead of a rough desert track, a smooth tarmac highway lined with willows and irrigated green fields led to Kabul; it had been built for Afghanistan in the early 1960s by the U.S. Army Corps of Engineers as part of a national highway encircling the central massif. (The Russians had built the sections leading southward from the Soviet border and, unknown to the Afghans, had designed them to carry tanks and serve as landing fields; but that would only become known many years later.)

What had formerly been a bone-breaking day-long journey now took only a few swift, smooth hours in a comfortable sedan. Instead of twisting over the old wearisome hump of the Lataband Pass, the new road ran through the breath-taking gorge of Tang-i-Garu —the Devil's Throat—where the Kabul River drops foaming over the rocks past the German-built hydroelectric dam at Sarobi. The canyon walls towered overhead, red and purple and ochre, a wild tangle of stony splendor.

From the depths of the gorge the highway darted up thousands of feet, then swooped down into the green Kabul valley. We sped across the valley into the city and pulled up in front of Joan and Abdul's house, where their kids came tumbling out to welcome me.

Kabul was both familiar and changed, mostly though not entirely for the better. Thanks to the Sarobi dam, the lights no longer flickered and dimmed in the evening; but the glow of the city lights diminished the brilliance of the starry night-time sky. The city was no longer quiet. The Russians had paved the main streets, and cars and beat-up taxis had replaced most of the horse-drawn *gawdis,* though donkeys and bicycles threaded their way among them. Some of the huddled old bazaars had been torn down, shaking out the clutter from the center of the city, replacing it with Pushtunistan Square, which was surrounded by small parks, government buildings, glass-fronted shops, two sizable western-style hotels, and the Khyber Restaurant, where the local jet set hung out.

In the side alleys, snack bars and grubby hostels catered to the mostly European hippies who had started pouring into Kabul in search of cheap drugs, shocking Kabul's citizenry, who associated drug use with bums. To their further dismay, these kids, decked out in fashion jeans, shorts, and low-cut blouses and toting expensive cameras, were pan-handling and teaching Afghan children to beg. I saw a man grab an urchin whining for "*baksheesh*" near a hotel and shake him. "What are you doing?" he shouted, "You're an Afghan! Don't you have any pride?"

Several movie theaters sported garish posters for popular Indian romance films or an occasional European film likely to titillate and enticingly scandalize local viewers.

The city was spreading out across the valley, grown to more than half a million or more. In the guise of foreign aid, it was being remodeled into a relentlessly functional facsimile of an Eastern European industrial suburb. The crumbling old adobe city had at least been rooted its own traditions; the grubby walls that turned their backsides to the street often concealed beautiful interiors and the streets were full of life.

On a hilltop outside of town, Bagh-i-Baala, the abandoned old palace of the Amir Abdur Rahman, had been restored and turned into a handsome restaurant surrounded by gardens (in one of which Kayeum had quietly and kindly buried our poisoned pet, many years before).

I walked over to our former home. The current residents were away and I couldn't go in, so I stood outside with memories. After the dogs were poisoned I had thought of sowing the yard with salt when we left so that nothing would ever grow there again, the way the Romans did at Carthage, but I didn't do it. Now, through the gate I could see greenery where Ahmed-jan had labored assiduously to create a garden in thankless clay.

But the great change was the presence of women: Kabul was no longer a world where women were visible only as shrouded ghosts in shapeless chadris. One now saw them shopping, or in the Khyber restaurant, or in clusters at bus stops, en route to school..

The chadri had not been banned; it had simply been made optional and had rapidly vanished. Sometimes in the bazaar one still saw a woman shrouded from head to toe, but (I was told) those were usually older women who had been veiled so long they felt uncomfortable without it; or poor women who did not want to reveal their shabby clothes. One day in the Da Afghanan, a man clapped his hands over his eyes until I had passed—a diehard, unreconciled to an unveiled woman.

Many women were still primarily occupied at home, but many of the younger women were working in offices, teaching, running a beauty salon or a telephone switchboard, or crowding into schools and the now co-educational university.

Old friends who had been minor officials or fellow teachers when first I knew them were now, like Kayeum, members of the cabinet or otherwise in the forefront of the constitutional movement. Marshall still spoke English like a book, but he had acquired an American degree or two and a cabinet portfolio. The very junior diplomat who had first given me a contract to teach in Afghanistan was Minister of Justice. I had known the prime minister as an official of the Ministry of Education, and three of his four successors would also be old friends. The American-trained physician who was now the leader of Parliament had been our family doctor. (Many years before that he had been the young boy for whom King Amanullah tore up the warrant for his rebellious father's execution.)

Some of my former students were in Kabul, though many were working in the Helmand or elsewhere around the country. Mohammad-jan, now an official of the HVA, came to say hello, still reserved and inward. "I told you I would come back," I said.

Others were scattered around the world, often studying for advanced degrees. Anwar and I had indeed met in New York; he was now at a major American university. A foreign colony is always transient, so everyone I had known there—diplomats and teachers —had disappeared, gone home or to new assignments. In any case, everyone had work to do and lives to live, and this time, I had no job to anchor me in daily life. So it was sometimes an unexpectedly lonely time.

But it was also a hopeful time.

From my window at the Kabul Hotel, overlooking the royal palace, I used to see the king driving his convertible out of the palace garage, alone, with the top down. Nobody on the street seemed to pay attention. Which suggested that, like the Scandinavian monarchs, he was popular enough not to need any bodyguards, and that change was being welcomed..

Afghanistan, under its new democratic constitution, was preparing for its first nationwide parliamentary elections, which were to be held by secret ballot and universal suffrage; women would be voting. An assignment to report on those elections was paying my way back to Afghanistan: thus did I get my introduction to Afghan politics. To my surprise, I was the only foreign reporter there. The Afghan reformers thought they were pioneering a new way for much of the Near East, but as usual, the world was paying little attention to what happened beyond the Khyber.

I interviewed officials who had been involved in writing the new constitution and were now laboring to make it work. I interviewed candidates for parliament in Kabul and in nearby towns and villages, who were struggling with the novelty of presenting themselves to potential voters, not as tribal or village leaders or *maliks* automatically entitled to authority but as individuals, facing what had hitherto been unthinkable, competition. Some of the novice candidates asked me about elections in America. One complained bitterly that his opponent offered tea and cake to potential voters. "Isn't that unfair?" he demanded. "Wouldn't it be illegal in America?"—and was dismayed to learn that tea and cake were not beyond the pale.

I was not aware that a secret Communist party had just been formed in Kabul, so when I interviewed a flamboyant candidate named Babrak Karmal who was agitating among the students at Kabul University, I didn't know that he was on the Soviet payroll. Still, it didn't take long to figure him out. He expounded on the need to bring the benefits of revolution to Afghanistan.

"Revolution?" I asked. "Like the Mexican Revolution?" That drew a blank stare. "Well, then, how about the French Revolution?" He had never heard of that one, either. That brought us to the obvious alternative, the only revolution he knew. He didn't seem to know a lot about that one, either—just that he favored it.

Nobody knew whether the election process would work or whether it would be peaceful, but work it did and peaceful it was. I visited the long lines of voters at polling places—both men and women, even a few women still wearing the *chadri*—waiting patiently to have their hands marked with indelible ink, indicating that they had voted. The process was not perfect, but it worked. All over the country, thousands voted, for the first time in Afghanistan's long history. The first reform government presented their resignations, to take effect when the new parliament convened in a week or two and confirmed a new government.

Meanwhile, I had other articles to work on. I arranged with the tourist office for a car and a guide to go north to see Mazar-i-Sharif and the Pamirs. Before, the north had been out of reach, beyond the barrier of the Hindu Kush; it took our students a week or more to arrive from Mazar or Faizabad when the school year began. Now the Russians had cut the world's highest road tunnel through the Hindu Kush at Salang, bringing the northern border to little more than a day's drive from Kabul.

The highway led through the familiar Koh-i-Daman valley, past Istalif and Charikar, where we used to picnic with Shaban when the flowering Judas trees were in bloom, and Gulbahar where unpaved side roads turned off to Panjsher and Bamian. The road began to climb past villages clinging to the cliffs among poplar groves, golden in the cool September sunlight. The Salang tunnel was at an altitude of almost twelve thousand feet in a world of stone: snow lay unmelted in the crevices of raw peaks and icy winds beat against the car.

Inside the dark, narrow tunnel, almost two miles long, trucks and busses vied for space with flocks of fat-tailed sheep; the air was cold and stale. We emerged on the other side of the mountains into the Oxus Valley, a different world where the air was mild and the mountains, dotted with pistachio trees, sloped down onto the vast steppes of Central Asia.

We stopped for the night at an inn in the small town of Haibak. The innkeeper was taken aback when I demanded the exclusive use of a room with three beds: there were men looking for a place to sleep. He was astonished when I agreed to meet his exorbitant terms and paid nearly four dollars to rent all three beds for myself.

The next day we passed the domed beehive roofs of Turkoman villages, quite different from the flat-topped houses of Pushtuns and Tajiks. Then more mountains loomed ahead and suddenly we were speeding through a canyon as narrow as a needle's eye, the canyon I had expected the Khyber to be, those many years ago. Beyond it lay Tashkurgan and the last of the ancient covered bazaars, a world of Ali Baba and Aladdin, where footsteps were muffled and one would hesitate to rub an old brass lamp. Dust motes floated in the shafts of pale light from skylights high above. In dim alleys, silversmiths or coppersmiths hammered out delicate designs and blacksmiths struck the red-hot iron on their anvils as small boys pumped the bellows of their forges. Elsewhere, boot sellers and tailors sat cross-legged in their shops, stitching silently, blanketed in dusty stillness. The walls of the teahouses were painted gardens of tulips and roses and caged nightingales.

Beyond Tashkurgan lay Mazar-i-Sharif, said to be the final resting place of the martyred Caliph Ali, son-in-law of the Prophet Mohammed, in whose footsteps the lakes of Band-i-Amir had sprung forth. In the fifteenth century Timurid rulers built a magnificent shrine above his tomb in the midst of the bustling market town. Flocks of white doves swooped around the vast azure-tiled domes and courtyards that spread out among rose gardens like fragments of the sky. I could only imagine how they must look during the great springtime festival, when the tulips were in bloom. Inside, beyond a carved screen of polished wood, a constant relay of mullahs endlessly intoned verses from the Koran. Around the velvet-draped cenotaph, ornamented with silver sickle moons, the faithful knelt and prayed.

Not far from Mazar, rising from the dusty plains, lay the vast ruins of Balkh, the ancient Mother of Cities, where Zoroaster's high banners flew. From the top of those mounds, one looked down into archeological digs like slices in a giant layer cake: a dozen layers of civilization, four thousand years of vanished living.

Nearby, I spent a morning watching the flying fingers of Turkoman women at a big horizontal loom, tying myriads of tiny knots to create the fabric of one of their beautiful crimson carpets. I spent an evening sitting on such carpets in a black felt nomad tent where women baked thin sheets of unleavened bread over open fires, drinking tea and listening to the sleepy bleating of sheep interspersed with singing commercials from Radio Ceylon on my hosts' portable radios.

From Mazar we turned east to Kunduz, heading toward Faizabad and the high Pamirs. I had an invitation to dinner from the governor of Kunduz. In his parlor, I was surprised to see a painting by the sixteenth century German artist Lucas Cranach. It was a family heirloom, he told me: his grandfather had been educated in Germany and married there. When he brought his German bride home to Afghanistan, she brought the painting with her. So here in a remote town in northern Afghanistan hung a painting by a Renaissance master, its existence probably unknown to art historians. I have wondered what happened to it in the tumultuous years since then.

Over dinner the governor expressed surprise at my travel plans. "If I were a reporter," he said, "I would go straight down to Kabul. Don't you know what's happened?"

No, I didn't.

Two days before, he told me, at the opening of the newly-elected parliament, a mob of university students had tried to storm the parliament building. The hapless, ill-trained police had been unable to control them, the army had been called out, shots had been fired, and several people had been killed. The installation of the new government had been postponed.

I cancelled the mountains and headed for Kabul, where I went straight to the post office and cabled the New York Times, "RIOTS IN KABUL STOP TANKS IN STREETS STOP DO YOU WANT COVERAGE?"

Thus I became, at least for a few months, a foreign correspondent —in fact the only one in town—and I didn't even own a trench coat.

The city, and the government, were in a state of shock. It had all started innocently enough: following the election, the government had announced that, in emulation of democracies elsewhere, parliament's meetings would be open to the public; but nobody thought about tickets or arrangements for the few visitors expected.

Babrak Karmal—he of the single revolution, one of four secret communists who had been elected—incited crowds of students to march on parliament and demand entry. They attempted to force their way in. Rocks were hurled. Doors and windows were smashed. People were injured. Hundreds more, summoned by agitators, joined the riot. In the end, several students and bystanders were dead.

The agitators tried to parade the dead students through the streets as martyrs and spread false stories of secret executions. Karmal, though uninjured, appeared at a window of the main hospital, theatrically bandaged, his arm in a sling, to harangue a crowd of excited student followers.

The prime minister resigned. A new government took office—but shakily, against a threat of upheaval emanating from the radicalized university. I reported on these events.

But eventually it was time for me to leave.

This time I made no promises. Once I had had a place in Kabul, had been briefly part of its life—but that time was long gone, and I had no illusions that it would return. Everyone had been more than welcoming, but now I was only a visitor. I might come again and always be welcome, but I would never be part of it again as before. So—old friends and new ones—we said au revoir and hoped to meet again, knowing that we probably would, but differently now.

We didn't know how differently.

Reportedly, during the riots, Karmal had shouted, "Tomorrow will be ours!" Kayeum, hearing that, is said to have murmured, "Not as long as I'm here." But over the next decade, Kayeum was not always there, nor were others who might have made a difference. The reformers were spread thin. Sometimes they were abroad as diplomats, or had simply stepped aside when, constitutionally, others took their places in new governments.

The world outside paid no attention and offered no significant assistance.

Nevertheless, over the next decade, considerable progress was made. Many of the modernists were hopeful: they foresaw development for their country and improved relations with their neighbors and the entire region. A border treaty with China was signed. A treaty on water rights removed a source of friction with Iran. A settlement for a long-standing border disagreement with Pakistan seemed possible. Some Afghan diplomats even foresaw a settlement of the regional clash with Israel; one told me that he hoped to be the first Afghan ambassador in Tel Aviv.

Many schools were opened, for girls as well as boys. Women continued to flock to the university and into the world. Some received scholarships to study abroad. They became teachers, doctors, were elected to parliament, held cabinet positions.

Former students and other friends continued to turn up at my home in New York. Many officials arrived every autumn for the opening of the United Nations General Assembly. That's when I dined and danced with cabinet ministers and ambassadors, old friends from the days when we were all junior nobodies.

A second national election was held, again by universal suffrage and secret ballot, and it was even more successful than the first. Five constitutional governments held office in that decade when Afghanistan reached toward democracy; unfortunately, their leaders were unaware that secret KGB-controlled Soviet agents were planted among them, even in their cabinets, and often subverting their efforts.

A third national election was scheduled for September 1973.

A few weeks before, while the king was visiting Europe, Soviet-trained and -directed Afghan air force and tank corps officers carried out an almost bloodless coup, overthrowing the monarchy and the constitution to install the former prime minister and strong man, General (and Prince) Mohammad Daoud in a newly-created office of President.

Soon many of my friends were in prison; some died there. Others were forced to leave the country. Kayeum's name was at the top of the list to be eliminated, but the Kayeums were in America: as a "vacation" after a decade of intense effort, Abdul had been given a less demanding assignment as consul general in New York. So he survived in exile.

Daoud himself was not a communist, though he admired the USSR and was known in political circles as the Red Prince. Ordinary Afghans knew him as the ousted king's cousin, so to the public his coup appeared to be merely a power struggle within the royal family. As a known patriot and former premier, he served, probably unwittingly, as cover for the first attempted Communist takeover, and he lasted for five years. Members of the Afghan Communist party and Soviet agents found places in his government. But when he flatly refused to take orders from Soviet leader Leonid Brezhnev, he was overthrown in another coup—this time a bloody one, carried out in April 1978 by the same officers who had put him in power a few years earlier.

Daoud and his family were gunned down in the presidential palace, and a red flag replaced the traditional Afghan tricolor, as the leaders of the two Afghan Communist factions, who had been forced together by Moscow in preparation for the coup, were installed together at the head of the openly Communist People's Democratic Republic of Afghanistan.

I knew both of them. Karmal, of course: he finally had his revolution. The other one, to my shock, was a former math teacher at Darul Mo'Allamein: Hafizullah Amin. He had been one of the teachers who came to my house for tea. Later he attended Columbia University for a while; but because of his radical activities, he was yanked home without his degree and began working underground. Amin had drawn in some Darul Mo'Allamein students. Dastagir Panjsheri, the boy who read his newspaper in class, had become a KGB agent. Mohammad Mansur, a shy, soft-spoken boy on the reading room committee, was somehow—I still cannot imagine how—transformed into a party executioner.

On that morning in 1978 when the first confused reports of the coup hit the front page of the New York Times, one of my former students, a U.N. staff member who happened to be in New York on business, sat with me over coffee, going down the list of the new revolutionary government, pointing to half a dozen names of former students, to my dismay:

"These guys have been trying to get me to talk with them," he said. "Now I know why. This is a Soviet takeover," he exploded, "but it won't work. They can do it with the Poles, they can do it with the Czechs, but they can't do it to us—we're Afghans and we'll fight."

I looked at him. He was not a Pushtun, one of the traditional warrior peoples of Afghanistan. He was a Herati, steeped in poetry, art and music. Hearing him say, "We're Afghans—we'll fight!" I knew that the war was on. Within weeks I was hearing of massacres of villagers who resisted clumsy efforts to replace religion with crude Marxist doctrine. Villagers began fighting with rocks and whatever old weapons they had. Russians in the ministry of defense were attacked. Schoolgirls were protesting in Kabul and being shot down. Thousands of people were being arrested, disappearing into torture chambers and killing fields established by a new secret police, as the entire generation of experienced non-Communist leadership was deliberately wiped out—killed, imprisoned, or driven into exile.

Thus began the long, terrible avalanche of chaos and destruction, outstripping even that of Genghis Khan, and the collapse of Afghan society, which have engulfed Afghanistan over the past three decades and left it prey to its neighbors' ambitions and those of its own worst elements and made it a pawn of international struggles. That tragedy has at times been reported (and mis-reported) on the front pages of the world. But in 1978, after those first headlines of an unexpected, ostensibly-indigenous coup, the world turned its back again and forgot.

It seemed obvious to me from the very first that—having tried everything else and failed—Moscow would eventually send in the Soviet army, and so they did, at the end of December 1979. A squad of special troops killed Hafizullah Amin and installed the ever-compliant Babrak Karmal as president. The world, surprised to learn that anyone found Afghanistan worth that effort, finally took notice.

By then, more of my friends had been imprisoned, tortured, killed, or driven into exile, and still more would be in the future. Some turned up in the United States, telling of desperate escapes with nothing but their lives, often on foot over the mountains. Others, I heard, found sanctuary elsewhere, in the Middle East, Europe and Australia. Still others simply vanished; I can only guess at their fates.

Hassan Kakar, universally respected for his integrity, tried to remain in Kabul, recording events with a historian's care, but he was arrested in 1982 for participating in the underground resistance. While the regime attempted unsuccessfully to enlist his support, he spent five years in the notorious Pul-i-Charkhi prison where many thousands died, meticulously using his imprisonment to gather information from his fellow prisoners for a future history of events. Finally released through international pressure, he managed to escape and get to America, where he and his family now live, and he has published two books on Afghanistan's recent history.

The Kayeums also live here. Their children grew up to be teachers, a banker, a businessman, a doctor. "Marshall" and his family escaped and found a new home at an American college; his daughter became the beauty queen for her state and an active member of the U.S. Army Reserve.

During the next dozen years I made more than one trip to Peshawar —as a journalist in 1979, and later as director of the Afghanistan Information Center at Freedom House in New York and an officer of a private charity I founded to provide humanitarian aid to war-ravaged Afghan civilians. I didn't go to Kabul. In 1979 I had a visa, but Afghan refugees told me that anyone I spoke to would be in prison the next day. Later, it was impossible.

But I did see Gul Baz Khan again.

He had retired to his village, an honored elder surrounded by admiring grandchildren. His hair was white, as was his neatly-trimmed and rather dashing short beard. Otherwise he seemed little changed. Still straight as an arrow, he had given up blue jeans for starched white *tomban* and *peron*—with of course a jaunty brown karakul hat.

Electricity had reached Nevekali village, so I bought him an electric fan for the hot weather and a heater for winter. He introduced me to his wife and invited me for tea. When I walked into his cottage I found, pasted on the wall and decorated with paper flowers, a dozen old snapshots from the days in Kabul—me, Chevy, Bill, the house, the dogs, Gul Baz himself with all of us. He had saved them all those years.

He told me, "Sometimes in the night my wife shakes me and makes me awake and he's say, 'You were laughing in your sleep. Why were you laughing?' And I say, 'I was dreaming about long-long time ago in Kabul, with Archer-sahib and Khanum-sahib and Doctor Chevy and everybodies.'"

Before I left, I again gave him some airmail folders addressed to me. Over the next few years I received one or two of them—just formulaic courtesies written by a letter-writer in the bazaar, but welcome as greetings.. Then one day in 1983 I got an envelope from Peshawar with an unfamiliar return address, and before I opened it I knew what it would tell me: Gul Baz Khan was gone. He had been killed in a bus accident. The correspondent, a friend of his from the village, told me that a few days before, he had taken out his copy of this book as he often did and asked to have his friend read him again the parts about himself.

The Afghanistan I knew is gone, and will not come again. The friends who filled the years I spent there are lost or scattered across the world. Many of the treasures of the Kabul museum have been smashed or stolen and the Buddhas of Bamian were destroyed despite international protest. Peshawar is no longer a tranquil oasis: Dean's Hotel has been pulled down in favor of an office tower. Instead of the placid clipclop of tonga horses, the streets are noisy with motor rickshaws. Hard-eyed, fanatical armed men shove their way through the bazaars, aiming to return their countries to a seventh-century world equipped with 21st century armaments.

The rest is gone, swallowed in disaster.

But a few years ago, I got a letter postmarked from Peshawar, from someone whose name I didn't recognize.

"Dear Madam," it began. "I am the grandson of Gul Baz Khan…"

It was not written by some letter-writer in the bazaar for a villager who could not himself write or read, but by the young man who signed it. He was an accountant, he told me, a college graduate who worked in a bank. I thought of those distant afternoons with a homemade alphabet book and a proud man learning painfully to print his name.

"I believe you have written about my grandfather in a book," the letter said. "Unfortunately, someone has taken that book from our home and has not returned it. Would it be possible for us to obtain another copy …?"

Well, yes, young man.

Here it is.